TABLE OF CONTENTS

Spirits of Texas

and

New England

Over 100 True Encounters

with the Supernatural

Also by Oscar De Los Santos

Fiction

Hardboiled Egg

Infinite Wonderlands 1: Sailing the Seas of Chronos

Infinite Wonderlands 2: Black Auras

Infinite Wonderlands 3: Kaleidoscope Future
(forthcoming)

11:11 – Stories About the Event
(co-author, writing as MOJO)

Non-Fiction

Questions of Science, Answers to Life
(co-author, with JJ Sargent)

Reel Rebels
(forthcoming)

Spirits of Texas

and

New England

Over 100 True Encounters

with the Supernatural

Oscar De Los Santos, Ph.D.

Fine Tooth Press

© 2004 by Oscar De Los Santos, Ph.D. All rights reserved. Printed in the United States of America.

First edition published 2004.

ISBN: 0-9753388-7-0

Cover photo by Hugh McCarney

Library of Congress Catalog Card Number: 2004110417

This book is printed on acid-free paper.

Once again, for Kelly

With all my love

(OK forever!)

Acknowledgements

I would like to thank my mother and sister, who experienced some of these events firsthand and shared their stories with me. I am also deeply indebted to the other relatives and friends who contributed their experiences to this collection (special thanks to Kelly L. Goodridge, and to my aunts Caridad Alaniz and Guadalupe Alaniz, three guiding lights). Kristine Falconieri and Jessica Nymann helped me proofread the manuscript (I appreciate your efforts, ladies). Finally, I extend special thanks to Sam Salas, JJ Sargent and Emily Olson for their story contributions, thoughtful commentary, research assistance, and unwavering friendship.

INTRODUCTION

A Voice from Beyond the Grave

The phone's ring shattered the silence of the April night. It was late – a little after two a.m., as a matter of fact – when the call came through, but I was still awake. I've always been a night owl. It was in the early 1980s and I was still living at home while I worked on my undergraduate studies at the state university in Corpus Christi, Texas. That night, I had wrapped up my latest batch of homework about a half hour before the phone started ringing. Still wired and unable to sleep, I cracked open one of the endless string of science fiction novels I zipped through when my school reading was finished for the night.

Then the phone rang.

The sound was jarring. To this day, I remember the ice water jetting through my veins as I bolted off the couch and raced to the extension in the kitchen. There's something about a phone call in the middle of the night that sets most of us instantly on edge. It's more than just the startling nature of the sound. It's the lightning-quick suspicion that such an intrusive call can only bring bad news. Sometimes we're lucky and it's just a wrong number. Other times, the news is anything but pleasant. Such was the case that long-ago night.

I picked up the phone extension shortly after the second ring. By then, my mother had picked up another receiver in her bedroom. I listened to a world of whirling winds and static. Somewhere behind the maelstrom, a voice asked for "Petra? Petra?"

The voice – distinctly aged and female – continued to plead for my mother to respond. And she did: "Yes, Mother? Mother? I'm here."

"Petra!" the voice cried out again.

And then, perhaps because I heard the urgency in the caller's tone and the anxiety in my mother's response, I spoke into my receiver. "Hello?"

The wind in the telephone shrilled, rose to a crescendo, then a sharp click killed the connection.

I met my mother in the hallway. She was hugging herself and she looked stunned. "That was Mother," she said.

I nodded. It had indeed been her mother, my grandmother. "Yes. That was definitely *Abuela*."

To have my grandmother calling us in the middle of the night would have been disturbing under any circumstances, but this call was far more sinister.

My grandmother had been dead for over half a year.

Why had she called? I'll never know for sure, but I suspect it had something to do with the death of one of my mother's brothers a few short weeks later. Perhaps my grandmother called to prepare my mother for the shock, since she was especially close to my uncle.

A Haunted Family

My grandmother's call from beyond the grave is far from an isolated incident of the paranormal manifesting itself in our family. Many Latinos have their share of supernatural stories to tell. We are part of a culture with very strong religious and spiritual ties. Our superstitions run deeply as well, but many of these superstitions have strong basis in facts and true incidents. To be sure, not all Latinos believe in ghosts and devils, but some families have so many encounters with the supernatural that it becomes virtually impossible to ignore it. Such is the case with my family.

Indeed, it is no exaggeration to state that I come from a haunted family. As I compiled a list of paranormal incidents to discuss in this book, I was struck by the plethora of stories that originated from my own relatives (particularly, those on my mother's side of the family). Some of us might be viewed, for better or worse, as conduits to the realm of spirits and paranormal phenomena. This is not always a welcome position to be in. In most cases, members of my family are very uncomfortable with this position. I am definitely an exception to the rule.

I believe that the more open you are to supernatural phenomena, the more likely your chances of having a paranormal experience. This doesn't necessarily make you a quack or fanatic or someone who will readily label any event supernatural in scope. Far from it. On the other hand, the opposite is also true. If you go through life ready to dismiss every single occurrence as perfectly rational and tied to the realm of ordinary existence, then you have de-railed your chances of experiencing something wondrous and extraordinary.

Student of the Supernatural

I truly believe that if you keep an open mind, your chances of having a supernatural encounter will greatly improve. That is what I have tried to do throughout my life. Although I can't explain why I've always had a love of things fantastic, I believe that part of it is certainly tied to my Latino root system. As a child growing up in South Texas, I heard countless stories (or *cuentos*) of apparitions walking lonely trails and haunting old ranches and abandoned homes in the wild Texas brush country. Television further fueled my interest in the world of ghosts and phantoms. I used to love to watch *Dark Shadows,* the 60s supernatural soap opera that featured vampires, witches and werewolves. Universal horror films and other "creature features" made for great Saturday afternoon viewing. Sometimes my mother would allow these screenings. On other occasions, I had to sneak in a viewing at a friend or cousin's house. And of course, there was also the library.

I've always loved books, even before I could read them. My mother read to me as a child. She bought me countless Little Golden Books and anything else she could afford on her meager household budget. And she introduced me to the library. I remember that I quickly outgrew the children's section and begged the librarian to let me check out the adult books. Mother seldom denied me much when it came to cultivating my imagination with a book. She checked out *The Strange Case of Dr. Jekyll and Mr. Hyde* for me when I was very young and then read me the book! Comic books further stimulated my creative fires. Along with Spider-Man, the Fantastic Four, Batman and other great super-heroes, I also read the lurid Warren horror comic magazines. *Creepy*, *Eerie* and *Vampirella* kept me awake on many a night. As I grew older, I turned to paperback fiction and fell in love with Ray Bradbury, Arthur C. Clarke, Robert A. Heinlein, Frederik Pohl and other grandmasters of the science fiction genre. Still, my love of horror never disappeared. Indeed, my reading in that area expanded, once I discovered the non-fiction section's "true life" texts full of ghost encounters, hauntings and psychic phenomena. I devoured these books as quickly as I could get my hands on them.

My interest in the fantastic is deeply imbedded in my root system. Today, I'm a writer and a professor at a university in New England. Physically, I'm a long way from my native Texas, but Texas is never far from my heart and soul. It was in the Lone Star State that my love of supernatural studies was born and it is in Texas where a substantial part of this text is anchored.

This book is a true labor of love. It focuses on my personal encounters with the supernatural. It also delves into the stories told to me by relatives, friends and acquaintances over the years. Most of the stories focus on South Texas, but other parts of the state are covered from time to time – as is Connecticut, my home for the past decade.

A word about the names of the individuals throughout the book: in most cases, I have avoided using last names and used real first names. Certain individuals, however, requested total anonymity, so I changed their first name. Every other word in the book is 100% true, to the best of my knowledge.

If you are intrigued by supernatural phenomena, you should find this text quite interesting and informative. If you are a skeptic, then I hope my stories make you reconsider your position on the paranormal. At the very least, I hope that *Spirits of Texas and New England* makes you ponder the possibility that the supernatural is alive and well in this realm of existence – and beyond.

PART I: TEXAS

CHAPTER 1

THE CREST DISTRICT: THE TALE OF A
HAUNTED TEXAS NEIGHBORHOOD

Haunted Summer

The summer of 1981 was, in many ways, a magical summer. I was nineteen and riding high on life and youth. At the time, I was a nighttime disc jockey for 95 KZFM, the number-one rated pop rock station in my hometown of Corpus Christi, Texas. (I use the term "hometown" affectionately. Truth be told, even then Corpus Christi was hardly a "town." Far from it. Today, the "Sparkling City by the Sea" is home to over three hundred thousand citizens, and in 1981, it was well on its way to hitting the three hundred thousand mark.) Because of the radio station's popularity, a long string of request lines never stopped blinking. It was on a quiet Sunday night that I picked up the phone receiver, hit one of those blinking phone lights and met Gail. She requested a tune, I played it and we stayed on the line, chatting away. Eventually, Gail invited me over to her place after my shift. I accepted.

That innocent phone call and tempting invitation soon led to more than I would have imagined. Along with a wonderful summer romance and my first real girlfriend, I soon found myself in the middle of a disturbing confrontation with the supernatural.

Originally from Houston, Gail was a voluptuous blond eighteen-year-old with a saucy personality and vibrant green eyes. She was spending the summer in Corpus Christi with her divorced father. Gail's dad was himself not a permanent resident of Corpus Christi. Rather, he worked for an oil drilling company that placed him at various locations throughout the state and sent him on day- and overnight-trips to inspect various drilling sites. Sometimes, Gail's dad would be gone from Corpus Christi for two or three days in a row. Needless to say, Gail and I had a lot of time to ourselves that summer. The set-up was ideal for a couple of lust-driven teenagers, except for one slight catch: my summer girlfriend lived in a haunted house (and, as I was eventually to find out, a haunted neighborhood).

Haunted House in the Crest District

When most of us think of haunted houses, Hollywood and great horror fiction by Ray Bradbury, Shirley Jackson and Stephen King have prejudiced our thinking. We likely envision a creaking, dilapidated Victorian dwelling rising three stories above a windswept cliff. Perhaps a violent surf pounds jagged rocks far below the mansion. Believe me when I say that Gail's house was the antithesis of the proverbial dark and spooky mansion. Indeed, it was just one of many homes in a then relatively new neighborhood in Corpus Christi. This area was known as the Crest District. To this day, most of the names of the streets in this neighborhood begin or end with the word "Crest" (Crest Meadow, Crest Haven, Crest Mont, Crest View, and Crest Terrace, for example). Gail's home was a three-bedroom, one-story brick ranch located on one of these streets. The home came complete with a neatly trimmed, postage-stamp lawn, a fenced-in back yard, and a two-car garage. Eventually, I came to discover that it also came with a bonus feature: an invisible presence that made itself known from time to time.

I can't say for sure when I first heard the voices in the house, but I know that I heard them several times that summer. The pattern grew familiar; if Gail and I were in one part of the house – the living room, let's say – I heard the sound of very faint, muted voices speaking in enthusiastic conversation with each other from a distant room. As much as I have been intrigued by the paranormal over the years, I have also kept a hardnosed skepticism about such matters. Even then, at nineteen, I tried to dismiss the voices as outside noise. Maybe, I reasoned, I was hearing the sounds of a neighbor's television or a radio turned up full blast. But this was summer and the central air conditioner was on at Gail's house at all times. Eventually, I ran out of plausible explanations. The voices persisted and grew impossible to ignore.

It always sounded as though there were more than two voices engaged in animated conversation. At times, it sounded like three to five people were having a rousing social encounter, but I could never quite understand them. They were incredibly faint most of the time, and even when the banter peaked, it was aggravatingly distant. One thing is certain, though: after hearing these distant conversations on several occasions, I could no longer dismiss them as anything other than voices engaged in lively talk sessions.

The voices became a regular part of the ambience I came to associate with Gail's home. At times, they could be deceptive, so real that I would have sworn they part of an actual conversation that was taking place in the house. For example, one day I was in the middle of washing my hands in the bathroom when I distinctly heard voices talking in the kitchen. Since Gail and I were alone, as usual, I presumed that friends had dropped in unexpectedly and she had asked them to step into the kitchen where she was cooking supper. However, when I joined her in the kitchen a few moments later, she was alone and the voices had once again disappeared.

These incidents put me in a quandary. On the one hand, I was very anxious to discuss the phenomenon with Gail. On the other, I knew that my new girlfriend spent a great deal of time alone in the house and I certainly didn't want to scare her. So I kept my mouth shut and continued to listen to the perplexing ethereal whispers – until Gail herself spoke of the voices!

A Message from the Dead

To reiterate, my interest in the supernatural has long been with me. I didn't panic when I heard the voices. Instead, I wondered if they truly belonged to spirits. If so, I pondered, would these entities communicate with us more directly if we gave them another means to do so? I still didn't bring up the voices I was hearing in her house, but one night, I told Gail about some remarkable experiences I had with a Ouija board when I was still in high school. I told her I still had the board and that it might be fun to try it out one evening. To my surprise, she was eager to give it a whirl.

A few nights later, I brought the board and a friend over. Mike was a fellow disc jockey at a rival radio station, but a good friend. Together, the three of us lit candles, dimmed the lights, and sat around the Ouija board on the living room floor. Gail and I agreed to work the planchet first. Mike sat beside us and watched. We were about to ask the first question when an uneasy feeling came over me. I listened but heard no voices. I shrugged and smiled across the board at Gail. She returned the smile and placed her fingers on the planchet. I did the same – then quickly pulled them away. A powerful vision slammed into my head and shook me up. In my mind, I saw a male figure, dressed head to toe in black leather, save for a white motorcycle helmet. Then the words CYCLE and CRASH superimposed themselves across the cyclist.

"I can't do this," I said. "I'm sorry."

My friends demanded answers. After a moment, I sheepishly described what I saw in my mind.

"That's too weird," Mike said softly.

"What?" asked Gail.

"I just lost a friend in a motorcycle accident last week," said Mike. "Someone back in California. I didn't mention him to you guys because you don't know him. But I've been thinking a lot about him. In fact, he's been on my mind all night."

That ended our first and only Ouija board session in the Crest Meadow home that summer. Perhaps this was for the best. Many people well versed in the supernatural strongly advise against such dabblings. William Peter Blatty, for example, works the use of the Ouija board into his tale of a possessed little girl in *The Exorcist.* Blatty based his novel on the now infamous case of a young Mount Rainer, Maryland boy whose dabbling with a Ouija board may have eventually led to possession. Given the preternatural energy that I believed to be a part of the Crest Meadow residence – an energy that would come to feel increasingly malevolent – it's likely to our benefit that our Ouija investigations went no further.

On the other hand, another investigation yielded other intriguing information. One night, I was browsing through Gail's father's bookcases when I came across a book that discussed the use of the Ouija board. Other titles in his collection revealed a keen interest in the paranormal. Ghosts, hauntings, exorcisms: these subjects were generously represented amidst the rows of books. Many of the texts focused on out of body experiences. The next time I saw Gail's father, I made it a point to ask him about his occult library, especially the books on astral projection. He claimed that he had practiced leaving his body for years. I asked if I could read one of his books but he warned me to beware of doing so lightly. "There's always the danger of another spirit invading your body once your own spirit has left it," he explained. This warning was enough to make me shelve the book and my interest in astral projection for the time being. (A little later in this book, I will discuss a friend's illuminating experience with this phenomenon.)

Night of Terror

One Saturday night, Gail and I attended a midnight screening of *Night of the Living Dead*, director George A. Romero's terrifying and graphic film of fleshing-eating zombies invading the United States. The low-budget shocker zeroes in on the plight of several individuals trapped in an old rural Pennsylvania farmhouse as the horde of flesh-eaters tries to break in and devour them. Was it prophetic that on that particular night we watched a film about a house whose inhabitants are threatened with supernatural infestation? In a sense, that describes our domain and situation when we got back to Gail's home in the Crest District. To this day, what happened that night still ranks as one of the most frightening experiences of my life.

It was late when we returned to the house. We headed straight to the bedroom. As we prepared to undress and get to sleep, I suddenly felt terribly uneasy. It was as if a wave of malevolent energy had enveloped me and refused to let me go. I slumped down on the bed and looked over my shoulder. Gail was across the room. She was looking over her shoulder as well and our eyes locked. I saw the fear in her eyes. Without a word, she walked over to my side of the bed and sat down next to me. Our hands locked and then, from down the hall and somewhere in the living room or beyond it, I heard the voices begin their incessant sibilant chatter.

Gail gripped my hand and squeezed it.

"Listen," she said. "The voices are back!"

Her comment shocked me almost as much as the disembodied chatter.

"Voices?" *Back?* "You hear them too?"

"I've heard them all summer," said Gail.

"But why didn't you say anything?" I chastised her. "I can't believe you've been hearing them, too."

"All summer," she repeated. "I just didn't want you to think I was crazy or something."

I then explained that I had also heard them, but concern for her had prevented my sharing the information.

"Have you ever seen anything in the house?" Gail asked.

"No. Have you?"

"No, but sometimes I've felt someone right near me," she said.

"Really?"

"Yeah, and once—" She paused, then continued softly. "Once I was in the bathroom and drops of water splashed across my face."

"Are you sure you didn't do it yourself?"

"Positive," said Gail. "I just walked into the bathroom and something splashed water across the right side of my face."

We sat there for another long minute or two, hoping the voices would fade away, as they usually did. They didn't on this night. I suspected they wouldn't; creepy as the sounds had always seemed, I'd never gotten a sense of danger from them. Tonight, whether it was the voices themselves or something else that accompanied them, an air of danger and extreme negativity accompanied the auditory presence. I felt it. Gail did, too.

After another minute, I decided I had to do something. Gail's father, a firearms enthusiast who recognized that his daughter spent long nights alone, left her with a loaded shotgun in the closet. He'd also given me lessons on how to operate the weapon.

Although hunting is a major sport in my home state and I have friends and relatives who love it, I usually steer clear of guns. However, I was grateful for the loaded shotgun on this particular night.

Of course, it's silly to think that a firearm blast would stop a supernatural presence, but there was great comfort – even if it was a false comfort – in holding a rifle as I searched the house from one end to the other. Every room and closet, bathroom, shower stall and bathtub, bed, and nook and cranny was given a thorough inspection. The voices seemed to mock us. Wherever we were, they weren't. As we moved to one side of the house, they took their talk to the opposite end of the dwelling.

Very soon, the entire house had been searched and we found ourselves in the garage. Above us, someone had left the attic door open. A black maw stared back at us. Soft whispers trickled down. I finally found my courage and a flashlight and peeked into the attic. It was completely empty.

Gail and I returned to the living room. The voices were talking at a frenetic pace from the back bedrooms. They were still too soft to understand but seemed to have more and more to say. We sat on the couch and felt the home's oppressive atmosphere hang heavily around us. I remember being scared nearly senseless when my eyes fell on the clock and I saw that it was exactly half past three in the morning. Many people claim that midnight is the so-called "witching hour." However, students of the occult know that evil often seeks to mock Judeo-Christian beliefs, including Catholicism's three-part deity (Father, Son and Holy Spirit). Dark entities often try to confuse and frighten with series of threes, such as three knocks, three scratches, three objects levitating or crashing to the floor. Three o'clock in the morning has also been recognized by many to be the true witching hour – the time period when humanity is most vulnerable to the forces of the demonic.

We should have left the house but I was young and stubborn back then. There was also the danger of Gail's father returning to find his daughter missing. He was due to return from his latest inspection work sometime that morning. In fact, I should have dropped her off after the movie and left, to be on the safe side. I hadn't planned to stay more than an hour. Yet here I was in the midst of something extraordinary and terrifying on a Sunday morning.

Something rattled against the patio door. Then a scratching sound.

"It's Candy," Gail said.

I rose and flung back the curtain. The German shepherd looked up at me, tail wagging, and scratched the screen again. They say that animals are hypersensitive to the supernatural. Did Candy know something unusual was going on?

"Bring her in," I said.

"But—" Gail began to protest.

"I know she's not allowed inside," I said, "but this is a special circumstance, don't you think?"

Gail agreed. She walked to the patio door and opened the blinds and the sliding door to let the large black and brown pet into the home.

Candy's happy, tongue-lolling, smiling face quickly changed to a close-mouthed, frowning gaze of concern. Her eyes focused on the hallway leading to the bedrooms. Then her body stiffened and she growled deeply and menacingly. All of a sudden, the dog barked once and shot past us. Candy raced down the hall, to the bedrooms.

Gail returned to the couch and we listened closely. Initially, I half-expected to hear more barks and the sound of a scuffle. Instead, silence greeted our ears as Candy made her unseen rounds in the back rooms of the house.

What did the dog encounter? I can't say. All I know for certain is that about a minute after she left the living room, Candy trotted meekly back toward us, head low, eyes frightened, tail tucked literally between her back legs. She jumped on the couch beside us, and cast a worried stare toward the hallway. After that, she refused to budge for the rest of the night.

Nor did we, for that matter. There we sat, two frightened teenagers and a spooked dog (perhaps literally), listening to soft conversation emanating from nowhere, waiting for the long night to be over. I've often heard it said that three a.m. is the true devil's midnight. That may be accurate. I know that particular hour was especially tough on the psyche that night in the Crest home. I remember praying intensely as the minutes dragged on. I also remember deciding that enough was enough around five a.m. I was about to stand and suggest to Gail that we head out to a diner and read the morning papers when I suddenly realized that this long night of terror was over. I checked my watch. It was 5:15. Beside me, I felt Gail relax. She untucked her legs from underneath herself and stretched. Candy jumped off the couch.

It was truly over. The voices were gone, as was that terrible presence that oppressed us for roughly three hours. Curiously, the phenomena didn't dissipate gradually. One moment, I was frightened almost to the point of nausea and the next, I felt a calmness wash over me. I knew – somehow, *I really knew* – that everything was okay again. At least for the time being.

End of Summer

This particular incident took place near the end of the summer. Very soon, Gail would return to Houston. Although we made vowed to find a way to be together, time sent us on separate paths. I think of her from time to time and I remember most of that summer very fondly. I wonder, also, if our sexual blooming had anything to do with the supernatural incidents we each experienced at the home in the Crest District. Many studies confirm that poltergeist activity manifests itself around the time of puberty in some children. Could it be that paranormal activity may result from the sexual blossoming of some individuals? I wouldn't rule out the notion that Gail and I exacerbated whatever paranormal forces may have resided in that house via our sexual experimentation. Moreover, perhaps my overt interest in the occult (recall my lifelong interest in the spirit world and our dabbling with the Ouija board that summer) combined with her father's interest in these matters (recall his occult library and his interest in astral projection) also helped to bring forth the spirits. Perhaps these combined factors caused the supernatural manifestations to be especially strong that summer. On the other hand, given what I discovered about the Crest District in the next few years, it is clear that we stirred up preternatural forces that were already residing there.

Initially, I thought I had discovered a haunted house. The next few years revealed that I was dealing with a haunted region.

A Ghost in the Shower

I was sitting in an ice cream shop the following summer. My friend Amy was working her way through a double-scooped strawberry cone. Amy and I always had fun times together. As usual, our conversation was lively that night. Something we had never previously discussed was the supernatural, but on this particular evening, summer scary movie talk eventually led us to ghost stories. I decided to tell her about my bizarre experiences at the house in the Crest District.

Amy stopped eating her cone and stared at me. "Back up a second. Where did all this happen again?"

"In the Crest District." I gave her the name of the street and Gail's old address.

"Oh my God," she said.

"What?"

"My last boyfriend Tony lived right around the corner," she said. She mentioned the name of the street. It was indeed very close to Gail's old home. "But here's the weird part. Every time we were on the phone late at night, he kept insisting that something was in his shower. He'd put me on hold over and over, go check the bathroom and come back and say it was gone. Actually, I thought he was just running to the kitchen for snacks. Or he needed to go to the bathroom and was too embarrassed to say so. Now I'm not so sure!"

That was the first time I met someone else who had a supernatural story to tell about the Crest District. Corpus Christi sprawls alongside a section of the Gulf of Mexico. Even with the Gulf Coast breezes, however, the city remains balmy most of the year, thanks to its South Texas location. I remember dropping Amy off and driving around the Crest District. It was a muggy night, as usual. My headlights tried in vain to cut through heavy fog, a staple around the city. Memories of Gail and the voices in her home melded with Amy's brief story about her ex-boyfriend and "something" in his shower. Two supernatural tales coming from one neighborhood.

I stopped the car in front of Gail's old home. Then I drove around the corner and checked mailbox addresses until I found Amy's ex-boyfriend's house. Fog swirled around my car. I didn't stop for long. The damp weather and my memories made that cruise most unsettling.

An Incubus Attempts A Rape

My oldest and best friend Sam still lives in Corpus Christi. We met as young teens working for the local Greenwood Public Library. While I eventually moved into college teaching, Sam stuck to library work. Today he is a reference librarian in a Texas library. In his younger years, Sam also did his share of restaurant work, including a long stint at the Sizzler restaurant in downtown Corpus Christi. While there, Sam met Juan and his wife, Maria. Juan managed the Sizzler, while his wife assistant-managed the eatery. Eventually, Sam learned that his bosses lived in the Crest District. Indeed, the couple owned a house on a street that intersected with Gail's old street.

One night, while Sam, Juan and Maria shut down the restaurant and worked on cleanup, the subject of ghosts and haunted dwellings came up. Juan joked that the only ghosts in the Sizzler were the few tourists who strolled in without a suntan. Sam eventually steered the conversation to the Crest District and relayed my story about the events that took place in Gail's old home. Juan put an end to ghost talk at that point, but Maria took Sam aside and promised to talk to him about "something very weird" another night, when her husband wasn't closing the restaurant.

"I'm almost relieved to hear about your friend and those weird voices in the house," she said. "We're practically around the corner from the house you're talking about and let me tell you, we've had some terrible experiences at our place."

Maria's assessment might be considered an understatement, when one considers that she was almost raped by a ghost!

Like most of the houses in the Crest District, the house that Juan and Maria owned was probably no more than three or four years old. Unlike Gail's ranch-style dwelling a street away, however, Juan and Maria's home was a two-story tanned brick affair, with dark brown wooden trim. The house hardly seemed like the sort of structure that most of us might envision when we think of haunted mansions. Still, looks can prove most deceiving.

As is often the case with paranormal cases, things began subtly and eventually escalated. Initially, it seemed that the couple had the sort of mischievous ghost often reported in homes where poltergeist activity is taking place. Items were often moved from one place in the house to another; some disappeared altogether, only to return at a later time. And there were also the rapping sounds that resounded from outside. Quite often, it sounded as if someone was knocking hard on the garage door or the front door. When Juan or Maria went to check, they found no one.

Slowly, the impish presence shifted its attention exclusively toward Maria. Now it was she whose items were missing and she who heard the outside rapping most frequently. Once, while dressing in the master bedroom upstairs, Maria heard a tremendous slamming from outside. It sounded as though someone had rammed a car into the garage doors directly below her window. Maria heard the slam again. She raced to the window. The driveway was empty.

It was at this point that Maria began to grow fearful of the events. No longer could all the missing items be easily dismissed as careless forgetting; no longer could all the startling sounds be brushed aside as the antics of prankster kids in the neighborhood. Indeed, the children in the area were well behaved and had never given Juan or Maria any trouble. Maria was a religious woman. Like her husband, she emigrated from Mexico, a country deeply ingrained in religion and supernatural beliefs. Maria grew concerned that something out of the ordinary had descended upon their quiet urban dwelling. A few nights later, her suspicions were proven correct when a phantom spirit accosted the young wife in her bed.

Tales of incubi and succubi permeate the horror genre. Poems have spoken of succubi, as have countless legends. Over the years, a series of disturbing paintings have pictured a demon-like entity crouched atop the bosom of a swooning woman. ("The Nightmare" by John Henry Fuseli is probably the most famous of these works; Fuseli himself did six versions of the painting and the great psychoanalyst Sigmund Freud had a print of one hanging in his office.) As she suffers through her fever dream, the lust-filled incubus prepares to consummate their union. Belief in incubi and succubi has existed for centuries throughout the world. Although they may come in many guises, the general consensus is that these entities are linked to the demonic. Allegedly, an incubus visits a female as she sleeps and tries to arouse her sexually in order to gain access to her spirit. Similarly, a succubus attempts to have intercourse with a male as he sleeps. The words are of Latin derivation and actually allude to the position of the entity at the time of its infestation. An incubus is said to attack from *above*, a succubus from *below*. On the night of her attack, an incubus attempted to have sexual intercourse with Maria.

It was a warm summer night and very late. Juan was already lost in slumber when Maria came to bed, threw open the curtains to let the bone-white light of the full moon shine into their bedroom. She got into bed and lay very still. The long hours at the restaurant usually made her fall asleep very quickly. Tonight seemed to be no different. She felt herself drifting off. All of a sudden, an oppressive force slammed onto her chest and pressed her deeply into the mattress. Maria cried out for Juan but he didn't respond. She yelled again, but her husband slept on. (Such failed attempts to awaken loved ones during moments of psychic infestation are not uncommon.) Maria realized that she was destined to fight this battle alone – *but what was she fighting?* Moonlight from the window revealed that nothing physical was holding her down – yet something clearly was restraining her! She couldn't budge off the bed. Again, Maria attempted to push the invisible entity off her chest. It was fruitless. Indeed, a moment later, her plight grew worse. Either the entity was extremely resourceful or he brought reinforcements to assist in his violation. Maria suddenly felt her ankles gripped by icy vises. Cold fingers caressed her calves. Then something pushed her left forearm onto the mattress and it was secured by another invisible flesh rope.

Perhaps only Maria's rock-solid religious faith saved her that night. The young woman raised her remaining free hand to her face and made the sign of the cross. The gesture is one of the strongest symbols of those steeped in Catholic dogma. Instantly, the weight on Maria's chest lifted and the frigid vices disappeared. The attack was over. Not surprisingly, so was Juan and Maria's stay in the Crest District. The couple sold their home and relocated to another part of the city a few months later.

Innocence Invaded

I learned more about the Crest District and its strangeness one night at the radio station. I was on the homestretch of a 10 p.m. to 2 a.m. shift and ready make room for my replacement. The phone lines were lively earlier in my shift, but the blinking bank of lights was dark now. Then Angela called up to make a request. I was tired. Between a yawn, I asked her what she was doing up. She said she was babysitting. I asked where and she mentioned the Crest District. I came wide-awake.

"Any ghosts in the house?" I asked, trying to sound as if I was joking.

"Not this one," she said seriously, "but down the road, yeah."

"Quit kidding," I said. She insisted she was serious.

"Okay, who lives down the road?"

"Nobody now, but I used to know the people who did." She mentioned the name of a Crest street. "The people that lived on that street had trouble at their house. A lot of trouble."

My shift was coming to an end so I asked Angela if she'd meet me for dinner the next night.

"No way," she said. "You're just trying to pick me up. I'm not sleazy."

"I know that. And I'm not trying to pick you up. Forget what you've heard about disc jockeys. We're *not* all alike. Right now, I'm more interested in your ghost story than anything else. I promise."

After much coaxing, Angela finally agreed to a rendezvous. We met at a local restaurant, picked an isolated booth in the back of the place and chitchatted until the waitress took our order. Then I asked her to tell me about the "trouble" she spoke of on the phone the night before.

"You'll think I'm stupid," she said, twirling her spoon around and around her glass of tea.

"Believe me, I won't." I finally convinced her to tell her tale with a promise to tell of my own experiences in the Crest neighborhood.

Angela used to know a woman, Sara, who was a native of Corpus Christi, as was her childhood sweetheart, Leonard. The couple spent their first married years living in a small apartment. Even after Michael was born, they continued to live in their cramped quarters. Then Sara and Leonard contemplated expanding their family. Could they afford it? Very likely, they reasoned, but a move would definitely be required.

Sometimes luck, both good and bad, arrives simultaneously. The same week that Leonard received a promotion in his job at the naval air station, Sara was browsing the morning classifieds when she spotted what sounded like the ideal home for rent. While Leonard was at work and Michael was at school, Sara went to check out the place. The house was located in the Crest District. Sara liked the look of the neighborhood: new and clean. A neighbor waved as she pulled up to the home with the realtor. It was a sprawling four-bedroom ranch. The couple wasn't looking for such a large house, but the asking price was reasonable and they wouldn't have to worry about moving again anytime soon.

Leonard's promotion allowed the family to move into the house. It also allowed Sara to quit her part-time job at the jewelry store in the Padre Staples Mall. Suddenly, the young woman found herself living the life she had envisioned in her best of daydreams. She was a stay-at-home mommy and devoted housewife. Her love for Leonard continued to grow, and he returned her affection in kind. On the surface, things couldn't have been better for the couple. Unfortunately, things changed within weeks after they moved into the Crest District.

The trouble started innocuously enough. One bright morning after her husband left for work and Michael boarded the bus for school, Sara returned to the house to work on a stack of laundry in need of pressing. She set up the ironing board in the living room and watched television as she ironed. Then, in the middle of pressing one of Leonard's shirts, Sara detected fleeting movement out of the corner of her eye. She glanced towards the direction of the movement. The hallway that led to the back part of the house was empty. Sara returned to her ironing. A few minutes later, she noticed the movement again. Once more she looked up and once more she perceived nothing out of the ordinary. Yet there *had* been *something* there, hadn't there? A quick shadow skipping across the hall, from one open doorway to another? Sara set down the iron and walked down the hall to investigate. As she suspected, her search yielded no trace of an intruder.

But the fleeting shadow did not disappear. Not permanently, anyway. A few days later, Sara was in the middle of putting groceries away when something distracted her. This time, she caught a better view of the shadow as it skimmed out of the open garage door and into the living room. Sara raced to the living room. It was empty. Her first glimpse of the shadow a few days before had left her feeling disconcerted; this latest incident rattled her nerves enough to call her old friend Angela and invite her to lunch.

"That's when I first heard about all this," Angela explained at our own dinner meeting. "I learned about it from the beginning, as it was happening. Actually, I was the only one Sara told during that time. She and Leonard kept it to themselves for years."

"Well, it sounds peculiar, I'll admit," I said, poking at the remains of my meal, "but maybe she just imagined it all."

"I'd agree with you, except for two things."

"What's that?"

"I've known Sara forever and she's not one to exaggerate. And what I've told you is just the very tip of the iceberg. Things grew a lot more disturbing."

Angela continued with her story.

The shadow became a permanent fixture in Sara and Leonard's house. It made appearances at the most inopportune times. Sara never caught a head-on glimpse of the entity, but as the weeks went by, she saw the shape out of the corner of her eye as it made its way all over the home in the Crest District. Walking into the house from the bus stop after seeing her son safely aboard, Sara caught glimpses of a black swath streak into the bathroom. Another time, while transferring laundry from washer to dryer in the garage, she detected a shadow slinking behind a stack of boxes. On still another occasion, she was setting the table when she saw an obscure form slump behind the island that separated the main kitchen area from a small eating nook. Of course, Sara investigated each incident and found nothing inconspicuous where seconds before she had seen the shadowy form.

These incidents pushed the young wife and mother into a constant, low-grade state of fear. She became very nervous. At times her fear escalated to veritable panic, especially on long afternoons when the entity made multiple appearances. The family wasn't religious but Sara often considered consulting a priest on a number of occasions. She felt trapped. She thought that if she told her husband, he would think her neurotic and an unfit mother. She couldn't tell her parents. Her father was dead and she didn't have a very close relationship with her mother and younger sister.

"So she told you," I said to Angela.

My new friend nodded. "Yeah, but she didn't go into a lot of detail. And really, when everything came out in the end, she was telling the wrong person."

If there is one person Sara should have confided in sooner, it was her husband. Leonard may have initially tried to dismiss Sara's stories as flighty fantasies, but his opinion would have quickly changed. It seems that the young husband was having experiences of his own in the Crest home. Sitting on the couch after dinner and reading the paper one evening, for example, Leonard grew certain – *absolutely certain* – that he spotted a man sitting perfectly still in the wingback chair to his right. He couldn't detect any features because he was looking at this figure out of the corner of his eye, but the silhouette was definitely tall, broad and masculine. It sat statue-like and stared straight ahead, its hands resting on its knees. Finally, Leonard could take the suspense no longer. He whipped his head to the right. Except for a cushion, the wingback chair was empty!

Other similar incidents plagued Leonard. A phantom figure appeared out of the corner of his vision while he was shaving. A glance in that direction turned up nothing. Admiring the backyard after mowing the lawn one morning, Leonard thought he saw a silhouette streak into the tool shed. Of course, the shed was empty when he checked it out. One lazy Sunday afternoon, Leonard had the house to himself. He read the newspaper until he grew drowsy, then decided to take an afternoon nap on the couch. As he awoke, his sleepy eyes detected a streak of *something* racing across the hallway, from one bedroom to the next (a move frequently spotted by Sara). Leonard raced down the hall, only to find a set of empty bedrooms.

Finally, one night, Leonard and Sara left Michael with a babysitter and indulged in a nice dinner. At the restaurant, Leonard made Sara talk about her nervous state. He asked if she was having an affair or if she was considering leaving him. Sara was shocked. Her husband's questions underscored how badly things had grown for her – for them – in the past few months. Sara broke down and sobbed. They left the restaurant. Outside, she gripped Michael's hands in hers. It was nothing of the sort, she said, then confessed her problems. As he listened to his wife, Michael felt both astonishment and relief wash over him. When Sara finished her story, Michael told his. Although they had no idea what to do with their information, they each felt tremendous relief over having related it to someone else. Before that night, Sara had confided only in Angela, and only revealed bits and pieces of the myriad incidents she experienced. Leonard had told no one until then. In the end, they decided to ponder their unorthodox problem for a few days, before making any move. Sara believed that dinner date to be as important as the night that Michael proposed to her. She felt a renewed dedication and deepening trust in her husband; she also sensed he was experiencing the same validations. They drove to another restaurant and enjoyed a fine dinner before heading home.

Unfortunately, Sara and Leonard's son wasn't spared from the hauntings that occurred in their Crest District home. Indeed, it was Michael's encounters with the supernatural which finally launched Sara and Leonard into action. The six-year-old had taken to sleeping with his parents. At times, he would crawl into bed with them in the middle of the night. Other nights, he would request to sleep in their bed as Sara or Leonard tucked him in his own bed. The couple usually acquiesced, but grew tired of the arrangement after one long stretch of days during which Michael had become a permanent fixture in his parents' bed. As he came into their bedroom yet again one night, mother and father gently protested.

"Why don't you go sleep in your own bed, sweetheart?" Sara suggested.

"Good idea," said Leonard. "You have your own bed in your own room, son. Use it."

"Well, I would," said Michael, "if it weren't for all those people in there."

Leonard and Sara stared at each other. One of the things they had agreed upon, after finally discussing their troubles with each other, was that they would under no circumstances discuss the incidents with their young son. Yet here was a seemingly related bomb dropped by Michael himself.

"What people, Mike?" Sara asked softly.

"The ones in my room," he said.

"Mike, don't lie," Leonard said. "There's nobody in your room right now."

"Not now," Michael said. "But they come at night. They fill up the room and walk around and they talk and stare at me all night and how can I sleep in there with all that talking and moving around going on?"

Little Michael's revelations proved to be the final blow. Their nerves completely shot, Leonard and Sara moved out of the Crest District a short time later.

"But you still live there," I said.

Angela nodded. "I'm putting myself through college and my parents aren't in a hurry to see me leave the house."

"But my point is, you haven't had any problems."

"That's right."

"No ghosts?"

"Nope."

"No voices?"

She shook her head.

"Not even a weird shadow?"

"Nothing," she said, "and I hope to God it stays that way."

"I hope so too."

Conclusion

Who or what haunts the Crest District? Quite often, the spirits of Native Americans who lived in a particular area are blamed for the manifestation of supernatural phenomena. South Texas is no exception. Before the Spanish landed along the Gulf Coast and invaded the territories around and to the north and south of what is now Corpus Christi, the region was inhabited by the Karankawa and, to a lesser extent, by the Coahuiltecans. The Karankawa were hunter-gatherer people who kept mostly to themselves and lived a peaceful existence near the sea. Fish was a major portion of their diet. For the most part, they were not an aggressive people. Reports of early Spanish conquistadors attribute cannibalism to the Karankawa. True enough, but studies reveal that human-flesh eating was reserved for magic ceremonies designed to bring the tribe good fortune and a bountiful year. Evidence of cannibalism may also be attributed to other tribes in the region.

The Coahuiltecans are also accused of haunting South Texas. At times, various historians have discussed the Coahuiltecans as being comprised of one specific culture or tribe. However, the "Coahuiltecan" is an umbrella term used to describe a number of diverse Native American people in the South Texas region. Like the Karankawa, the varied bands of Coahuiltecan Indians are said to have practiced cannibalism. However, the images of mass human massacres for the sake of consumption are grossly erroneous. Once again, when human flesh was eaten, it was tied to ritual. Although some Coahuiltecans resided along the area that would one day be Corpus Christi, their domain spread further west and north. The Coahuiltecans were also similar to the Karankawa in that they were by and large a pacifist hunter-gatherer people. This changed to some extent as the region grew more populated in the mid-1700s, especially after the more aggressive Comanche in the north drove the Apache further and further south, into Coahuiltecan (and to a lesser extent, into Karankawa) territory. The Coahuiltecans suffered many losses. By the late 1800s, both they and the Karankawa were all but gone, defeated not so much by the invasion of other Native American tribes as by the diseases brought over by the Spanish.

It would be very easy to blame Native Americans for haunting the Crest District, as they have been accused of haunting so many other areas. However, some things don't add up. First of all, among the many people who have shared their Crest District stories with me, I have never heard anybody mention seeing a ghost or apparition that resembled a Native American. Second, the Crest District hauntings are often accompanied by foreboding feelings of danger and maliciousness. These are not spirits content with making their presence known from time to time or who simply wish to reside in passive coexistence with an area's human inhabitants. The feelings of danger and oppression that accompany so many of the tales told about the Crest District indicate that the hauntings are the result of aggressive spirits bent on tormenting the current residents of various Crest homes. To reiterate, the Native Americans who made this part of the state their home were, for the most part, a peaceful people. Still, something deeply unsettling and evil seems to be residing in this region. Maybe it is trapped there. Unfortunately, what that *something* is may forever remain a mystery.

Today I live in New England but from time to time, I return to Texas to visit with family and friends in Corpus Christi and throughout the state. When I do find myself in my hometown, I make it a point to drive around areas that are linked to my past. The last time I was in town, my old friend Sam and I drove down Chapman Ranch Road, another hotspot of paranormal activity in years gone by. Those who trek up and down the Chapman Ranch Road in the wee hours have long told tales of apparitions, often attributing the entities to the spirits of car-crash victims. As we came to the end of the road, I spotted a street sign in the distance. It read Crest Glen. I turned down this street and we drove around the Crest District once again. As the city has grown, so has this neighborhood. The District used to be built near the outskirts of the city. Acres of empty fields have suddenly been developed into more and more neighborhood streets, convenience stores, and gas stations. I marvel over the fact that everything looks so different. To me, it seems that the landscape has changed in the wink of an eye; the reality is that over twenty years have passed since my experiences in the Crest District. Of course, everything is relative: if things look so different to me two decades later, how stark would the changes seem to Native Americans who dwelled on this very land two centuries ago?

As I drove along with Sam, I questioned my belief that South Texas Indian spirits are not the haunters of this region. I was forced to admit that every group of people has its negative exceptions and renegades. Perhaps a few wandering souls from the old tribes continue to wreak havoc on a few unfortunates who today reside in the Native Americans' old domain.

Another possibility: Is the Crest District built atop ancient burial grounds? The answer seems far too cliché, too pat. Hollywood has often resorted to this solution to explain a haunting. And yet negative energy seems to be situated around the Crest District. Why? Who can really say?

As dusk descended upon us and we left the Crest neighborhood behind, Sam and I talked about the old stories. "The one thing that comes most to mind when I think of those times," my friend said, "is that all those occurrences were happening hot and heavy, around a particular stretch of time. It felt like, all of a sudden, we were experiencing or hearing about all these stories one after another."

Sam was right. Once we started to query people whom we found associated with the Crest neighborhood in some way or another, many had an offbeat or quirky story to relate. I have covered the most significant of the stories here, but there were plenty of quick "one liner" anecdotes told in passing. For example: "Oh, my cousin lives on Crest Meadow and she's often complained of crashes in the house." Or "My friend refuses to stay in her house on Crest Terrace when her folks are gone."

"Then," Sam continued, "either we backed away from the stories or they just stopped as suddenly as they sprang up."

We were young at the time. We were still stretching. We were intrigued by the events in the haunted neighborhood. Then life kicked into high gear and we grew too busy tackling the tail end of our teens and the first taste of our twenties to keep obsessing on one neighborhood.

We moved on, but the Crest District and its stories and spirits remains.

CHAPTER 2
MORE FIRSTHAND ENCOUNTERS
WITH THE SUPERNATURAL

Haunted Youth

My experiences in the Crest District certainly rank as some of the most disturbing encounters I've had with the unknown (see Chapter 1). Also striking are my experiences in New England, particularly the times I've felt portentous feelings come over me in an area that is purported to be haunted (see Chapter 3). However, these are not my only forays into the realm of the fantastic. Growing up, I was very quickly attracted to the stories my relatives told one another on warm summer nights, while gathered around the porch of their rural Texas homes. If I were given a choice between a western and a horror flick on the television, the tale of the vampire, the werewolf or the giant tarantula always won out. If I had to choose between a Hardy Boys mystery and a juvenile's condensed version of Stoker's *Dracula* or Stevenson's *Strange Case of Dr. Jekyll and Mr. Hyde*, I always chose the macabre text.

Many children are attracted to the horror genre. However, my love of the subject extended beyond childhood and remained with me when other kids abandoned ghosts, witches and warlocks on all nights but Halloween. I remember meeting the great science fiction and horror writer, Ray Bradbury, a few years ago and admiring his tie, a navy blue number with hundreds of bright orange pumpkins splashed all over it. Bradbury threw his head back and laughed heartily. "Every day is Halloween at my house," he exclaimed. I feel exactly the same way.

Maybe one of the reasons I was so engaged to the unknown is because I would rather face ghosts and spirits than the true life devils that made my early and middle school years a living hell. I lived in a rough Latino neighborhood. Fights broke out incessantly in my elementary and junior high schools. Sometimes these fights continued in the parking lot or a nearby playground. Other times they carried on into the streets. Older and tougher boys frequently picked on me. I remember being accosted on a number of occasions and pummeled for no other reason than the fact that I scored higher grades than they did, that I preferred the library to the football field (although I played a pretty fair game of Little League baseball) or that I had a flair for drawing. Truly, I was haunted by the physical world in a more aggressive and insidious fashion than by the spirit world. I knew that I was powerless to go against entire gangs of bullies, so I channeled my energies into my great loves: science fiction, horror and so-called "true-life" ghost stories. I became a silent investigator, ever on the lookout for the fantastic.

Cryptozoology 1: Goat-Man and Big Bird

Cryptozoology is a term used to identify the study of unusual creatures rumored to exist in various locations throughout the world. These animal and amphibian life forms manage to evade widespread public scrutiny. Nevertheless, a few eyewitness reports – together with the occasional (often blurry and grainy) photograph, film, video recording or sound byte – hint that these fabled beasts do exist. The Loch Ness Monster and other sea monsters (such "Champy," the beast that supposedly lives in Lake Champlain), Bigfoot and other mammalian anomalies fall into the realm of cryptozoology. Texas has its own history of sightings that defy animal and aquatic life as we understand it. Two of these are the goat-man and Big Bird.

When I was a child of eight or so, there was a great deal of talk about a goat-man running around South Texas. The goat-man was strictly a nocturnal entity. Witnesses claimed to have encountered this abomination while driving down lonely back roads between Corpus Christi and Kingsville; between Kingsville and Benavides; and between Robstown and Alice. The goat-man – or "el chivo" (*chee-vo*) as he was known in Spanish – was said to have the face of a bearded man with a wild mane of hair, broad muscular shoulders and goat horns sticking out from his forehead. The man-beast was said to have a strong and bare barrel chest. There the similarities between this creature and human stopped. From torso on down, people swore, this being was no man; instead, fur was purported to cover the creature's lower stomach, below the navel. This fur trailed downward and grew thicker, covering his legs, which were, incidentally, not the legs of a man but the shanks and hooves of a large goat!

The speed with which this creature was said to move was also remarkable. Most of those who saw the goat-man spotted him as they drove down lonely highways. The man-beast was usually standing out in a field, or by the side of the road. Then, as the witness streaked past in his automobile, the abomination gave chase! Many witnesses claimed that the creature managed to keep pace with their car for a good quarter mile or more! A few brave witnesses did the opposite of speeding up. Instead, they slowed their cars and trucks down to get a better look at *el chivo*. The goat-man then scampered into nearby woods.

Curiously, the description of this goat-man is very similar to the description of a similar creature said to attack residents around Lake Worth, Texas in the late 1960s. Maybe there were two such creatures or the goat-man made his way down from the Fort Worth area to South Texas. Maybe it was just the rumors that traveled.

I was a kid when the stories of the South Texas goat-man materialized. As soon as I heard them, I grew quite interested and kept a razor-sharp lookout for him on out-of-town trips. I even talked my father into going on special goat-man scouting expeditions. They yielded nothing substantial but they further fueled my interest in the extraordinary and its occasional invasion in our everyday lives.

A similar wave of sightings hit South Texas when I was a little older, this time involving another perplexing creature. Almost overnight, talk of a "Big Bird" became the rage in the mid-1970s. Scores of residents in Robstown and surrounding areas swore they saw a giant bird with a tremendous wingspan hovering around the region. Drivers often spotted the winged creature on isolated roads or on the outskirts of various towns. Once again, my father indulged my curiosity and drove me around the Robstown area in search of the Big Bird. Not surprisingly, these amateur cryptozoological expeditions yielded little more than an ever-growing desire to probe the supernatural. On the other hand, it wouldn't have been my first encounter with such a presence. Somewhere in between talk of a goat-man stalking South Texas and Big Bird flying over the Lone Star State's skies, I experienced two shocking and perplexing supernatural encounters in one day. These incidents greatly enhanced my interest in the supernatural – and each continues to haunt me, in its own unique way.

A Demon at Daybreak

One Saturday morning in the summer of my ninth year, I woke up very early. Of course, I was up early most Saturdays since it was cartoon day, but on this morning, I was up before the sun. I even beat my parents to the punch, a rarity. It was the weekend and they'd decided to catch a few extra snoozes. I was too excited to sleep in. We were going out of town this morning, leaving Corpus Christi behind for the weekend and heading to the small town of Benavides, Texas, where my parents grew up from their teens through their thirties. Many relatives still lived there. For the next two days, we would visit my grandmothers, aunts, uncles, and cousins. I always enjoyed the Benavides trips and I suspect it was eager anticipation that awakened me to the still and dark atmosphere of our home that early dawn. Or it may have been the demon.

To this very day – even as I type these words in my well-lit office – I still see the very image I encountered in that long ago pre-dawn light as I lay in my bed. The door to my bedroom was open. I rolled over and gazed at the living room. From my position, I could see the right frame of the door which led to the kitchen. And from the kitchen, I detected a black silhouette peeking out and looking my way. I saw only head, shoulders and part of the demon's chest. Its posture was dramatic. It seemed to be craning its body far out into the living room, but keeping its legs concealed. And it seemed to be staring right at me. I use the term "it" instead of "he" because that's the way my young mind registered the entity. To me, it resembled a demon. It was a large black shape with a huge inverted triangle of a face and – most disturbing of all – the silhouette had horns sticking out of its head!

What I saw couldn't be real, I told myself. Even as a kid, I was pretty good at keeping my wits about me. I tried hard to convince myself that I was imagining things. I blinked once, twice, a third time. I shut my eyes and opened them again. *The demon was still there!* Still, I refused to believe what I saw. It had to be some trick of the pale dawn light filtering its way through closed curtains. I sat up in bed. The demon continued its silent vigil by the kitchen door. I blinked again and the vision remained. I remember a fresh wave of fear washing over me as I forced myself to get out of bed and walk to my bedroom door. I got as far as the hallway. The black shape refused to dissipate. It continued its stony stare. Standing by the door to my room, I suddenly realized that it was impossibly tall. A man craning his torso around the door as the abomination before me was doing would have had to be seven feet tall or better.

A second later, the black bulk seemed to shift and lurch. This proved too much for this nine-year old boy. I raced back to my bed and yanked the sheet over my head for a good ten minutes. Finally, and with great reluctance, I peeked out. My room and the hallway were brighter. The living room was also better lit as dawn approached. But the black demon kept its vigil! Worse, the coming light didn't make it vanish, but lit up its face. I saw bushy eyebrows raised above saucer-round black eyes. I saw a thin and elongated nose. I saw a mouth pulled back and frozen open in sardonic laughter. And above all the grotesquery, I saw its pale horns stretching toward the ceiling.

I thought I had been scared before. Now I was terrified, truly on the brink of madness with fright. I threw the sheet over my head again and lay there, too scared to move, barely breathing. Then I heard a shuffling sound in the distance. Someone was walking down the hallway. Someone (*something?*) was in my bedroom! Something shook me!

I strangled a cry as the sheet was pulled back and I stared into the face of my mother.

Mom told me to get up and get ready to go. I didn't need to be told twice. More than ever, I was anxious for us to leave the house and start our trip to Benavides.

Vision of the Virgin Mary

Before I was born, my parents lived in the small South Texas town of Benavides. Many years before I was born, scores of residents of Benavides and such nearby towns as San Diego, Freer and Alice came forth with a series of remarkable stories. These people claimed to have witnessed a holy vision. Specifically, some citizens claimed to have seen the Virgin Mary! The Holy Mother of Jesus Christ was glimpsed both fleetingly and for long periods of time. Some claimed she appeared on their property; others insisted they saw the Virgin in the wild Texas brush country, at ranches and around other rural locations. Her manner of dress was always the same: simple, long flowing robes and a cover for her head. The reported colors of these garments often varied. Some described Mary in blue and white robes with a cream-colored head cover. Others saw her dressed all in white. Still others saw the Virgin dressed in the red, greens and yellows often associated with the Mexican version of Mary – *"La Virgen De Guadalupe"* – that allegedly appeared to Juan Diego in Mexico.

The Virgin never spoke during these sightings, nor did she look directly upon the witnesses. Most people who claimed to have seen her remember Mary looking away with an expression of complete serenity on her face. Several witnesses remember her hands held together in prayer. All agreed that the apparition caused an immense feeling of tranquility to blossom within them.

Why should the Blessed Virgin suddenly be sighted in South Texas? For one thing, Texas is a state with strong ties to the Catholic religion. Moreover, in South Texas, Catholicism has centuries old roots that reach back to the Spanish friars who came to bring Christianity to the New World. These friars built missions and worked to convert Native Americans to the Catholic faith.

As a religion, Catholicism is quite unique in the sense that a female holds a key role in one of its most important stories. The Virgin Mary is revered as the Mother of Jesus Christ. As a female, she redeems the role of Eve, who enticed Adam to sample forbidden fruit, resulting in the duo's expulsion from the Garden of Eden. To reiterate, the Mexican version of Mary is also known as Our Lady of Guadalupe. Guadalupe means, "Stone serpent trodden on" and further underscores that the power wielded by Mary can crush Satan, who appeared to Eve as a serpent in the Garden of Eden.

Over the years, Mary has been cast in a number of variations. The darker-skinned and bright-robed *Virgen De Guadalupe* who appeared to Mexican peasant Juan Diego (also known as Our Lady of Guadalupe) is quite different in appearance from the fair-skinned, light-blue and white robed Mary often worshiped by Caucasians. Statues of the Virgin Mary are popular among Catholics. Talented artists and sculptors have created countless varied images and icons of the mother of Christ. In her traditional guise and other variations, Catholics "Hail Mary" throughout the world. Some worshippers devote a substantial portion of their prayers to the Mother of Christ.

Because Mary is so much a part of the South Texas Catholic faith – so much of a living entity to many faithful – witnesses' sighting stories were seldom doubted in the 1960s. Whenever someone came forth claiming to have seen the Virgin in the nearby brush country or at a neighbor's ranch, word spread rapidly and eager spectators soon flooded the region. Some of the curious claimed to see the Virgin moving around the location as soon as they got there. Others saw nothing. Were these new "witnesses" pulling everyone's leg? For that matter, were the initial reporters of a Mary sighting also telling tales? It is hard to say, but one thing is certain: a great many people claimed to have seen the mother of Jesus Christ roaming around South Texas during the 1950s. Reports of such encounters eventually grew more rare, but in the early 70s, there was fresh talk of the Virgin making a new wave of appearances around the Benavides, San Diego and Alice regions.

On the Saturday that began with my seeing a demon in my home, my family traveled from Corpus Christi to Benavides to visit relatives. Two of my closest cousins, Gladys and Diana, accompanied us on the visit. Gladys is my first cousin and a year younger than I; Diana is a few years older. Their father was my mother's brother and my uncle. I was very close to *Tio* (Uncle) Cruz. In many ways, he was like a second father to me. At the time, he was in the hospital, having suffered a setback in his ongoing battle with heart trouble. My ever faithful and diligent *Tia* (Aunt) Lupe remained by my uncle's bedside, but both parents insisted their daughters accompany my family to Benavides in order to pay a visit to their grandmother, aunts, uncles and cousins.

During the course of the day, while visiting the homes of my grandmothers and various relatives, we learned of several new sightings of the Virgin Mary in the area. To reiterate, Gladys and I were very close. More than first cousins, we were best friends. The stories of the Virgin Mary sightings amazed us and fueled our imaginations. Gladys attended Catholic school throughout the week and received a steady dose of religion study. I was enrolled in public school; nevertheless, I attended weekly religious instruction classes and Sunday Mass. I remember that Gladys and I took long walks through the hot streets of the small town, longing to see anything out of the ordinary. I remember saying on more than one occasion that I would love to see the Virgin. I wonder if I would have kept repeating those words if I had known that my wish was hours away from coming true.

The roads between Benavides and Corpus Christi are dark and lonely in the wee hours. My family drove home late that Saturday night. My parents were in the front seat of the car, my mother cradling my younger sister Iris in her arms. Cousins Diana and Gladys rode with me in the back seat. I had the window seat behind my father, who was driving. Gladys had the other window across the way. Poor Diana, older than the two of us, was stuck in the middle, since Gladys and I insisted on having a window seat.

A few short minutes after leaving Benavides behind, I gazed out the window and was awed by the striking starscape far above. The night sky in these small South Texas locales is blacker than any I have encountered, thanks to sparse population and the absence of big-city lights. That particular night, the stars above shone with uncanny brilliance.

I was still staring at the constellations when it happened: all of a sudden, I spotted an oval-shaped yellow light high above. In some ways, it was like a tiny fat cigar standing vertically. If I had extended my hand to the light and measured it between the tips of my thumb and first finger, it would have probably measured an inch from the top of the oval to the bottom. Gradually, the blob-like light became more defined. Now I saw that the yellow oval encircled an equally bright green ring. I stared at the light, mesmerized, yet too self-conscious to holler "UFO!" just yet. I tried to dismiss what I was seeing as nothing more than an optical illusion. First, I leaned forward in my seat, pretending I was restless. I had a motive behind my movement. My eyes combed the aqua colored glow of the dashboard lights in front of my father's steady driving hands. Nothing remotely like the colors I was witnessing outside my window came close to being cast by the instrumentation of the car panels. I finally sat back in my seat and stared straight ahead for some time before I allowed myself to look out my window again. When I finally gave in, the light was still there! Moreover, the brilliant oval orb had gained another color: now the incandescent gold of the outer rim and the vibrant green of the inner ring encircled a shimmering crimson innermost ring! As I watched, the triage of colors stabilized and the object lost some of its blurriness and grew more distinct. What I saw made me turn away from the tiny bright light and refuse to double-check its presence for many long miles. I still see that vision to this very day: a woman, her head partially obscured by a deep green shawl and wearing a bright red robe, staring serenely at the ground, her hands palm-pressed together in prayer. Around this woman shimmered rays of gold.

Earlier in the day, I had heard many stories of the Virgin Mary and her past and more recent appearances around the area. While walking with my cousin, I had made numerous declarations professing a desire to see Mary. And now, it seemed, my wish had come true. The Virgin hovered in the night sky above me. So why was I so scared? Other witnesses spoke of great joy in their hearts after their encounter with the Virgin. Yet I was feeling anything but elation. Quite frankly, I was terrified. It was all I could do to sit calmly and act sleepy. Finally, my cousin Diana sensed that something wasn't right and asked if I was okay. I whispered that I thought I was seeing the Virgin Mary. I felt terribly embarrassed. I remain thankful that Diana didn't scoff or accuse me of blasphemy. She simply told me that I was lucky and advised me to say a prayer in Mary's honor. I did and I felt a little better, but not by much. Then I shut my eyes and tried very hard to sleep. It was fruitless.

The drive between Benavides and Corpus Christi is only about an hour and fifteen minutes long. This particular trek seemed endless. Every now and then, I'd squint my eyes open and check for the presence of the Virgin. She – or whatever the light was – was still there, a tiny image of the Madonna hovering in the night sky and keeping pace with our car. Finally, as we entered the city limits of Corpus Christi – which is Latin for "The Body of Christ," incidentally – the image winked out. It was that fast: there one moment, gone the next.

Demon at Daybreak, Holy Vision at Night:
Lessons of a Lifetime

What a day!   In the first light of morning, quite unexpectedly and without any kind of conscious desire to do so, I saw something with the visual characteristics of the demonic, complete with horned head. That night, I saw something that can easily be classified as the antithesis of evil. I have reflected on this strange series of events for four decades. Although I have no definitive answers, I have reached some conclusions about what may have occurred on this extremely significant day in my life.

Curiously, Good and Evil seemed to have violated some of the usual symbolic trappings we place upon them. Morning brought a demon into my home. Yet, don't such entities lose their power by day? Or at the very least, don't we most often hear about evil spirits making their appearance by cover of darkness? And what about the Virgin Mary? Why did an entity that is so closely associated with goodness and light appear to me at night? I do not believe I imagined what I saw. And yet, why was I so frightened by her appearance? I believe both experiences comprise harbor lessons from the spirit world. After years of assessing the wondrous encounters, I recognize that the first incident involving the demon in daylight taught me that Good and Evil are not bound by time as we measure it, nor by such constructs as day and night. I suspect that spirits are all around us, regardless of time of day and position of the sun. Books teach us to read symbolically: we associate Good with light, bright colors and white. Similarly, we align Evil with darkness, shadows and black. We affix many other symbols and suppositions to the positive and still others to the negative and we are not entirely wrong in doing so. However, Good is not always found radiating light and vested in bright raiment. Likewise, Evil is not always couched in darkness and black cloak. Recall the saying: "One may smile and smile and still be a villain." Quite true. That was the first lesson I learned that day. Beware – literally, *be aware* – at all times. Evil can strike at dawn and Good can visit you anytime, day or night.

Lesson Two might also be summed up with an old adage: "Be careful what you wish for; you may get it." That's exactly what happened to me on the day that I heard the stories of the Virgin Mary. Perhaps because I was rocked by the disturbing presence of the demonic in the morning, I longed to be visited by one of the most positive representations of the spirit world to offset the earlier encounter. I'd like to think so, but I don't think that's accurate. Instead, I was young, undisciplined and lacking respect for the supernatural realms that lie beyond our existence. I heard the stories of the Virgin and, not fully comprehending the extreme assault on the psyche that such experiences can generate, I unthinkingly but quite sincerely expressed a desire to see the Virgin Mary. This was not a request borne out of extreme religious devotion or awe of that revered position which she represents in church dogma. Rather, I was a young kid looking for kicks. To my astonishment, the Cosmos called my bluff! I got what I asked for and learned a lesson the hard way. Unprepared, I felt no elation at the vision but instead suffered a second major scare that day. The power of Good in the cosmos is immense. We should not call upon it lightly or take it for granted. It's a lesson I've never forgotten.

A Mother Visits Her Son After Death

I began this book with the story of my grandmother's beyond-the-grave phone call to my mother. My father's mother – I affectionately called her *Ma Grande*, a literal Spanish translation of "grandmother" – also made an appearance of sorts in my home. This occurred about 1985, a year or so after my first grandmother rang up my mother. Once again, the event took place late at night; once again, I was up late, working on an essay for a literature class at the university. I didn't have a computer at the time, so I was doing it the old-fashioned way, hammering away at a manual typewriter, a bottle of white correcting fluid by my side. As I whipped one sheet out of the typewriter and prepared to scroll in another, I discovered I was out of paper, so I went to retrieve some more in the bedroom where I kept school supplies. At the time, my father was sleeping in this particular bedroom. I opened the door and walked in softly, trying hard not to wake him. The bedroom was dark but I knew my way around. The first thing I noticed upon entering was the strong odor of tobacco. Nobody in our immediate family smoked but I was very familiar with that particular tobacco odor. The room smelled of lit Salem cigarettes and tobacco. As I quickly retrieved the paper, I remember thinking, *It smells exactly like Ma Grande in here.* My grandmother used to love to smoke her Salems (and considering the fact that she lived into her mid-80s, I'd say she got away with her lifelong tobacco habit pretty effectively). It was only upon shutting the door and moving down the hall that the full implication of the experience hit me. Ma Grande had been dead for several months! I turned on my heel and raced back into the bedroom. My father slept on in the dark room. I filled my lungs with air and walked softly around the room. The smell had completely disappeared!

It seems to me that my grandmother came to visit her son that night. Moreover, the incident allowed me to experience clairsentient phenomena for the first time. If clairaudient people *hear* the supernatural and clairvoyant people *see* the supernatural, people who are clairsentient *smell* the permeation of the supernatural in a given location. This is the only time that I can recall actually smelling the presence of the supernatural, although it may have happened on other occasions and I simply wasn't aware of it. Still, I believe I interrupted a supernatural visit that night.

Psychic Dream: A Friend In Need

Can dreams prophesize the future? Many people swear this to be the case. Countless stories throughout the world speak of people glimpsing a future event while in the arms of Morpheus. These nocturnal visions are not always focused on grand earthshaking events. Sometimes the incident that is prophesized might almost be described as mundane. The dream just happens to come true a short time later. Many such dream encounters are rooted in family experiences. Cassandra Eason has written *The Mother Link*, an excellent study that describes the psychic links between mothers and their children. In some of these cases, parents recognized impending danger for their child via dream messages. Likewise, some children were alerted to events in their parents' lives via dreams. This psychic communication is not restricted to relatives. Sometimes we receive messages about close friends in our dreams. This happened to me shortly after I graduated from high school, when I was going to school full-time and working a full-time graveyard shift at the radio station. Looking back, that kind of crazy schedule was a major mistake. For one insane semester, my schedule ran something like this: work the overnight shift (in the studio at 10 for advertising and commercial work; deejay from midnight to six a.m.), rush home, shower, eat breakfast, head to the university, attend classes until around one, eat something light, then hit the sack until around eight, get up and do homework and then head out to the radio station to start the cycle again. I was less than successful at this breakneck venture and scaled back on the number of classes I took in future semesters.

One late afternoon, though, my mother awakened me after only a few hours of sleep. My friend John was on the phone, she explained. He said it was urgent. I stumbled to the phone. Even before I got to it, I knew what he wanted. John had a reliable automobile, but when my mother awakened me, I was in the middle of a dream in which John's car had broken down and he desperately needed a ride to work. So rather than say, "Hello?" when I picked up the receiver, I cut to the chase and said, "Hi, John. You need a right to work, right?"

I heard silence on the other end of the connection.

"Right," I continued. "I'm on my way."

I got to John's house a few minutes later and he dashed out to the car. I had been right about his needing that ride.

Ouija: the Deadliest Board "Game"

Many parapsychologists warn of the dangers involved in tampering with the Ouija board. For years, individuals have made up their own boards and planchets, while others prefer to buy the popular version of the board game that is sold by a major toy company. However, most serious students of the supernatural know that whether one chooses to use a makeshift board or the official board "game," the Ouija board is not to be used flippantly.

There are countless tales of individuals who experimented with the Ouija board and regretted doing so. The biggest problem that many paranormal experts attribute to the Ouija board is that its users never know what kinds of spirits they will contact. Just as there are both good and evil human beings in the world, there are good and evil spirits. When a person uses a Ouija board and invites contact with one specific soul, there is no way to tell if one is indeed fooling oneself into believing that contact with the spirit world has been established, whether one is speaking to the loved one, or whether one has been tricked by a potentially dangerous entity. Even in cases in which the users of Ouija boards do not ask to speak to a specific entity, there is still the danger of the board acting as a conduit between its human users and malevolent entities. These spirits often begin to interact with the Ouija board users in a fairly innocuous, friendly fashion, but as time passes and the session continues, the entities often grow more aggressive in their responses and demands.

Worse yet, learned students of the occult believe that using the Ouija board is tantamount to casting an open invitation for the spirit world to visit the board user's location at anytime. This is something that amateur practitioners do not realize and often live to regret. At times, Ouija users have reported hearing the sound of the planchet skating around the board on its own, even after the board has been put away. People have also found it extremely hard to get rid of Ouija boards. I have met several individuals who swore that they had tried to dispose of their Ouija by throwing it away, only to stumble upon it days later, in a closet, attic or basement.

To sum up, it seems that if you use a Ouija board, you may open yourself up to a negative visit from the spirit world. Your use of the board is an open invitation to all entities, *good and evil*. In the worst of scenarios, there have been horrifying cases of possession reported in association with the use of Ouija boards. The Robbie Manheim case is probably the most famous incident that is at least partially associated with Ouija board use. In the first half of the twentieth century, the young Maryland boy suffered months of possession before he was cured via multiple exorcism rituals. (See Thomas B. Allen's *Possessed* for a non-fiction account of the case; see William Peter Blatty's famous novel, *The Exorcist* for a fictionalized tale that was directly inspired by the Robbie Manheim case.)

The longer I study the paranormal world, the greater respect I have for it. There was a time when I was far more naïve to the dangers of tampering with the occult. In my teenage years, I actually owned a Ouija board but I have used this instrument only on three occasions. (Recall that I aborted the Ouija session in the house in the Crest District even before it started, so I will not count that session.) I was a sophomore in high school when I purchased my "official board game." Naturally, I had to experiment with it immediately. I waited until late that night, then unwrapped my new purchase and began a solo session.

"Is there a spirit present?" I asked the empty room around me. I felt rather foolish, until I felt the planchet lurch beneath my fingers. It slid to the word YES in the upper right-hand corner of the board.

For a long time, I simply stared at my fingers poised lightly over the planchet. Had I caused the heart-shaped object to move? I thought not, but I had to be sure. I slid the planchet back to the center of the board.

"Is there someone here?"

Once again, the planchet slid beneath my fingers. YES, the board declared.

"Who are you?"

The spirit didn't waste time. The planchet moved left, right and back again, spelling out a name: ISOBEL WALKER.

"Where do you come from?"

I expected the name of a Texas city or town to be spelled out for me. Instead, I got NEW ORLEANS.

I continued to converse with ISOBEL. She spoke in short sentences and one, two and three word answers. I learned that she lived in the New Orleans area all her life. She claimed to have died there in the late eighteen hundreds. (She gave me a year, but I no longer remember it.) She had been married, but unhappily. Her life was a sad one. She still felt sadness.

After a while, I stopped receiving messages, but I was hooked. I wanted to learn more about this ghost from a bygone time. The next night, I pulled out the Ouija board once again and dimmed the lights. Immediately upon placing my hands on the planchet – even before I asked a question – the planchet slid to HELLO. I was taken aback.

"Isobel?" I asked.

The planchet slid toward YES.

She spoke anxiously tonight. The planchet was on the move again, spelling out I COME SEE YOU.

I come see you?

"I don't think so," I muttered. "Let's just talk."

Once again, the planchet moved swiftly. I COME SEE U, it insisted.

Fear crept over me. I took my fingers off the heart-shaped pointer and put the Ouija board away.

My friend John's father (the same John who needed the emergency ride to work; see "Psychic Dream," above) was a reporter and had a features column for the Corpus Christi *Caller-Times*, my hometown's newspaper. I asked John's dad if there was any way to determine if an Isobel Walker had lived and died in New Orleans in a certain year. I gave him the year. John's dad said he would make some inquires and he kept his word. He called and wrote the New Orleans Hall of Records and inquired about the mysterious name. A letter soon arrived from a record keeper in New Orleans. The note explained that there was no mention of an Isobel Walker living or dying in the city or the area in the given year. However, the note went on to explain that a fire had destroyed some of the area's earlier records and there was roughly a ten-year span of time with spotty holes in its history. Therefore, just because they couldn't find an official record substantiating the woman's presence in the area during the time in question didn't necessarily mean that she had not lived there during that period of time.

After receiving the information from John's father, I pulled out the Ouija board one last time. Once again, I had no sooner placed my hands on the indicator than it started moving here, there and back across the board. This time, whatever was contacting me made a request: LET ME COME SEE YOU NOW.

"Isobel? Is that really you?"

I received an emphatic reply: I COME 2 SEE U.

I don't know if this was Isobel speaking or some other entity. I suspect the worse, however. The entire tone of the presence changed dramatically from one night to the next. On the first evening that I spoke with Isobel via the Ouija, I had the sense that I was engaged in peaceful interaction with someone. On the second and third occasions, the tone of the entity (or entities) speaking through the Ouija was very different. Indeed, it sounded as though something was trying desperately to capitalize on the open doorway to the physical realm. Perhaps this new presence was trying to masquerade itself as Isobel. In any case, today I am grateful that I stopped tampering with the Ouija board after this incident. While a part of me still wonders what would have happened if I had replied, "Yes, come see me," I am thankful that even though I was young, I had enough sense to protect myself and cut off my experimentation.

I didn't throw the board away, though, and that brings up a perplexing epilogue to this tale of the Ouija. I stored the board atop a stack of other games in one out-of-the-way corner of the living room. This particular stack of games was near a large fan that I usually kept going until the wee hours most evenings. One morning, shortly after I had put the Ouija board away, my mother chastised me for leaving the living room fan on all night. I apologized and made it a point to turn off the fan the next night. The following morning, it was my father's turn to admonish me for leaving the fan on and in the middle of the path between living room and kitchen where someone could run into it and hurt themselves. This was frustrating news. I was quite certain that I had turned the fan off and rolled it out of the way and against the wall before going to bed. The next night, I made absolutely certain that the fan was off and out of the way before I went to bed. Sure enough, the following morning I was scolded for my negligent ways with the living room fan!

That was the last night the Ouija spent inside the house. That board is history – and so far, it has yet to come back.

We will hear about other disturbing incidents involving the Ouija board in Chapter Four of this book.

UFOs and the Supernatural

I couldn't have been more than eight years old when this happened, but like so many of the past events I experienced in this text, I remember the incident with stark clarity. I was driving around the small town of Benavides with an aunt and two cousins one warm summer night. All of a sudden, a white ball of flame shot across the heavens and disappeared into the thick woods beyond the horizon. A silent explosion of light followed. One moment the world was black, the next it was lit with daylight intensity. I remember seeing a cobalt blue sky, the shiny green leaves of a copse of banana trees and the white paint of an old ranch house. This brilliance lasted no more than a second or two, then darkness returned to the world. Very likely, what I saw that night was a small meteor's final burnout trail and impact on the earth. I'm almost certain that's what the light was, but a part of me still wonders. That was the first time I witnessed something perplexing making its way across the night sky, but it wouldn't be the last.

In 1992, I was working part-time as a pool attendant in an apartment complex in Columbus, Ohio. One sweltering afternoon, I was sitting by the sign-in table, reading. I put my book on the table for a moment and stretched and craned my neck back on the chair. Something was coasting across the brilliant blue sky high above: it was an oval-shaped, silver object. Although it had the same basic shape as a Goodyear blimp, it was far too slender and long to be such a craft. Further, the curiosity was traveling higher than any blimp would ever cruise. More than anything, the object resembled a bright bulbous needle. I could detect no sound whatsoever coming from the craft. When I stretched my arm up full length and pinched my fingers for a rough size estimate, the object was about half an inch in length from one end to the other. Given the incredible height at which the craft seemed to be traveling, this would have made its actual size enormous. Yet there it was in the sky above, moving slowly and serenely toward a distant eastern cloudbank. I watched it for a good two minutes before it finally disappeared.

I've often pondered over this particular UFO sighting. When the flying saucer craze was at its national peak in the 1950s and 1960s, the majority of the craft were reported to resemble the flat ovals of a plate – hence, their name. As time passed, UFOs with slightly different appearances were reported. Some resembled children's spinning tops, while others were shaped in the form of silver cigars. Did I see one of these slender anomalies hovering over the skies of Columbus, Ohio on that sunny summer afternoon? It seems so.

I've spotted several UFOs throughout my life. There's nothing remarkable about this fact. I simply attribute it to the fact that I am ever on the lookout for aerial anomalies. What is interesting is that each of my sightings has violated the classic pie-plate appearance of the classic flying saucer. I do not claim that any of the aerial puzzles I have spotted were extraterrestrial in origin. However, each has been quite fascinating, especially the one I spotted on a dark road between Sinton and Corpus Christi, Texas one cold winter's night.

People who work in the media are a clannish, good-natured lot. I feel I'm qualified to make such a statement because I worked as a disc jockey in the Corpus Christi radio market for about eight years. The public sees only the façade that the media puts on for the public, but behind the microphones and when the cameras are off, things are much different. Many disc jockeys and TV personalities who work for competing broadcast stations are good friends. Even though they wouldn't be caught dead broadcasting on their rivals' airwaves, the same on-screen competitors often meet up at houses or bars and talk shop throughout the night. Such was the case when several of my close friends and I were part of the Corpus Christi radio market. At one period, a close-knit group of five of us worked for five different radio stations! As I reflect on those times, I'm still very grateful that Ruben and I worked for different companies in January 1981. Although I enjoyed Ruben's company and would later work with him at one station, the fact that we didn't work together that winter led to a most remarkable UFO sighting.

At the time, I worked for rock station 95 KZFM (Z95) while Ruben worked for KSIN in Sinton. I've always loved to stargaze but the Corpus Christi city lights usually obscure most of the night sky. One Monday morning, I received word that I had the night off and wouldn't have to report for my usual evening shift. I asked Ruben if I could tag along to check out the night sky at the tiny country music radio station where he worked. Ruben did the six-to-midnight shift at the rural station. Because the broadcast building was so isolated, he welcomed the company.

Imagine my disappointment when the night turned out to be misty and gloomy. Still, I had promised to accompany Ruben that evening and there was always the chance that the weather might clear up. It never did.

Unlike my KZFM, which broadcast twenty-four hours a day, Ruben's KSIN went off the air at midnight. So after my friend signed off for the evening, we headed home. The cold drizzle continued as we drove down dark roads that would lead us out to the highway and the trek home.

A few minutes after leaving the radio station behind us, I glanced at Ruben as he drove. Through his side window, I noticed a bright light far out in the darkness. We continued to converse, but I kept an eye on the light. It seemed to be stationary and yet I knew that given the inclement weather, I wasn't seeing a star. Another minute passed. Finally, I could no longer resist calling Ruben's attention to the bright dot in the sky. I asked what he thought it might be. Like me, he said his first guess would be a star, if not for the weather. He continued to glance at it and I finally asked him to pull over so we could check it out more carefully.

We got out of the car and stood by the trunk area. The light grew larger, then larger still. I extended my arm, held up my hand and "squeezed" light between my thumb and forefinger. It never got enormous, but it grew large enough for me to extend my thumb and finger about half an inch in order to cover the area of sky that it occupied. It also grew close enough and clear enough for us to see that we were looking at three lights, not one. These orbs made up a triangular shaped configuration. Two lights formed the top and a smaller red light completed the upside down triangle on the bottom. Try as I might, I couldn't tell whether there was any solid object connecting the lights. However, the front white light had two small beams or streams of light shooting outward from it.

Ruben and I watched the object(s) grow bigger and move across a field, toward our road. At most, it was about five hundred yards away from us. Amazingly, it seemed to be flying quite low. As the object prepared to glide across the road, it sailed over a small utility shack and a light pole. I would estimate it to be cruising approximately seventy-five feet off the ground.

Most remarkable of all, however, was the lack of sound. Indeed, *there was no sound whatsoever emanating from the vehicle, whatever it was!* I believe that if it had been a plane or helicopter or some other flying object with which we are familiar, it would have made a detectable and distinct noise. But the night seemed unnaturally silent during the time Ruben and I had our close encounter.

There's an interesting postscript to this story. When the object finally disappeared behind dense woods in the distance, we took off and headed not for home, but to our friend Michael's apartment. We knew he would be awake and just getting home. Michael worked the six-to-midnight shift for yet another radio station in the area, this one in Robstown. Like the rest of us, though, he made his home in Corpus Christi. Michael listened as we told our story. He was fascinated and asked us to keep him posted with any updates. Instead, it was Michael who came up with the update.

A day or so later, Michael had a most surprising and welcome gift for us. An item came over his radio station's AP teletype wire that talked about the "at least 41 people" in "La Vernia, Texas" who "claimed they saw a UFO" the night before! Although La Vernia is located a few hours northwest of Corpus Christi, the town's UFO reports are remarkable to me because witnesses describe the object flying over La Vernia as triangular shaped, with two white lights and one red light. Their description matched exactly what Ruben and I saw the same night!

I have often wondered about what I saw that dreary winter night. As time goes by, I have been tempted to dismiss whatever it was as something ordinary (perhaps a plane flying toward Corpus Christi International Airport). Still, I don't let my rational mind debunk my sighting completely. There are key indicators that suggest the object was not an airplane: the ghostly silence, the fact that Ruben corroborated my sighting and also found the object inexplicable, the reports from La Vernia from people who saw a very similar object – perhaps the exact *same* object – *on the same night, within hours of our sighting.*

Even in moments of crisis, I try to remain open to the world of Things Fantastic. At the same time, I try hard to look upon events objectively. I do not stretch the truth but neither do I deny the presence of the extraordinary when it manifests itself. The mind is the most wondrous part of our being. It is kin to our sensibilities, but it can also be overly protective. Often, it resists our moving into uncharted territory. Curiously, the more time that passes between the period when a supernatural event took place and the present, the more the mind works to convince us that nothing strange occurred. Why? I believe our brain goes into Overdrive Protection Mode. The supernatural rarely makes an appearance in our daily existence. (Reflect on the word itself: super-natural; consider too, its kin: extra-ordinary.) When it does (usually fleetingly) invade our lives, it ruptures the comfort zone and the rational checkpoints that we erect, sometimes consciously, often unconsciously. Some of us, however, wrestle to keep our minds open and receptive to the supernatural. I can no more completely dismiss this UFO sighting casually than I can dismiss the other mysterious phenomena that I've encountered. In fact, I give this particular UFO incident prominent status because it ranks among those rare cases where I encountered clear visual confirmation that something extraordinary was taking place.

You may be wondering what these UFO accounts are doing in a book about haunted Texas. For one thing, I would not discount a connection between UFOs and the supernatural. Taking the term at its most literal, supernatural does not necessarily have to deal with ghosts, spirits or other wonders most often associated with the occult. To say that something is supernatural in scope means, literally, to claim that it falls into a category that is beyond everyday laws that govern the world. Certainly, then, we can assert that some UFO sightings fall into the realm of supernatural phenomena when they perform feats that defy our current understanding of the laws of physics and existing technology (streaking away at speeds that defy explanation, moving about the night sky in zigzag fashion, executing 45-degree angle course changes, operating without any detectable sound).

Many ufologists have tried to crack the UFO mystery. Science tells us that traveling to our planet from any other that we have discovered beyond our solar system would be impossible. Not only would the trip exhaust all known modes of fuel supply, but life support systems and supplies would also be taxed. Moreover, even traveling at the speed of light, such an interstellar journey would take so long that any beings arriving on this end would be dead. Of course, in most cases, scientists have extrapolated these theories from a Terran perspective, with Terran science and technology as their cornerstones. The vast size of the universe is almost too great for the human mind to fathom. An often-cited example still conjures up the best image to help us comprehend the size of the cosmos: if every grain of sand from every beach on Planet Earth were tossed into the air and made to represent a star, there still wouldn't be enough grains of sand to represent each star in existence! Add to that the myriad planets that might be revolving around those stars and the scenario becomes truly senses staggering. Isn't it fair to assume that on at least one of those planets besides our own, the chain of events necessary for the spark of life to evolve has occurred? Moreover, couldn't we speculate fairly that such life would differ – perhaps slightly, but likely radically – from life on our own planet? If such is the case, then our own laws of existence may not govern such life. Indeed, the life forms on other worlds may differ so dramatically from human life that their own food, fuel and storage problems in need of being overcome before making an interstellar voyage may not be the same as ours. Further, their technology may be supremely advanced when compared to our own. That which we consider supernatural may to them be a simple thumbprint of their elementary physics. It seems only fair to keep an open mind about the possibility that extraterrestrial life might be visiting us from time to time.

Those who are ready to dismiss all UFO sightings as terrestrial in origin should consider several factors. Of course it is natural to assume that many sightings are actually terrestrial in origin. Other sightings can be blamed on atmospheric conditions, a trick of the light or other natural anomalies. However, the sheer variety and volume of UFO sightings makes it impossible for the open-minded investigator to dismiss *all* sightings as misidentified airplanes, hoaxes or curious weather phenomena.

Some of the most engaging UFO theories have been posited by investigators who speculate that these craft move around space and time in ways that transcend humanity's understanding of physics. Thus, these beings seemingly materialize in our world and then disappear with such speed that some people say the UFO they were tracking became a sudden streak or simply winked out of existence before their eyes. Perhaps witnesses are seeing a UFO bend space and time as it jumps from one pocket of space to another. Moreover, since space and time are connected (see key treatments by Einstein, Carl Sagan, Stephen Hawking and others on this subject), some of the more imaginative – but not entirely dismissible – explanations for UFOs have centered on the possibility that *we are piloting these vehicles and visiting ourselves!* In other words, it is fair to speculate that UFOs may come not from elsewhere but from else*when*. (For more on the latter discussion, see Whitley Strieber's absorbing journey into the realm of ufology. In a series of books that begins with *Communion*, Strieber discusses his many encounters with beings that he labels "visitors." Strieber's follow-up studies include *Transformation* and *The Secret School*; all are worthy of close examination. Another book which touches on the subject and raises some fascinating theories about the origin and modes of transportation of extraterrestrials is *Night Siege: The Hudson Valley UFO Sightings*, co-written by Dr. J. Allen Hynek, Philip Imbrogno and Bob Pratt. Dr. Hynek was a diligent scientist and UFO investigator. He was responsible for coining the term, "Close Encounter," and for writing one of the most significant works on the subject of unidentified flying objects, *Close Encounters*. In effect, Hynek provided the title for Stephen Spielberg's classic film on the subject of extraterrestrials; Hynek also served as a consultant to Spielberg during the film's production. Today, Phil Imbrogno continues to investigate UFOS and the paranormal and has written a number of thoughtful treatises on the subjects. See my appendix/bibliography for more information.)

Finally, there is this point to ponder: UFOs have been known to make frequent appearances in areas that are supposedly haunted by ghosts. This connection remains unresolved but it is well documented.

Unfortunately, there have been many people who have attempted to capitalize on the UFO craze over the years. Some have made up stories, while others have gone so far as to stage fake alien landings, photographs and sightings. These people have tarnished the efforts of serious investigators (often referred to as ufologists). The best policy when it comes to UFO studies is the same policy that applies to serious investigation of any supernatural phenomena: keep an open mind.

A Box of Cursed Books

In the late 1980s, a syndicated TV show appeared with the unsavory name of *Friday the 13th: the Series*. It was produced by Nick Mancuso, Jr., who was largely responsible for launching one of the most successful – but eventually tiresome – film series in horror film history. After John Carpenter directed the extremely effective *Halloween* in 1978, a string of slasher films followed. (Ironically, the original *Halloween* is hardly a slasher or "body count" film, but rather a harrowing study in psychological horror that shocks largely through *implication* and suspense-building rather than graphic displays. This mattered little to the flood of imitators that followed, as they ripped off the idea of the crazed stalker and substituted increasingly explicit gore and violence in place of a good story.) Among the Michael Myers imitators was Jason of the long *Friday the 13th* film series. For most of the series, Jason was a vicious, machete-wielding mountain of a man in a hockey mask. Like Michael Myers in the subsequent *Halloween* sequels, Jason was imbued with supernatural powers; he became literally unkillable. The visage of the hockey masked, machete-armed serial killer became as recognizable a horror icon in the 1980s as the elongated white-faced visage of the black robed ghoul did in the late 1990s, thanks to horror maven Wes Craven's chiller, *Scream*. However, Mancuso's *Friday the 13th: the Series* TV show differed considerably from his *Friday the 13th* big screen series. For one thing, this was no serial killer series; no Jason stalked the night hacking people up from week to week. Instead, the show focused on the extremely inventive premise that an antique shop owner made a pact with the devil before he died and in so doing, extended his life but cursed everything in his possession, including all objects in his shop. When the antiques dealer disappears, two unsuspecting relatives sell off all the goods in the shop. Each object is cursed in a unique way and brings temptation and death to those surrounding it. The bulk of the series focuses on cousins Mickey and Ryan's attempts to track down and retrieve all the cursed objects that were unwittingly sold in order to secure them in a vast vault built in the basement of the antique shop. The notion that objects may be imbued with negative or positive energy is highly intriguing. People often talk about a place having good or bad energy. Why not objects? If what happened to me over a period of time is any indicator, I am inclined to believe that some objects are capable of harboring positive and negative energy. Unfortunately, in my case the latter seemed to be the case.

In 1983, my friend Sam helped our buddy John inspect an abandoned rental home. John's grandmother owned a number of small properties and the tenants skipped out on this particular house after they got behind on their rent. John had a key to the back door of the house, located in an old neighborhood in Corpus Christi. According to Sam, the moment they entered, he knew trouble lay ahead.

The back door led into a small storage area that in turn eventually led into the kitchen. When Sam and John entered the storage room, the first thing they noticed was that floor and ceiling, walls and windows had been painted black. In the center of the room stood two thick, purple and well used candles, their bases affixed to the floor with melted wax. Sam thought the room felt creepy, but he wasn't sure whether to blame his feelings on residual evil phenomena or the mere surprise of encountering such a room.

His mood would only grow worse, however, as he and John moved through the rest of the small house. Although the place was empty and hadn't been painted black, another disturbing sight awaited them in the living room. On one of the walls, a painting of The Last Supper hung, the right corner "chewed or gnawed away" (Sam's description). He walked up to the painting. Virtually one-third of the illustration was gone. He detected what looked like teeth marks on its ragged corner.

Sam and John found two other items in the house, both in the master bedroom closet: a Ouija Board on the upper shelf and a box of books on the occult and witchcraft on the floor. Sam took the books, knowing I'd be interested in them, and let John dispose of the Ouija board.

The next time I stopped by Sam's house, he told me the eerie story and gave me the box of books. I took the box and put it in the trunk of my car. I meant to look the books over immediately, but I was working full-time and the radio station had us involved in a number of after-work public relations appearances. I was also going to college part-time during this period. As a result, I never got around to checking out the books and actually forgot about them for a time. I would come to regret this oversight.

I've been a book lover all my life. Today, I make a living teaching books. I write books. I love books. I do not believe in throwing books away – but there are extreme exceptions to this rule, and this is one instance where I believe the books should have been destroyed. I believe that box of books was responsible for a series of misfortunes that befell upon me during that period of time. Why I didn't put two and two together is something that I still ponder. I must chalk it up to my extremely busy schedule.

About a week after receiving Sam's gift, I was sitting at a stoplight. The light changed to green and I started rolling again. All of a sudden, a black truck smashed into my left side. The driver's side panel, from front bumper to front door, was completely smashed in. I was shaken up but unhurt. My father knew a body-shop worker and once the insurance companies took care of business, he did a beautiful job of restoring my car. However, no sooner had I gotten the car back – about a week and a half, tops – than I was plowed into by another car! This time the other driver begged me not to get the insurance companies involved. It was his second accident in the company car in the past few months and he wanted desperately to keep it hush-hush. He promised to repair my vehicle. Of course, the safe thing to do would have been to call the cops and get an official accident report written up. Had this stranger decided to back out on his agreement, I would have been in a bind. I blame youth on my decision to trust the gentleman, who luckily turned out to be just that – a gentleman and true to his word. Sure, driving back to the auto-body shop was embarrassing but once again, my father's friend did a superb job of restoring my vehicle. I wonder if he would have bothered if he knew that two weeks later, he would be seeing my car again.

The third time my car was hit, I wasn't even in the vehicle. It's a good thing, too. I was standing in a grocery checkout line when I heard an announcement over the P.A. system. Would the owner of a blue Mercury Zephyr come out to the parking lot immediately? Was that my car? It couldn't be, I thought. No way. But the license plate they announced confirmed that it was indeed my car.

I walked out into the parking lot in a daze and couldn't believe what I saw. My car had been spun completely around, smashed into by an out of control car on one side, scrunched up against the front grill of another vehicle on the other. The term accordion comes to mind when I remember what was left. An elderly gentleman lost control of his old clunker, mistook his gas pedal for his brake and charged full-throttle into my poor Zephyr. Surely this was the end of my car, I thought.

Incredibly, three weeks later, I was cruising down the streets in the same car! (My father's friend must have had a touch of the supernatural himself – or had wizards working for him – so talented was he at refurbishing "sick" cars.) When the car was towed to the body shop for its third repair, the damage was so great that I was asked to remove everything from the trunk before the shop worked on it. The moment I opened the trunk, my eyes fell on the box of books. It was the first time I had seen them or thought of them since I placed them in there the night Sam gave them to me. My mind did a quick juxtaposition: car wrecks/books. There had to be a connection, considering the house where the texts were found.

A short time later, John discovered that his missing tenant was a practicing witch, heavily involved in the black arts. Good riddance to her, whether she skipped out on a few months' rent or not.

And good riddance to her books. This is the only time in my life that I can consciously remember throwing books away.

11:11

Is there something supernatural about certain numbers? Those who believe in numerology ascribe great powers to some numbers. The number 1 has long been a part of my life and the sequence of numbers 11, 111 and 11:11 intersect with my everyday existence with uncanny frequency. It's been over twenty years since this phenomenon began. Imagine my shock a few years ago, when I learned that several of my friends also run into 11:11 (which I pronounce "eleven-eleven") all the time! A couple of years ago, I invited three friends and fellow writers – JJ Sargent, Emily M. Olson and Heather Margaitis – to join me in forming an 11:11 writing group. JJ, Emily and Heather also experience 11:11 sightings quite often in the course of their everyday lives. The 11:11 writing group's goal would be to produce a collection of short stories linked – and inspired – by the numbers 11 (eleven), 111 (one-eleven) and especially, 11:11. For almost a year, group members devoted every Friday night to sharing and critiquing each other's work. Our efforts paid off. We didn't plan it, but exactly eleven months after launching the writing group, we finished our collection. Shortly thereafter, *11:11 – Stories About the Event* was published under the pseudonym of MOJO (Heather Marie Margaitis, Oscar De Los Santos, JJ Sargent, and Emily M. Olson). Recently, I was interviewed about the amazing saga of eleven-eleven. The exchange underscores the origins of the phenomena for me, as well as the extent to which these numbers are present in my life:

Q: Let's begin at the beginning. When did you have your first encounter with the numbers that you and the rest of MOJO have chosen to label "The Event?"

A: I remember the very moment: I was driving down the freeway in my hometown in Texas one fall evening in 1980. A rock song came on the radio and the DJ said, "It's eleven-eleven." For some reason, my eyes fell to the icy blue digital numbers on the car's dash radio for confirmation. Four pillars stared me in the face: 11:11. That did it. I was hooked. It was all I could do to tear my eyes away from the clock and put them back on the road where they belonged.

Q: And after that?

A: I saw 11:11 everywhere. If it were just numbers on clocks, well, I might say that my mind had affixed itself to some visual pattern. But no. Even today, over twenty years later, I'll go to the grocery store and purchase several items and the total will be 11 dollars and 11 cents. I can't tell you how often that's happened to me. Or my change will be 11.11. Or at the end of the day, I'll find myself with eleven dollars in my wallet and eleven cents in my pocket. And while we're talking grocery stores, how about this: sometimes I'll come home and the expiration date on several of my canned goods will be 11/11! Or I'll email a letter to someone and without intending to do so, zing it off at exactly 11:11.

Q: That's crazy!

A: But true. All too true. Try this on for size: I was part of a small team that spent over two years radically revising the undergraduate and graduate English curriculums at my university. There were countless brainstorming sessions, writing pow-wows and conferences, but at long last, we were down to one final meeting. A committee had to approve the programs before we could implement them. Over two years in the making, mind you. Can you guess the actual time that the final vote was cast to green-light the programs? You'd be right if you answered 11:11. I checked my watch and was stunned.

Q: So it seems to me that you're alluding to a supernatural connection to the phenomenon. Is that correct?

A: Well, not exactly, although I don't think that you can completely dismiss that possibility. On the other hand, if you define supernatural as an event or phenomenon that goes beyond that which has been determined to be a regular and natural part of everyday existence, then I'm more comfortable associating the term with 11:11. After all, I do find it somewhat perplexing that this sequence of numbers seems to find its way into my day-to-day affairs far more often than any other pattern.

Q: Is it true that you've found many others that are also intrigued by 11:11?

A: [*Laughs*] Oh, you better believe it. Rest assured, the gang that comprises MOJO – Emily, JJ, Heather and I – isn't the only group that is being "haunted" [*laughs again*] by the numbers eleven-eleven. I can't tell you how many people have been floored when we get into discussions of the quirky and they reluctantly reveal that they've detected the 11:11 pattern in their own lives. It's very bizarre. JJ and I were best friends for years until one late-night conversation led us to discover that we both see 11:11 everywhere. Mind you, JJ grew up in New England and I did my stretching in South Texas. In some ways, we couldn't be more different; in others, we're very much alike. Still, we didn't know just how similar we were until we shared our eleven-eleven stories with each other.

Q: Bottom line: what does 11:11 mean to you?

A: Well, I can sit here and dwell on the strange dimensions that seem to be associated with the numbers. Some people even fixate on certain negative aspects of the phenomenon, but ultimately, for me they are a springboard to creativity. I'm a teacher, a writer and a critic. 11, 111, and 11:11 have fueled my imagination and enriched my stories. 11:11 gave birth to a book project and MOJO. In so doing, the numbers further solidified my friendship with my fellow book writers. For me, the positive far outweighs the negative. I hope 11:11 continues to motivate me and fuel my creativity.

ESP

Studies in extrasensory perception (ESP) indicate that some people may actually have the ability to read the minds of others. Some individuals seem more adept than others in this area. Tests indicate that a few rare subjects can divine information concealed behind walls, sealed envelopes and other obstructions. Many studies in ESP have been conducted under rigorous conditions and controlled settings. The results are often extraordinary. Some experts believe all of us are capable of developing our psychic abilities but too often we choose to ignore signals that hint at our capabilities in these areas. Many people are frightened by the notion that their own mental capacity might extend beyond the ordinary. They quickly dismiss any clue that indicates they have tapped into extrasensory capabilities. Once again, the importance of keeping an open mind is vital. If more of us kept ourselves open to the possibility that such mental feats are possible, who knows where our exploration might lead us?

Like most of us, I have not made it a point to test (let alone, exercise) my psychic abilities very often. Still, I probably do so more regularly than the majority of individuals. At least a few times a year, I engage in a simple experiment with friends. One of us will act as a *sender* and the other, a *receiver.* The designated sender will choose a number from 1 to 9 and try to project it into the mind of the receiver. The receiver, usually with closed eyes, tries to *see* the number the sender is projecting and identify it. The results are often remarkable. Sometimes senders identify seven out of ten numbers correctly. Other times the results are less than spectacular. It's important to recognize that not all senders make good receivers, and vice versa. Over the years, I have found that I am a far better sender than I am a receiver. Friends often think that I am pulling their leg and simply agreeing to whatever number they call out. Then I show them a written record of the session and they grow more impressed – and uneasy (more proof that anything that transcends normalcy tends to shake us up). However, while ESP may certainly be categorized with the supernatural, I don't think we need fear it. Nor do I think that this ability has much to do with apparitions, ghosts, hauntings or any kind of spirit intervention. Experts in the field of ESP concur that when we experience moments of heightened awareness, we have likely tapped into a type of mental ability that the human race has yet to learn to control. Human beings use no more than ten to twenty percent of their brain. The rest is still uncharted territory.

I encourage everyone to try the basic sender/receiver numerical experiment in psychic projection at least once At various periods in my life, I have engaged in these tests more often than others. Like most tasks, practice does improve one's capability to either send or receive. (A few tips: If you are the sender, it's a good idea to jot down the number that you are projecting. Keep the number hidden from the receiver until the experiment is over. Also, keep track of the number of hits and misses in a given session. A systematic record of successes and failures from session to session will let you know if you are improving or staying neutral in your efforts.)

Another form of testing can be accomplished with psychic cards. These cards may be purchased but a crude set may easily be drawn at home. They consist primarily of geometric shapes (circle, square, triangle, three horizontal wavy lines drawn atop each other, and star). The sender attempts to project these shapes into the mind of the receiver. I have used such cards on a few occasions and the results have been average – except on one occasion. During one session in the early eighties, one of my friends acted as a sender and projected the shapes to me. We kept a careful record of the session. On this occasion, I got an amazing seventeen hits out of twenty-one attempts! I wish I had kept up with this young woman and we had engaged in more such sessions. Her ability to send was uncanny, especially when I consider the fact that I'm usually a very poor receiver. Unfortunately, we lost track of each other.

I am convinced that many people experience moments of ESP without even realizing it. After all, people are more comfortable attributing moments of uncanny intuition to coincidence than to the supernatural. However, when several such incidents fall upon the heels of each other in rapid succession, the entire series of strangeness may be worthy of more consideration than most people are willing to devote to it. To reiterate, I think that most people are too ready to dismiss the highly unusual from their lives. The alternative – to admit that one has had an encounter with the supernatural –

is tougher to accept, primarily because we tend to fear the unknown. At the same time, most of these cases are likely just a sign that our mind is capable of doing far more than we are currently aware.

How far does the power of the mind extend? Certainly it is one thing to read the thoughts of another person, and quite another to actually use the mind to move an object. Yet that is precisely what may be happening in cases that involve telekinesis. (For more on this subject, see the section in Chapter Three entitled, "Telekinesis, Psychic Energy or Signal from a Spirit?")

Onward

It's time to shift our focus some twenty-six hundred miles northeast of Corpus Christi, Texas. Before I married my ex-wife – a lifetime New Yorker – she took a map of the United States and drew a horizontal line across it, cutting the country in half. She vowed never to live underneath the line. That ruled out my home state. The irony, of course, is that we now lead separate lives. Yet even though we're divorced, I've grown firmly entrenched in this part of the country. I fell in love with it the moment I arrived. Maybe some part of my unconscious always knew that I would end up in this part of the United States. Indeed, my mother still reminds me that when I was young and obsessing on the old *Dark Shadows* TV show, which was set in Maine, I used to vow to live in New England someday. The odds of that occurring seemed remote when I was a little Latino kid running across sun-scorched South Texas fields. Yet destiny works strangely. Certainly, New England is as much a hotbed of paranormal activity as Texas – perhaps even more so. New England is a much older part of the nation than my native Texas. As a result, it's as easy to run into someone who knows a good scary story up here as it was in the Lone Star State. And as you will soon see, many New Englanders have told me disturbing tales that they've lived firsthand.

Part II: New England

CHAPTER 3

PARANORMAL INVESTIGATIONS
IN NEW ENGLAND

Adventures in Supernatural Sleuthing

Late one night when I was about eighteen, I stopped by a 7-11 in Corpus Christi, Texas and gave the paperback rack a spin. Nothing looked very tempting until I knelt and went through the bottom pockets of the rack. There I found a copy of *The Demonologist* by Ed and Lorraine Warren and Gerald Brittle. Such was my introduction to the Warrens, arguably the most famous "ghost busting" team in 20th century America. Ed is a demonologist – a man who knows more about the supernatural and the ways to combat it than anyone I've ever met. Lorraine is clairvoyant. She senses paranormal entities, both benevolent and malevolent. In *The Demonologist*, the Warrens' first of many books, I read about some of their most famous encounters with the unknown, including tales of a possessed Raggedy Ann doll that wreaked havoc upon the life of one young woman, Ouija boards that tore apart the psyche of another victim and the Warrens' firsthand investigation of the now infamous "Amityville horror" case. Over the next few years, I read each of the Warrens' books as they appeared. Imagine my surprise, years later, when I ended up practically living in their backyard! I mean this literally; without intentionally doing so, my ex-wife and I bought a house a few short miles down the road from the Warrens in New England. Frequently, I would encounter Lorraine at the grocery store and I attended their seminars on the paranormal on a regular basis.

My first face-to-face meeting with the Warrens made me think about my mother's recollections regarding my childhood vow to one day live in New England. The ghost-busting duo came to lecture at Western Connecticut State University, where I teach. I attended the lecture and afterward, I went up to meet the couple. The first thing that Ed said as he extended his hand and gave me an enthusiastic handshake was, "We've met before." I was sure we hadn't, but Ed was insistent. Then I walked over to Lorraine and she said the exact same thing; she asked me how I'd been and what was new. I was flattered but a little thrown off. Having read their many books half a continent away, I *did* feel as though I knew the Warrens. Could they have picked up the same sort of energy from me? Who knows. I recalled my mother stating that as a child, I was sure I would live in New England someday. Maybe that explains why Ed and Lorraine Warren felt they already knew me.

One of the Warrens' books focuses on Union Cemetery, which many people claim is the most haunted graveyard in America. Ed and Lorraine have logged countless hours and unearthed (no pun intended) scores of disturbing stories about this cemetery, located off Route 57 in Easton, CT. I cannot recommend the Warrens' texts highly enough. They are a veritable storehouse of facts and insights into the world of the supernatural. Further, the Warrens and their son-in-law, a fellow psychic sleuth, lecture throughout the New England area. Their talks are supplemented with fascinating photos, audio and videotaped images of haunted homes and folk. Just as I never would have believed that I would one day end up living near and getting to know the Warrens, I never would have thought that I would also find myself living a few short miles from Union Cemetery. I'd read a great deal about Union over the years. Naturally, when I discovered I was living very close to "the most haunted graveyard in North America," I had to check it out for myself. I'm glad I did. My friends and I had two strange encounters with *something* at the site.

A Crackle in the Wind and A Bird in the Pocket

It was a little after eleven one summer night when JJ Sargent and I finally decided to put our work aside. We had been doing some writing at my university office in Danbury, Connecticut. Now it was time to save our data onto a computer diskette and shift gears, from literary critiquing to supernatural sleuthing. For some time, JJ and I had been meaning to visit Union Cemetery, but time and schedule constraints kept forcing us to put off the investigation. Tonight was the night and we were ready, camera in hand and minds prepared to face the unknown.

It took us about forty-five minutes to drive from Danbury to Easton. The graveyard is quite isolated and, at the time, free from most artificial lights. I swung the car through the graveyard gates and my headlights cut swaths across ancient tombstones. It was a good night to investigate: cool and clear, with low humidity. Above us, the sky was a black velvet blanket strewn with bright stars. It was so clear, in fact, that we could see the Milky Way Trail streaking across the sky. Even if we struck out in the ghost department, JJ and I decided, the nocturnal visit to Union had already paid off aesthetically. (A friendly bit of ghost-hunting advice: If you decide to venture into the world of "ghost busting," it's extremely important to make sure that the weather is cooperating. Ideally, I have found, clear nights work best for such inquiries. This way, if you should be lucky enough to capture something extraordinary in a photograph, you can rule out inclement weather as a contributor to your ghostly picture.)

JJ and I wandered about the cemetery. Every now and then I would snap a photo. We didn't rush through the experience. Instead, we tried to acclimate ourselves to our mysterious surroundings – and allow anything that was present to acclimate itself to us. Then, as I wandered about the tombstones I suddenly hit upon what can best be described as a *cold pocket*. This area that I stepped into was positively *frigid* compared to the rest of the cemetery. I snapped a picture and called to JJ. As he was moving toward my location, I suddenly felt something scamper up my arm.

"Damn spider," I muttered and brushed it off with my left hand. As I did, I discovered that whatever I felt on my arm was no spider or insect. My arm crackled and snapped sharply as my hand brushed my forearm from wrist to elbow!

"What the hell!"

"What is it?" JJ asked.

"My arm!" I switched hands and shot my right hand up my left arm. Once again, I heard faint sizzling and crackling. "Both of them! They're electrified or something."

I know that sounds funny but my rattrap memory still remembers exactly what I spouted at the time.

"What do you mean?" JJ asked. Then he didn't need further explanation. He mimicked my motion and the results were even more astounding. If my arms crackled softly, JJ's sizzled loudly as he repeated the forearm-brushing movements!

JJ moved slowly about the cold pocket region. When we left it, the cold disappeared, as did the surprising electrical reaction of our bodies to the area. Yet when we were in the cold pocket, JJ played a jarring symphony of electronic snaps and sizzles as his hands did slow sweeps of his forearms. I shot a few more pictures and then we hurried out of the cemetery.

A trip to a diner was in order. JJ and I sat and discussed the incident. Both of us had heard about Union Cemetery for years. Both of us had read about it. We had each listened to Ed and Lorraine Warren expound upon it with great insight. We had studied some of the Warrens' amazing photographs of the place, but neither one of us had ever visited the graveyard before this evening. While we had approached the investigation with open minds, we weren't expecting tremendous results on our first visit. How wrong we were! The night's experience more than fulfilled our wildest expectations.

Everything seemed alright until JJ's eyes suddenly went saucer round and an expletive flew out of his mouth.

"What now?" I asked.

"Our work, man," he said, pulling the computer diskette out of his pocket. "The two hours of writing that we did back at the university! Flushed down the drain!"

He was right. Electromagnetism destroys software data. If we had indeed experienced some kind of electromagnetic psychic phenomena at Union that night, the computer diskette was history. Then I smiled. "That's great!"

"You're crazy! What do you mean?"

"Don't you see," I said, "that's the placebo! That's the little bird in the cage. Get it? That's the birdy we carried into the mineshaft – Union Cemetery – with us for safety and warning. That disk was fine before we left my office. You know it and I know it. We double-checked it. If there's a problem with it now, that means we really experienced something supernatural tonight. I already know we did. You do, too. But that's our backup – our double-checking device."

We raced to JJ's home and popped the disk into his computer. The glowing message on the screen both elated and spooked us all over again. It read: "ERROR! CANNOT OPEN FILE. MAGNETIC DAMAGE TO DISK."

The Mad Monk and Company

To reiterate, JJ Sargent and I collaborated on *11:11 – Stories About the Event*, a book of short stories written with two other writers (see Chapter 2, "11:11"). When it came time to shoot a picture for the back cover of the book, we decided to pick a location that embodied our love of the quirky and strange. Off we headed to Union Cemetery.

It was a gray fall day, cloudy but without a trace of rain in the area. The four of us shot many photos on several cameras. JJ was in full monk's regalia. (JJ's wearing the monk's robe shouldn't be considered a sign of disrespect. He has firm religious ties and is an ordained minister.)   Shortly after we arrived, I asked JJ to mug for a test shot. Ever the flamboyant individual, he spread his arms wide and took a dramatic stance. Little did we know that a host of ethereal entities would be captured in that one particular photo!

Once I got the photos developed, I scanned them into the computer and studied them carefully. It's amazing what the big vibrant electronic screen brings out in a well-taken picture. Most of the photos are fairly innocuous. They capture our writing group in various poses and moods, from the serious to the silly. JJ's mug shot, however, is unquestionably troublesome. As I studied it, I thought I detected curious shadows among some of the tombstones. Were they phantom faces? I couldn't be sure. I pointed out several of these anomalies to JJ. He agreed they could be comprised of something other than shadows.

"Take a look over my right shoulder, though," JJ said. "There's no doubt about that one."

I studied the picture once again and I was rocked by what I saw. There, perfectly visible behind JJ, was the leering mustached and cowl-faced image of an entity I have chosen to call "the mad monk." This monk may be mocking JJ's more serious use of the monk robe. The ghost of the mad monk stares directly at the viewer with dead white orbs.

"Now, check out the figure near the mad monk's left shoulder," JJ said. Once again, I was completely shocked by what I saw. "I call him the fair-faced man."

There, to the left of the monk, is another cowled figure, this one with a pasty white visage.

There was one more surprise in the photo. This discovery was made by my friend Lisa. One night, I booted up the picture on the computer screen and proceeded to tell her about the entities clearly visible in the photograph. Before I could even point them out with the pen in my hand, Lisa pointed to the photo herself and said, "Oh, yeah! Right there! That's so *creepy!*"

It was creepy all over again for me, too. Instead of pointing to JJ's left shoulder, Lisa pointed to the space directly above JJ's right hand. There, floating on air and clearly visible, was a figure with a sardonic face, complete with pointed ears! How could we have missed this entity in the first place? I have no answer to this question. In many ways, the entity that Lisa spotted looks like a cross between a demon and the wide-eyed classic visage that twentieth century culture has come to recognize as a "space alien." For that reason, I've chosen to label him the Alien Devil. (This photo and others may be viewed on my website – http://www.loonyscribe.com.)

As this book was going through its final revisions in summer 2003, one final and disturbing entity was found by Janet, Valter, Katie, and Jessica, a group of paranormal enthusiasts with whom I shared the photo. This particular monstrosity is to the left of the Alien Devil. It resembles an old hooded hag, but its body looks like that of a fat black bird. Two slender legs allow it to perch atop a tombstone.

I have no idea how JJ and I could have missed this creature after studying the photo so closely. I am just as puzzled by the fact that the day following the group's discovery of the black "Hag Bird," I was riding with JJ down a Connecticut country road and telling him about this discovery, when all of a sudden a huge black bird dove right in front of JJ's car and was crushed beneath its wheels!

Haunted Vortex

My second dramatic moment in Union Cemetery took place by day. My old friend and fellow Texas "Crest District" investigator Sam came up for a fall visit a couple of years ago. Sam requested to see Union and I drove him out to the cemetery. Once there, we tramped over leaf-strewn aisles and shot pictures of tombstones. The afternoon was crisp and cold and the weather, cooperative. This particular visit yielded nothing on celluloid; nevertheless, something very unsettling occurred after we had been at the graveyard for about a quarter hour. All of a sudden, the wind rose up around us and began to whip at our jackets and the leaves on the ground, stirring them up and sending them swirling higher and higher. I stared at the incredible display as the wind rose higher and whined around trees and tombstones in whirlwind frenzy – literally. We gazed up as the leaf-vortex grew taller and thicker, way over our heads, rising twenty, thirty, forty, fifty feet. I could hardly believe it but we were witnessing a mini-cyclone coming alive and growing stronger before our eyes. Sam and I were at opposite ends of the inverted triangle of wind. As we watched leaves doing lazy circles high above and the twister begin to dissipate, we looked at each other in wonder. Could this have been nothing more than a curious natural anomaly? Certainly. But the odds of that being the case while the two of us stood at Union Cemetery makes it seem unlikely to me. I believe that the twister was another case of the spirits that reside in "the most haunted graveyard in America" greeting their respectful visitors.

The Graveyard Mystery Continues

I am certain that I have encountered the unknown at Union Cemetery. The incidents I have focused upon are the most striking, but seldom do I venture to that particular graveyard and come away "empty handed." In fact, sometimes my spirit seems to anticipate the visit and begin unconscious preparation for the journey. For example, I remember getting ready to make a quick trip to the cemetery one October afternoon to shoot some pictures. I was married at the time and living a short distance away from Union (about a fifteen-minute drive). As I loaded the camera with film, a little song came into my head for no reason whatsoever. I've never heard the song or melody, but I started to sing it softly: "Let's go out to the pumpkin patch, let's go out to the pumpkin patch, let's go out to the pumpkin patch . . ." I kept repeating the phrase as I left my study and bounded down the stairs. Suddenly, my wife shot out of our bedroom and asked me what I was singing. I paused for a moment and had to think about it. "Nothing," I said.

"Yes, you were."

"Oh, it's just a silly song I made up," I said, embarrassed.

"How does it go again?"

Now I was really red-faced. "It's really nothing."

"Sing it again," she said.

I did. "Let's go out to the pumpkin patch. . ."

My wife looked downstairs at me, a perplexed expression on her face. "You didn't see me come in from shopping earlier, did you?"

"No. Why?"

"Look what I just bought." She disappeared from the top landing for a moment, then returned with a pretty vest in hand. "I was just hanging it in the closet when I heard you."

My ex-wife loved vests. Draped on a hanger was a colorful orange, black and green assembly with a black silk back. The front is what intrigued me, though: splashed on either side was a plethora of cats doing wild springs and summersaults over acres and acres of pumpkins nestled in a moonlit patch! Was my psyche so charged up for my impending trip to Union Cemetery that I picked up vibes from my then wife? I don't know, but I've long puzzled over this particular incident.

Photographing the Dead

Over the years, I have shot many photographs at Union Cemetery. Some of these pictures seem to offer proof that the graveyard is haunted by beings from another realm of existence. I have detected a pattern in photographing curious anomalies and I offer another tip if you are going to engage in this kind of activity. It's a good idea to walk around a location before you really start shooting. Further, pace yourself as you take the photographs; consider shooting more than one roll of film. Chance are that if you shoot an entire roll within your first few minutes of arriving in a supposedly haunted site, you will get a bunch of good pictures but not necessarily pictures that capture any sort of paranormal phenomena. Take a little time to acclimate yourself to a location – and allow any phenomena in the location to grow acclimated to your presence – and you stand a better chance of capturing something out of the ordinary. At times I have shot photos at Union Cemetery and with the progression of the roll, I find more and more hovering globules of light invading my photographs. Paranormal investigators frequently refer to these luminescent anomalies as "spirit lights." Supposedly, these lights are actually spirits making their presence known via dancing balls of energy.

Rest assured that not every outing to a haunted site yields successful data. Indeed, there are many occasions when the paranormal sleuth comes up empty-handed. I have shot my share of photos at many paranormal locations that have been quite unremarkable. (This is why digital cameras are such valuable tools for the contemporary "ghost buster." It's possible to shoot virtually hundreds of photos on digital camera and load them up into your computer without sending them out to be developed. These digital photographs are as sharp as – and in many cases, even sharper than – the photos taken by many film cameras.)

Quite often, a number of factors come into play in the success or failure rate of a paranormal photo shoot. Most important is one's frame of mind. If you approach such an outing in a stress-free and open-minded mode, you are far more likely to capture something of interest. Second, pay attention to your feelings throughout your stay at a haunted location. Keep your wits about you. If you begin to feel extremely uneasy or filled with heightened awareness, it is likely time to start snapping a few pictures. There have been several times when an uneasy or agitated feeling invaded me in the midst of checking out a haunted site. I've tried to act quickly during these moments and snapped several photos in rapid succession. Sometimes every photo in the roll will be normal except for one or two shots taken when the disturbing feeling came over me. On one such occasion, I shot thirty-five sharp but undistinguished photographs of graves and monuments in a cemetery on a very clear night, but in the middle of the roll, I captured a massive streak hovering over two tombstones.

I encourage anyone who visits a supposedly haunted domain to take a camera and try to capture the paranormal on film. The cost of such a venture is relatively inexpensive and photos can substantiate any strange experiences you have at the site. Not everyone is successful at photographing ghosts and other unusual phenomena. Like anything else, some people are more psychic than others and some people enter these investigations with a more open mind than others. Even "true believers" in the paranormal do not always have success in photographing spirits. At times, however, the rewards can be both gratifying and disturbing.

Haunted New England

New England has had several centuries to build a history of hauntings. Union Cemetery is but one of many haunted places that I've investigated during my time in this region. My friend JJ Sargent and I have trekked up and down state roads locating countless other hotspots of paranormal activity. For example, deep in the woods of Litchfield County are the remains of Dudleytown. Residents still refer to the area by that name. Many stories have circulated about the ancient settlement and the people who lived there. Legend has it that some of Dudleytown's residents went stark raving mad overnight. Others say the town was simply abandoned because of bad energy emanating from the countryside itself.

JJ and I took a hike into these woods and found the remnants of Dudleytown. Ultimately, what struck us as most baffling about this investigation was not what we saw or photographed but what actually occurred in the course of our hike. It took us a good hour and a half to circumnavigate our way through the dense foliage and find the ancient remains of the village (cellar foundations; dilapidated chimney structures; a few rotting wall frames), but our return trip to the car took us just over twenty minutes! This was incredible, considering that we followed the same route out of Dudleytown that we took to get to it. Even allotting for a few minutes of looking around, how could we have trekked the same distance away from the site in a third of the time it took us to get there? This is the only time I've encountered time displacement in the course of my paranormal investigations. It still makes my head reel when I think about it, and I'm glad I had a witness there to substantiate the event. Even before I said anything upon reaching the car, JJ had a puzzled look on his face. We both agreed that even though the remains of Dudleytown turned out to be less than spectacular, getting there and back was truly extraordinary. While this is my first and only experience with so-called "missing time," JJ had a previous encounter with temporal displacement. His other story will be discussed in the next chapter (see "*IT* Runs in the Family").

Another night found JJ and I investigating the woods surrounding the town of Moodus, where echoing moans have long been heard emanating from beneath the earth. One day, we drove across the Cornwall Bridge, where apparitions are said to materialize quite frequently. And on still another occasion, we explored the forgotten, dilapidated wing of an infamous hospital long known for housing some of the state's most mentally disturbed citizens. As we made our way through the ancient, labyrinthine wings of the hospital, I was shocked to see ancient manacles dangling from the walls of small rooms. These patient rooms more accurately resembled jail cells than hospital settings. Another part of the hospital looked, for all intents and purposes, to be a crematorium. It was in this building that JJ used his arms to play a repeat performance of the unsettling electromagnetic symphony we first heard at Union Cemetery.

One of the great things about living in New England is the fact that you can state-hop very rapidly. I live in Connecticut, but because of the close proximity of other states in the area, I have been able to investigate the paranormal in other parts of New England. Still, it's a big area and there are many stories worthy of checking out. Too many for one person. I'll leave it to other sources to fully explore haunted Salem, Massachusetts. Suffice to say that the Salem witch trials themselves are a blemish on our country's past and they underscore the gullibility and narrow-mindedness of many individuals. However, although I believe the people who were put to death for being witches and associating with the devil were innocent, I also believe that this tragedy may have imbued the area with the presence of the spirit world. Ghosts haunt the Salem area not because they are the souls of witches who will not rest, but because they are the spirits of innocent people falsely accused and robbed of their corporeal existence on this earth.

Rhode Island is steeped in history, paranormal and otherwise. Newport is one of my favorite places to visit. Just as there are the official mansions tours and self-guided walking tours along the rocky coastal cliffs, there are unofficial ghost tours of Newport. Although there have been a few slim volumes written about Rhode Island hauntings, this area is still in much need of further investigation. The same might be said for the many lighthouses dotting the New England coastline. Lighthouses are notoriously haunted sites. There are many stories to be found in these structures.

New Hampshire has its share of ghostly dwellings. In the summer of 2002, I took a trip to the "Old Man of the Mountain" state and investigated Danvers State Mental Hospital. This gargantuan gothic structure is located off New England Interstate I-95, just north of Danvers, Massachusetts. The hospital is now abandoned. It is truly one of the most foreboding sites I have visited. The dilapidated hospital sits on hundreds of acres. It sprawls castle-like atop a hill, mammoth in size. Many ghost sightings have been reported on the grounds of these gloomy premises. Perhaps this is due to the cemeteries residing on the grounds of the Danvers hospital. Until recently, these graveyards were weed-infested and neglected. Even today, hundreds and hundreds of tombstones are still marked only by numbers. Who were these seven hundred-plus people? Are their souls crying out for attention?

It is no surprise that Danvers Hospital inspired horror grandmaster H. P. Lovecraft to write at least one of his most disturbing tales, "The Thing on the Doorstep." Moreover, the hospital lives on, in some ways, thanks to D.C. Comics. Several comic book writers and critics insist that Danvers State Hospital is the inspiration for Arkham Asylum in the D.C. comic book universe. Super villains such as the Joker, Mr. Freeze, Poison Ivy and others are routinely housed in Arkham. Other critics and fans insist that Arkham Asylum is derived from Lovecraft's stories. Even if the latter is the case, then the seeds of Danvers Hospital are buried in the comic books' Arkham Asylum. Most recently, Danvers Hospital served as the setting for a disquieting horror film called *Session Nine*. In this story, several men who are renovating the hospital fall prey to malevolent spirits. The setting of the ancient hospital enhances the story's horrific elements.

During that same trip to New Hampshire, I visited "America's Stonehenge." This place resonates with the energy of people who walked and lived in ancient rock dwellings thousands of years ago. That same energy can be found in Celtic ruins located in the woods of Southern New York and in the stone believed to be a dolman for long-gone inhabitants of the area now known as South Salem, New York. I never miss out on the opportunity to explore such ancient sites. Even when nothing overtly supernatural manifests itself while I visit, even if all the photographs I take turn out to be no more than beautiful shots of nature, these sites are steeped in history. Each in its own way sings the songs of ancient days and peoples.

Given my propensity to experience psychic phenomena, I'm not surprised – but very gratified – that I've had some amazing encounters with the spirit world in New England. As long as such experiences remain non-malevolent, I hope they continue.

Telekinesis, Psychic Energy or Signal from a Spirit?

It's probably no surprise that I go "all out" when it comes to decorating during Halloween season. My house becomes a veritable haunted dungeon, with a wide variety of curios and props set up in the TV room. This is not only a throwback to my childhood and my lifetime love of ghost stories, monster movies and the like, but a part of my Spanish-American and Mexican-American heritages. In South Texas, the Halloween rituals are tied to Mexico's Day of the Dead. While many Americans celebrate Halloween strictly on the night of October Thirty-First, Mexico honors its dead with a celebration that begins on the Thirty-First of October and runs through the Second of November. The first day of November is celebrated as All Saints Day. It is also known as *El Dia de los Muertos.* November Second is known as All Souls Day. In many regions, November First is reserved for remembering the deaths of infants and small children. On All Souls Day, the souls of dead adults are honored. Both days are reserved to acknowledge that at one time these dead men, women and children were once a very special part of the family in the world of the living, and that they are still remembered fondly and missed. In Mexico, families host a variety of parties, celebrations and picnics on All Saints Day. Food and pastries are designed to resemble skeletons and coffins. Piñatas are used at birthday parties throughout the year. At All Saints Day parties, children bang piñatas shaped like skulls, cadavers, witches, or werewolves until the macabre representations crack and rain sweet treats down on them. Throughout these days, those who have died are lauded. At lunchtime, families head to the cemetery and carefully clean up the gravesites of loved ones. Tablecloths are spread out and massive picnic baskets are unloaded. Beer and wine are poured liberally. People eat their feasts close to their departed. Naturally, plates of food are prepared for loved ones and left near their tombstones. Children play around the cemetery or *campo santo* (literal translation: *sacred camp*). Neighbors visit with each other and their departed friends in the earth. In the evening, hundreds of candles are lit and the celebration continues. All Saints Day reminds believers that physical death is but a transition from one form of life to another. On this day, the coming afterlife is celebrated, along with the abandonment of our physical trappings.

I always leave my Halloween decorations up a few days into November to remember All Saints Day and All Souls Day. My props honor the many souls who have passed on, but I reserve special reflection for my departed father. I'm also wishing him a happy birthday, since he was born on All Saint's Day, November First (hence his name, Santos De Los Santos – Saint of the Saints).

Halloween season 2001 was initially no different than other Octobers past. Throughout the month of October, I watch horror films whenever I get a chance. I also host a party and all-night fright-film fest on Halloween night. For me, however, Halloween reached its apex a little earlier than usual in 2001. About a week before October Thirty-

First, I had a most remarkable run-in with the fantastic. Most people simply get to read about such incidents or see them depicted in horror films. I was inches away from the real thing.

A few days before Halloween, my friends Don and Tara stopped by my New England home for dinner and a movie. I'm a pretty good cook but Don spent years working in the restaurant and country club business before becoming an editor for an academic press, so I stepped out of his way and fell into the role of assistant kitchen gofer (as in "Go for this. . ." and "Go for that. . ."). One excellent meal later, we stepped into the living room where I asked my friends to pick out a movie from my extensive collection. They chose *The Craft*, an interesting film about modern day teen witches. Although the powers these girls obtain are more closely associated with the forces of earth and nature, *The Craft* is an excellent study of what can happen when too much power is acquired by the undisciplined. Supernatural power corrupts several young characters in the film; similarly, undisciplined power may have been the cause of events that occurred in my home that night.

Within minutes, Don, Tara and I were riveted by the movie. Don sat on one end of the couch, Tara curled up on the opposite end and I slouched into a rocker near the TV. The lights in the room were dimmed, the DVD print was sharp and letterboxed, and the sound was pristine as it filtered out of my stereo system. There are several moments in *The Craft* when spells are recited by the characters. There is also a scene in which the girls play a game called "light as a feather." I've never met any males who played this game, but over the years, I've met several women who claim to have played this game at various slumber parties in their youth. The object of the game is for two or three girls to gather around a "victim" and chant "light as a feather, stiff as a board" and raise the supine volunteer into the air. The chanters lift the body using only one or two fingers from each hand. Some former players swear that they had spectacular results playing the game as kids.

In *The Craft*, the "light as a feather" experiment is successful: three of the girls raise a fourth as they chant "light as a feather" and use a couple of fingers from each hand to elevate her.

Then, as the scene neared its climax, my TV did something it has never done before: the channel suddenly switched from the one used to transmit the DVD signal to a dead, noisy, static-filled channel.

Don and Tara whipped their heads my way. They thought I was monkeying with one of the remotes that run my electronic set-up but as they could see, the controls were nowhere near my chair. I raised my open hands in an "I'm innocent" gesture, got up and found the right remote to switch the TV back to its proper channel. We continued to watch the film. During another tense moment in the film, as spells are being chanted, the same thing happened. This time, I grew a little uneasy but I simply turned the TV back to the right station and allowed the film to roll on. Finally, during one of the movie's most tension-filled moments, as three of the characters gang up on their former friend and have a showdown with her, one of the candles on the coffee table before us leaped into the air and rolled underneath the table!

I can't emphasize just how remarkable an incident this is in the context of a lifetime of investigating the paranormal. I've felt the presence of the supernatural, I've photographed it, I've seen entities appear before me (the demon at dawn, the image of the Virgin Mary at night), but seldom have I ever witnessed such a blatant textbook example of paranormal phenomena. Moreover, I had witnesses who saw the same thing!

Tara screamed when the candle leaped into the air. After all, the object was sitting directly in front of her before the incident, resting atop a heavy metal base. Off to the side and at a 45-degree angle from Tara, I too could claim a front row seat to the candle when it jumped. Even Don – a born skeptic when it comes to the supernatural and the only one of us who didn't have a straight view of the candle – acknowledged that he saw it leap into the air because it was placed between his seat and the TV screen. Indeed, after a good half hour of talk and investigation, it was skeptical Don who asked that we finish the movie. As he put it: "We can sit here all night trying to figure it out but we're not going to get anyplace. And the more we talk about it, the more it's starting to freak me out." This admission came from a staunch cynic when it comes to the supernatural!

But what happened? What made the candle leap into the air as it did? Is it fair to say that a spirit was making itself known in my New England home that night? I don't think so. I think that something else flung the candle into the air and that something is the collective energy that Don, Tara and I mustered up on this particular night. First of all, the entire month of October is charged with positive vibes for me. I see it not as a time to revel in negativity but a time to celebrate the idea of another life that awaits our physical existence. Another important factor: the rapport established between the three of us who were present. There was camaraderie and the spirit (no pun intended) of genuine friendship in the air, as there often is when we get together. Finally, I believe we chose the right movie for something like the candle levitation to occur. I distinctly remember casting a surreptitious glance at my friends and reflecting on just how deeply all of us were engaged in *The Craft*. I assert that our combined positive vibes and our intense focus on the picture resulted in the paranormal activity we witnessed as the film progressed. I have no hard proof to this effect, of course, but part of *The Craft* deals with the harnessing of one's own untapped powers and channeling them to do extraordinary things. The girls in the film cast spells and get others to do their bidding. They levitate a friend using very little physical exertion. They learn to tap into their psychic potential and use it to move objects mentally. This is what may have happened on the night that Don, Tara and I screened *The Craft*. We tapped into that unexplored cerebral territory that I mentioned earlier. Perhaps we hit upon some collective form of telekinesis and performed a variation of the "light as a feather" experiment, without the use of fingers. The TV fluctuations from live channel to dead air were the first intimations of things to come. The levitating candle may have been the fruit of our unknowing but combined efforts mimicking that which was unfolding on the television screen before us.

Unquestionably, something extraordinary took place that night. We pushed the envelope of normalcy and moved into supernatural territory, but I believe it was some power residing in us which caused the amazing manifestations that we witnessed, not a ghost.

I have devoted this chapter to New England paranormal experiences I have experienced or investigated firsthand. It is time to shift the lens to others in the region. One of the things I have discovered is that almost everyone has a story with supernatural overtones or undertones buried in their repertoire. Much of the time, all you need do is ask and the stories flow forth. Some are more reluctant to share their tales, but they will often tell you about a friend of a friend who saw a ghost or moved into a haunted house or—

But enough of the hypothetical scenarios. Read on and you'll see exactly what I mean.

CHAPTER 4

NEW ENGLAND FRIENDS FACE
THE UNKNOWN

"I swear this happened to me one night. . ."

I live a long way from Texas these days but I've been fortunate to meet some great friends in New England. The following section is devoted to their encounters with the unexplained. I have found that in New England as in Texas, most people have at least one curious story to tell – one particular incident that they or a relative or a friend has experienced – one occurrence that cannot be easily explained, given our current knowledge of the world and its laws of operation. Most people who have experienced an encounter with the unknown are eager to tell their story, once they sense a genuine and open-minded interest on my end. And with a little coaxing, even those who don't have their own incident to relate are usually willing to tell a tale that happened to a friend or relative. This isn't too surprising. Since the birth of oral storytelling, tales of ghosts, haunted houses and supernatural phenomena have been popular throughout the world. They are often our first step toward inquiring whether some form of life beyond the realm of the physical world actually exists. And at times, as some of the following stories underscore, these tales seem to offer proof that such is indeed the case.

Spirit in the Park

Two of my university colleagues shared some remarkable stories with me. The first colleague I'll call Michelle, a gifted playwright with a keen interest in Things Fantastic. Michelle tells me that she is the most open-minded and spiritual of her family members but that on one occasion, her son had a remarkable experience at Ninham Mountain, near the Hudson Valley, in New York. Michelle's son and a friend were in the middle of a two-day hiking trip around Ninham Mountain Forest one fall day when they began to lose daylight. They found a good location and set about pitching their tent and gathering wood for a small campfire. One of the two young men was near the base of the mountain when he turned around and looked over at the pile of sticks to determine how much more wood needed to be gathered for the fire. What he saw froze him in his tracks. Beyond the tent and campfire-in-the-making, a Native American crept slowly through the underbrush, moving closer to their campsite.

Michelle's son was near some fallen tree branches when he heard his friend call out. He turned and immediately spotted the intruder.

"You seeing that?" his friend asked.

Michelle's son nodded. "Absolutely."

Dusk was upon them, but they saw the Native American clearly as he made his way closer to their location. The day quickly lost its warmth with the setting sun and a chill invaded their domain. Yet the Native American wore little more than a pair of pants made out of some animal skin. The two young men stared at their approaching visitor. Then, upon arriving at the unlit campfire, he grew transparent and vanished. The duo was understandably shaken and decided to pull down the tent and abort the overnight campout.

Many stories of Native American spirits circulate around Ninham Mountain and nearby Fahnestock Park, near Cold Spring, New York. Perhaps these hauntings are linked to the mineral energy many believe slowly seeps out of the mountain and surrounding landscape. People who hike certain parts of the area regularly report sudden headaches, nosebleeds and unexpected menstruation when they trek through areas around Ninham Mountain and Fahnestock Park. There have been myriad ghost sightings in the area and reports of active and residual hauntings. Not all of the supernatural activity witnessed around the Hudson Valley plays itself out like a recorded image. People have actually reported interaction with ghosts on the mountain.

Another possible explanation for paranormal incidents in these locations might be the stark evidence of a Celtic presence there that dates back thousands of years. Phil Imbrogno and Marianne Horrigan's *Celtic Mysteries in New England* provides an in-depth analysis of the mysterious chambers around Ninham Mountain and Fahnestock Park. The authors also discuss the possible connection between the paranormal activities in the area and UFO sightings around the Hudson Valley. The incident experienced by Michelle's son is but one of countless similar tales reported to have take place around the Hudson Valley. This region is worthy of hours of further investigation by professional and amateur paranormal enthusiasts, as well as those interested in exploring the mystery behind unidentified flying objects.

A Dead Man Phones for Help

Another colleague had a paranormal experience in her office at the university – in broad daylight! Elizabeth was between classes one afternoon and holding office hours. She had just finished seeing a student when the telephone rang.

"Elizabeth? How are you? Listen, it's George."

"George!" Elizabeth was happy to hear from her old friend. Only days before, he had been quite ill. In fact, a mere day before, George braved emergency surgery. Elizabeth considered it a miracle that she was speaking to her friend. "My goodness, this is a surprise, but it's I who should be asking *you* how you're doing!"

"Not good," George said. "I don't know where I am. I'm so confused."

"George, what do you mean? Surely they haven't released you already?"

"Released me from where? Dammit all, Liz, I can't find my way around here. I don't know where here is. I need help."

Suddenly, my colleague grew very concerned. Her friend had obviously managed to get up from his bed and was wandering undetected in some obscure corridor of the hospital. She knew it was important to get George help, but she also wanted to reassure him. Elizabeth put on her calmest voice. "George, you be still and stay put. I'm going to make sure everything's okay. Stand by."

"Oh, would you, please? Thank you, Liz. I'm so lost right now."

Elizabeth soothed her friend again and hung up the phone. Quickly, she dialed the hospital's main number and explained her friend's predicament.

"You need to attend to your patient immediately," she admonished the operator. "And shame on you for not watching him closer! You have a very sick man wandering your hallways and need to find him."

The attendant put Elizabeth on hold. A few minutes later, a no-nonsense sounding gentleman came on the phone and asked Elizabeth to identify herself. She did and once again admonished the hospital for being negligent and letting George wander the halls. The voice on the other end of the phone cut her off.

"Either this is a very sick prank or you're telling the truth and I'm at a loss as to how to proceed," said the man on the phone.

"What are you talking about?" Elizabeth asked. "Go find my friend – your patient – immediately."

"Ma'am, I know exactly where he is right now."

"Then you found him?" Elizabeth was growing exasperated.

"He was never lost. His body is downstairs. He's awaiting pick-up from the funeral home. Ma'am, your friend passed away shortly after eight this morning. I'm very sorry to break the news to you this way. It seems that somebody has played a terrible joke upon you."

Elizabeth hung up and worked hard to compose herself before her evening class. Fear and fresh concern washed over her. It had been no joke; she was certain of that much. Elizabeth had known George for over thirty years. It was his voice on the phone a few minutes ago, no doubt about it. She looked up at the clock. It was a few minutes past five. Yet the hospital supervisor said that George died a little after eight that morning. Not one to readily embrace superstitious beliefs or stories of the supernatural, Elizabeth found she had no choice but to accept the astonishing fact that she received a phone call from a ghost!

The Persistent "Wizard" and Company

Not everyone wants to experience the paranormal. Sometimes being open-minded or close-minded doesn't even factor into whether or not the spirit world invades our space. I dated a woman who never gave much thought to so-called "true life ghost stories" and the like. While she didn't read paranormal studies, this woman was a voracious reader of fantasy novels by such writers as J.R.R. Tolkien, Anne McCaffery, Pierce Anthony, Raymond Feist, and Robert Jordan. One night, when I was compiling true stories for this book, I called Lindsey and asked her to 'fess up about any supernatural incidents that may have occurred in her life. I had asked her once before, while we were dating. At the time, she blew off my question and made light of it. I sensed her reluctance in discussing such matters then. This time, it took a little coaxing on my part, but Lindsey finally agreed to grant me a short interview. I'm glad she did because she told me a most remarkable story.

"There are three things that happened to me many years ago," she began. "To this day they remain puzzles in my mind. The first occurred in my grandmother's house in the state of Washington. I was about ten years old and visiting her with my parents. My parents and I were sleeping in separate upstairs bedrooms. All of a sudden, I found that I was wide-awake, although I don't know what woke me up. I looked at the small alarm clock on the bureau. The green radium hands on the clock told me it was shortly after three in the morning. Then I heard a deep, hollow sounding voice calling out my name very softly from the hallway. I got up and stood by the door, thinking it was my mom or dad calling me, but their bedroom door was shut. The deep echoing voice called me again, then a third time. It became clear that the voice was coming from directly across the hallway, from a bedroom that was used for storage by my grandmother. There wasn't much in there, just some old boxes full of junk, and a mattress and box spring propped against one of the walls. The voice called to me again. I got really scared and ran back to bed. I don't know how or when I fell asleep but all I remember is the voice persistently calling my name in a weird sneaky way even as I drifted off again.

"The next incident took place in my folks' home. They live in the small town of Derby, Connecticut and have owned the house where this happened for many years. I was much older then, a high school student. I remember being totally consumed by the fantasies of J. R. R. Tolkien at the time, as well as those written by more recent fantasy writers. One afternoon, inspired by all I was reading, I drew a funny little caricature with a white beard and a pointed hat and flowing robes. Next to this figure I stenciled out the words, "THE WIZARD IS IN" and then I hung the sign on my bedroom door. That night, as I was about to drift off to sleep, I rolled over and faced the wall. All of a sudden, I felt three sharp and painful taps on my right shoulder. It was as though someone had jabbed the tip of a thick finger into my shoulder to get my attention. I was positively terrified. I knew that nobody was in my room. My door was closed when I snapped off the light just a few minutes earlier. Also, that door always used to squeak loudly. I would have heard it swing open if someone had tried to sneak in to scare me. But who would have done that, anyway? It was just Mom, Dad and me. Then I felt the three taps again, blunt, insistent and painful. I squeezed my eyes shut and tried to convince myself that I was experiencing muscle spasms. I wasn't, though. These jabs were real, human-like, bullyish. I didn't dare roll over to check one way or the other. The taps came again. And again. I started to pray silently. That seemed to drive off whatever had been bugging me. After a half-hour of solid praying, I rolled over and found the room empty and my door closed. I sprung out of bed, opened the door and ripped the wizard sign off my door. That was the end of that. I never felt those jabs again.

"The final incident takes place in the same Derby, Connecticut home, in the same room, in the same bed, but a few years later. I was home from college and totally hooked on a book. Yes, another fantasy. Sometime in the early morning hours, I shut off the lamp and laid back, ready to fall asleep. All of a sudden, my entire bed frame and mattress lurched forward and back again. For all intents and purposes, it was as though some giant underneath the bed had tossed it forward and then slammed it back against the wall. I know what you're thinking: that I was in some kind of half-sleep, half-awake state of consciousness and I did it myself, right? We've all had that happen. We're about to drift off and then we start to dream. Maybe in the dream we're walking down a broken sidewalk and we stumble and our body reacts and we shake ourselves awake. That's what I would be thinking if you told me this story. But that's not the way it happened, I swear it. I was still wide-awake. I mean, the span of time between the moment I shut off the light and laid back and the moment my entire bed was violently rocked back and forth was maybe fifteen seconds, tops. By the way, I stayed up the rest of the night. I flicked on my TV and watched re-runs of *The Honeymooners* until dawn!"

Children are often more receptive to the paranormal than adults. Maybe that's why the very young Lindsey experienced the unexplained in her grandmother's house. In her teen years, Lindsey may have provoked the spirit world with her "Wizard" sign. Certainly, fantasy novels that include wizards are not to be regarded as evil texts. However, Lindsey didn't clarify what kind of "Wizard" was "in" her bedroom. Malevolent forces often seek any kind of invitation to invade one's physical domain. Lindsey's decision to ignore the mysterious entity's finger-poking seems wise. She may have opened a door to something sinister but she quickly closed it by ignoring the entity and ripping the sign off her door. Ignoring and rejecting the presence of an entity from which we sense danger are arguably the best ways to handle such paranormal infestation.

A Wife's Not So Subtle Messages from Beyond

My friend Heidi lives in Northwestern Connecticut. She shares her home with her father, two Labradors – and a ghost.

When Heidi and I met about a decade ago, one of the first things she told me was that that her mother still visits the house from time to time. Footsteps can be heard pacing up and down her attic quite regularly. These clear, distinct footfalls move from one end of the house to the other. When she musters enough courage to go upstairs and check things out, she finds the attic space cluttered but empty of human intruders. Sometimes Heidi hears kitchen cabinets and doors opening and closing in the wee hours. When she gets up to check, she finds the kitchen in order. Today, Heidi works as a private investigator but the sounds in her house seem destined to remain a mystery. Of course, there is the possibility that these noises are being made by whatever remains of Heidi's departed mother.

For many years, the phantom sounds were restricted to rare footfalls echoing from the attic above and the occasional noise emanating from the kitchen. More recently, however, the paranormal incidents have increased substantially. They have also increasingly involved Heidi's father, Mitch. In winter 2002, Heidi's father engaged in a full renovation of the family bathroom. At Christmas time, Heidi and her brother gave their father a new medicine cabinet, which he mounted after painting and wallpapering the room. A few months later, Heidi awoke one morning to find her father in a very bad mood.

"How could you?" Mitch asked his daughter.

"How could I what?"

"How could you give me a present only to destroy it?"

Heidi was perplexed until she went into the bathroom and found that the door of the new medicine cabinet was practically wrenched off its hinges. It refused to shut correctly and Mitch had to wire up a makeshift latch to keep it closed. Except for their two dogs, father and daughter live alone in the house. (Heidi's brother moved to Dallas shortly after her mother died in December 1989.)

Naturally, Mitch quickly ruled the dogs out as culprits in the medicine cabinet mystery, which left Heidi to blame. Heidi swore she didn't damage the door of the cabinet.

"Then who did?" her father demanded to know.

There the matter rested, unresolved and still disconcerting, until a new puzzle overshadowed it a few mornings later. Once again, Heidi awoke to find her father in an uproar.

"What did you do with my favorite frying pan?" he asked her.

"What's wrong with it?"

"I don't know. I can't find it. What did you do with it?"

"Dad, why would I hide your frying pan?"

"I didn't say you hid it but you must've used it and misplaced it. Where is it?"

"Dad, what would I want with a skillet?"

"You tell me!"

"Do I even cook around here?"

Mitch had to admit that she didn't. Although Heidi lives in Bantam, Connecticut, she works in Danbury and eats out on most occasions.

"Besides," Heidi said, "we have other skillets."

"So you *did* lose it!"

"No," said Heidi. "I'm just pointing out that we have other cookware. Use another skillet."

"But I want my favorite!"

"Well, it doesn't look like you're going to use it this morning, does it?"

Nor the next morning, for that matter. To this day, the frying pan remains missing.

The kitchen mysteries didn't cease with the pan's disappearance. When Heidi got home from work about a week later, she was greeted by a stern look from her father. He was holding a teakettle in his hands. Before he even spoke, Heidi saw the huge dent on the side of the kettle.

"I suppose you're going to tell me you didn't do this, either."

Heidi stood slack jawed, staring at the dented teakettle. "Did you drop it?"

Her father sighed. "No, but you must have."

"I didn't," Heidi insisted, "but it looks like somebody sure did."

"I think it was you," said Mitch, "then you put it back on the stove. You're not going to tell me that Bouncer or Aspen dropped it, are you?"

"That's probably what happened. The dogs did it, right? Did you find it on the floor?"

Mitch shook his head. "It was sitting on the stove, atop its usual burner – but it was dented when I picked it up. It wasn't dented the last time I used it."

"When was that?" asked Heidi.

"Last night."

"And it was on the stove that way?"

Mitch nodded.

"Then it really couldn't have been the work of the dogs. They might have been able to reach up and knock it off the stove, but neither one could put it back."

"Exactly. Which means you must've done it."

"Dad! I didn't!" The conversation ended in stalemate.

Things remained quiet until the following weekend, when Mitch was tinkering in his basement workshop on a Saturday afternoon. As the dinner hour approached, he heard the sound of the front door open and shut, and footsteps echo over his head. He heard the dogs shuffling about and a woman's voice talking affectionately to them. After a while, he decided to run upstairs to say hello to his daughter, who had obviously gotten home from an afternoon outing. When Mitch got to the ground floor of the house, Bouncer and Aspen looked up from separate corners of the kitchen, where they were snoozing. He called out to Heidi, then searched every room. The house was completely deserted.

Heidi has heard evidence of a phantom visitor from time to time since her mother's death, but why has this activity increased lately? And why has the activity moved from being strictly auditory to becoming more mischievous and poltergeist-like in nature? Poltergeist activity is often found in the homes of people with youngsters approaching puberty. Paranormal experts stress that a substantial amount of the paranormal activity manifested in the homes of adolescents isn't the product of spirits at all but of the youngsters' expanding consciousness and sexual development. Still other students of the paranormal assert that spirits are indeed visiting the homes of such adolescents but that it is these youngsters' very psychosocial instability that attracts the spirits to the house. The youngsters are emotionally and socially immature, sexually in flux, and thus more susceptible to psychic influence. Poltergeists try to take advantage of such turbulent states. Admittedly, much of the phenomena being experienced in Heidi's house has the distinct ring of poltergeist activity: disembodied noises, objects seeming to move of their own accord. Heidi and I pondered the incidents for some time. She is a realist while I tend to venture beyond black and white to search for clues that are not necessarily fully entrenched in the so-called "real world." Neither one of us came up with a sound reason for the events that have taken place in her home.

Enter my friend Kelly, who upon hearing the story of the hauntings in Heidi's house, quickly hit upon a plausible explanation. In the past year – for the first time since his wife's death – Mitch has begun to date again. Could it be that Heidi's mother has returned to give him her blessing, or to voice her disapproval of some of his prospects? This may very well be the case, especially since so much of the recent paranormal activity is focused on Mitch.

One final incident that occurred during this time underscores the idea that the spirit of Heidi's mother seems to be trying to communicate with her husband. Since her death, Mitch has refused to throw away any clothes that Heidi's mother bought for him. One of his favorite items is a lightweight blue and gray checkered outdoor jacket that Mitch dons while doing outdoor chores in fall and winter. For years, Mitch kept this jacket hanging on a peg near the basement steps. That jacket recently disappeared off the peg, leaving Mitch frustrated and furious. Heidi and her father spent long hours searching every corner of their house for the jacket. It remains missing.

From Mental Hospital to Haunted House

Are ghosts more prone to haunt certain locations than others? It seems likely, considering that some places acquire solid reputations for being haunted, while others remain free of any tales of the supernatural affixed to them. While it is true that some places have gained a reputation for being the prototype of haunted dwellings – old houses, for example – one of the things I have discovered in the course of my supernatural investigations is that virtually any location – urban or rural, densely or lightly populated, high traffic area or isolated – may acquire a reputation for being haunted. I believe that it is ultimately a question of *who* lived or worked in the dwelling and *what* took place there at a certain time which determines whether or not a place becomes haunted. In the previous section, we learned that Heidi's home frequently manifests supernatural phenomena. However, hers is not the only haunted house in the family. Indeed, certain occurrences in her late grandfather's house are equally disturbing and perplexing.

Heidi's granddad owned a house that can easily be regarded as a prime dwelling place for troubled spirits. The sprawling dwelling is located in Litchfield County, Connecticut, in the small town of Lakeside. It is over a hundred years old. In the past, the home was used as a sanitarium as well as a recovery home for people with tuberculosis. Heidi's grandfather eventually purchased the house and turned it into the family homestead. He raised several children there, including Heidi's father, her four uncles and her aunt. Heidi explains that when her father was growing up in the house, her grandmother forbade the children to go up to the third floor. When they asked her why she was so adamant about this rule, Heidi's grandmother refused to elaborate but the children knew there would be dire consequences to face if they were ever caught sneaking up to the third floor of the house.

One of the strangest occurrences involves Heidi's grandmother and the family dishware. Over the course of several weeks, Heidi's grandmother noticed that some of her dishes were disappearing. At first it was just a dinner plate. Then a saucer. A day or two later, a cup was missing. Then another saucer, and so on. She questioned the children repeatedly about the missing dishes. Had they broken the items accidentally? Were they hording the dishware to play house? None of the kids claimed to know anything about the missing tableware. One afternoon, Heidi's grandmother heard noises coming from the rooms located on the third floor of the house. She raced up, expecting to catch the kids where they didn't belong. Instead, a shocking sight greeted her. When Heidi's grandfather purchased the house, there was a great deal of furniture left over from the home's hospital and care-home past. Much of that furniture was put to mysterious use that afternoon, to the grandmother's astonishment. The woman entered a large room in which a long dining-room table had been set up to accommodate a vast number of guests. Each of the places on the table was set with the proper dishware and utensils. Heidi's grandmother recognized her missing dishware. In fact, most of the items came from her kitchen! Most disturbing of all, the children turned out to be out of the house on this day; they were playing at a friend's home. When they returned, each vehemently denied having anything to do with the dining room set-up on the third floor.

When Heidi's grandfather bought the house, its windowless downstairs parlor room was painted a dark red color. To this day, the family has kept the room painted the same color and calls it, simply, "the red room." (The name calls to mind another infamous "red room" described in Jay Anson's terrifying case history, *The Amityville Horror*.) Several incidents have involved the red room in some way or another. For example: Heidi's grandfather passed away in the mid-1980s. When he was in failing health, Heidi's cousin Ellen arrived for an extended visit at the house to attend to her grandfather. For many years, curtains served as the only doors into and out of the red room. One night, while Ellen was reading in the living room, she felt a sudden chill come over her. She rested the book on the couch and scanned the living room and the hallway beyond. Then her eyes fell on the doorway of the red room. To her astonishment, something parted the curtains and protruded from the darkness beyond. Ellen felt a fresh surge of fright when she realized what she was seeing: a wrist and hand, palm upward, fingers curled inward, except for one, which was moving forward and back, in a hook-like beckoning motion. Her grandfather lay in bed upstairs. No one else but Ellen was in the house. Yet here was someone summoning her into the red room!

Ellen stood up. Her impulse was to run out of the living room – out of the house itself – but she was determined to get to the bottom of the mystery. All at once, wrist, hand and beckoning finger shot into the red room. Helen raced to the curtains, whipped them aside and turned on the light.

The room was empty.

Another incident involving the red room took place several years later, after Heidi's grandfather died. The second incident involves Heidi's uncles. The two brothers were sitting in the red room. They had long heard stories about the house and the very room itself, but had never witnessed anything out of the ordinary. As Heidi's uncles engaged in animated conversation, they grew conscious of the fact that the room itself was growing increasingly vibrant. Then one of the uncles looked up and tapped his brother on the shoulder. Together, they watched as two red orbs descended from the ceiling and floated at separate corners of the room. Spirit lights have often been seen in houses, cemeteries and lonely roads (see "Photographing the Dead" in Chapter 3, and "Spirit Lights" and "Phantom Flames" in Chapters 6 and 7) but they are most often described as glowing white lights. Crimson balls of light, on the other hand, are extremely rare. The brothers stared in amazement as the light globes descended further, hovered, then began to spin steadily. Then, in perfect unison, the orbs ascended back into the ceiling and disappeared.

A third uncle has also witnessed something weird in the house. Heidi's Uncle Lonny had a frightening experience in the home when he was a little boy. One day, Lonny found himself alone in the house, having stayed home from school because he was feeling ill. Lonny wasn't playing "hooky." The boy was sick enough to spend most of the day in his bedroom. His bed was situated in such a way that he had a clear view of the staircase leading to the third floor. To this day, Lonny stresses that what happened that afternoon was not the product of a fever dream or any other sickness-induced hallucination. As he lay in bed, reading, Lonny saw a woman appear in the hallway. She was dark-haired and beautiful, dressed in a long white dress. Lonny watched the woman walk up the staircase and disappear as she reached the third-floor landing. Who was this woman? One of the nurses that walked the home's hallways when it was a hospital? A long-forgotten patient that convalesced at the hospital? The possibilities are varied.

Heidi's aunt remembers that when the home was a hospital, a Native American hanged himself in the house. Other people who suffered from tuberculosis also succumbed to illness in the dwelling. This is a place that has had heavy human traffic flow over the years. More important, many people have resided in the building during extremely stressful times in their lives. Some of them never made it out alive. To this day, Heidi and her family maintain that the house remains infested with troubled spirits.

Mothers Beckon from This Life – and the Next One

Why would the spirit of a mother attempt to contact the world of the living if it is untroubled? Various reasons come to mind. For example, I began this book with the story of my grandmother's late-night phone call from beyond the grave. My mother's mother died peacefully and no one in the family has ever doubted that her soul is at rest. However, it seems too coincidental that one of my mother's brothers died mere weeks after she received a paranormal call from her dead mother. I suspect that this call had nothing to do with my grandmother's spirit being ill at ease. Instead, most of us in the family are convinced that my grandmother called to prepare the family for its forthcoming loss.

I suspect that there are instances in which deceased parents call out to their children simply to let them know that all is well. Quite often, we grow comfortable and familiar with family and friends and the roles various people play in our lives. Even if we do not take each other for granted, there is a wonderful pattern of familiarity that is often well established between a parent and child before the parent's passing. Often the patterns change as time passes, but we grow into familiar routines that bring us great satisfaction and strengthen the bonds we feel between ourselves and others. These patterns are forged even in times of illness. In Texas, my Aunt Cari took care of my grandmother for many years before her death. My grandmother wasn't in the best of health those last few years. She was often in and out of the hospital and bedridden for long periods of time. Throughout these times, she would often call out to my aunt. Months after my *abuela's* death in 1979, my *Tia* (Aunt) Cari often heard her mother calling out to her in the same familiar fashion that had been so well established before her death. A similar story concerns my friend JJ, whose mother lost a long and tough battle to cancer a few years ago. JJ and his mother shared the same apartment for a few years and he often attended his mother when she called for assistance. Long after her death, JJ insisted that he would still hear his mother suddenly calling out to him from time to time.

JJ's mother found other ways to contact him, including the use of a clown hat! JJ's nickname is "Jester." As a result, he has collected a number of jester hats over the years and hung them throughout his apartment. One afternoon, JJ was preparing to go to work when he turned around to discover one of his jester hats sitting in the middle of his bed. This was truly mystifying to him. Moments before, the hat had been hanging at its usual spot: on one of the corners of his bureau mirror. Even if the hat had fallen from its perch, it wouldn't have landed across the room and atop the bed. The only way it could have moved to its new spot was if it were tossed there – or moved by invisible hands. This occurred shortly after JJ's mother passed away and during the time when he heard her calling out to him on a regular basis. Perhaps she was "jesting" with her son on this occasion and letting him know that all was well with her spirit – and that he should work to enrich his own.

My friend Mary also claims that her mother's ghost has visited her. However, Mary has not only heard her mother, she has *felt* her presence – literally. Mary explains that since her mother's death, she has gone through some extremely tough times in her life. It was during these extreme moments of crisis that Mary received a comforting visitor.

"I felt her sitting at the foot of my bed as I lay there," Mary says. "The room was dark but I felt someone literally sitting there and I didn't need the light on to tell me that it was Mother. Another time, I actually felt her standing by my bed and then I felt her hand – her palm and fingers – resting on the side of my head. She spoke to me on that occasion. "Everything's going to be alright," she told me. "Everything's going to be just fine."

Mothers may return to warn living members of the family of impending death and danger. They may return to assure loved ones that they have crossed into the spirit world successfully and are at peace. And as Mary's story demonstrates, mothers may also return from the dead in order to comfort their loved ones in times of stress. As a later story in this book underscores, the old adage rings true: a mother's love *is* eternal.

"Nan" Saves the Day

Throughout this book I have included stories of ghosts that return to say goodbye, to visit loved ones or to prepare family members for an impending death. However, another reason ghosts visit the world of the living is to warn loved ones of danger. Such is the case with my dear friend Kelly, who received a timely visit from her grandmother on her mother's side. Shortly after her passing, Kelly retrieved a number of items from her *Nan's* house. Other family members regarded some of the items Kelly chose as worthless, but the trinkets Kelly chose were mementoes that triggered precious memories of times shared with her grandmother. To Kelly, the items were priceless. It's a good thing that she had special regard for one particular item – a sewing basket – because that object may have ended up saving her life.

As Kelly explains, "I loved my Nan's sewing basket, so that's one of the things I definitely wanted to keep. The box was made of wood but it had a small opening in the back, big enough for a nail. I hung it in my laundry room and I used it quite regularly. I still do. A few years ago, around 1997 or 1998, I was busy doing laundry and cooking at the same time. All of a sudden, I heard a tremendous *CRASH* from the laundry room. I raced over, opened the door and my heart hit my stomach. There on the floor lay my Nan's sewing basket. All the drawers were flung out of it and materials were scattered everywhere. I was sure at least some of the drawers or the wooden panels that comprised the structure would be cracked, but upon inspecting it, I found the box to be intact. I gathered up all the materials and began to put them back. As I crouched there, I was shocked to see the laundry basket pressed up against the baseboard heater. The plastic basket was disintegrating before my eyes! The plastic was all warped and melting. It looked like a surreal Salvador Dali painting in the making. Even worse, the basket was full of dirty clothes and they were smoldering! All of a sudden, I knew why the sewing basket fell at that particular moment. My grandmother knew of the impending crisis and she did what she could to alert me to it. I said, 'Thanks, Nan,' pulled the warped basket and singed laundry away from the baseboard heater, then continued to put the sewing box back in order. There was one more big surprise awaiting me. I looked all over the floor and under the washer and dryer for the thick nail I'd used to hang the basket in the first place. I couldn't find it. When I got up to retrieve another nail and a hammer, I couldn't believe what I saw. There on the wall, hung where I hammered it in several years before, was the nail I'd been looking for! That made me even more certain that Nan had come to rescue the family. There's no way that sewing box could have leaped off the thick nail. I hung it back on the wall and it's been there ever since."

Now Entering the Spirit Zone

Some ghosts are said to haunt certain homes or buildings, but how far does their area of influence extend? In some cases, only a certain room or floor of a home will be haunted. In others, psychic manifestations occur throughout a residence. And in still other cases, the area of paranormal influence seems to reach beyond the domicile or edifice and encompass the surrounding yard and property. For example, my friend

Mary believes she ran into supernatural energy that extended well beyond an allegedly haunted house built in Torrington, Connecticut. Before I get into the incident involving the house in Torrington, however, I wish to explain the manner in which Mary and I met. In the conclusion of this book, I provide an extensive discussion of "Synchronicity and the Supernatural," but I don't have to wait that long to touch on such a phenomenon. I need only explain my introduction to Mary.

Mary is a realtor who lives and works in Waterbury, Connecticut. I met her when I was in the market to buy a condominium. Granted, there are countless realtors in the business, so I was completely lost about where to begin and whom to trust. When I received pre-approval on a mortgage, I asked my loan officer for a realtor recommendation and he put me in touch with Mary. Again, I wish to stress that I could have simply picked up the phone book and called a random number in the real estate section. Moreover, my loan officer could have recommended various people to me but he mentioned Mary.

My first meeting with Mary proved to be a classic case of synchronicity. Not only are Mary and I diehard Elvis Presley fans, but like me, she is also a great admirer of President John F. Kennedy. Elvis fan that I am, I took immediate note of Mary's "1 ELVIS" license plate and had to ask her about it. Mary revealed her love for the king of rock and roll, that she had actually received a rare letter written from Elvis himself and that she treasured this letter as much as her personal note from John F. Kennedy. After she mentioned JFK, I knew I was in good hands. Mary was surprised when I confessed my love for Elvis but floored when I revealed that I teach a composition course structured around the JFK assassination! As if this weren't enough, during email exchanges, I revealed that I am a paranormal investigator. Mary confessed that she is fascinated by the world of the unexplained. In a previous section of this chapter, Mary talked about being visited by her mother during times of crisis (see "Mothers Beckon from This Life – and Beyond"). The following incident proved far less comforting to my friend.

According to Mary, she and a friend experienced something fantastic on a cold, clear and blustery December evening. The stars sparkled with the sort of diamond vibrancy they reserve for the most frigid of winter nights. Mary and Laura set out from Waterbury for an evening at the home of mutual friends in Torrington. Christmas gifts rested in the back seat. Mary and Laura were in good spirits and chatted as Mary drove them down the highway. As they reached Torrington, Mary paced her way around winding roads and hills. "All of a sudden," says Mary, "there's this wall of white up ahead. It was huge and wide. It wasn't fog. I know because the night was crystal clear and very windy. Then suddenly there's – well, *that*. This thing was absolutely huge. Both Laura and I were shocked and frightened but it was too late to stop the car. And then I realized that the thing – I hate to call it that because it actually seemed to be pulsing and *alive* – was actually shoving the car back. I was pushing down on the gas pedal, so scared, and yet the car was slowing down, struggling to get through this white mass. I actually felt my car struggle and lurch and slow way down. Then we were out of it. I can't tell you how scared I was."

Somehow, Mary composed herself enough to drive the remaining distance to her friends' house. The minute they saw Mary and Laura, they knew something was very wrong and made enquires. Reluctantly, Mary and Laura revealed what had just occurred. The Torrington residents quickly asked where the incident took place and Mary gave them the street and closest intersection. The hosts didn't seem surprised. Mary and Laura had their strange experience in front of a house long reputed to be haunted, the

Torrington residents explained. Loud noises have often been reported coming from within the empty house. Many witnesses have seen lights go on and off in the home (even when the electricity has been shut off). Most disturbing of all, entities are said to float within the home – and around it. If such sightings have been reported taking place in and around the property, why not on the part of the street situated directly in front of the house?

Mary had one of the baffling experiences of her life on that December evening. It seems that she and Laura entered a supernatural zone – an area that harbors paranormal energy. Perhaps this energy is residual and emanates from the house. Or perhaps the reverse is true, and the house may be haunted by the energy around the property upon which it is built. In any case, the atmosphere outside that particular house in Torrington was anything but ordinary on the night that Mary drove through an energy cloud.

The Ouija Board and Possession

In Chapter Two, I discussed my own experiments with the Ouija board. I consider myself lucky to have gotten away with such foolishness. Two of my closest friends also tried using a Ouija board when they were much younger. Kelly's results are startling, while JJ's nearly ended his life.

As children, Kelly and Dee-Dee were the best of friends. One girl or the other could frequently be found bicycling to the other's homes, her bike basket full of Barbie and Ken dolls and accessories. Kelly and Dee-Dee's friendship endured as the girls moved into their teens and Barbies were abandoned for books, boyfriends and board games. Early one evening, Kelly arrived at Dee-Dee's house and found her in a state of excitement. Dee-Dee had used part of her birthday money to purchase a new game and she was quite anxious to share it with Kelly. In fact, this particular game worked best with two players, Dee-Dee explained.

Kelly stared at the Ouija board resting on the floor of the bedroom. "Do you think it'll work?"

"Let's try it," said Dee-Dee.

The girls settled down on the floor, the Ouija board between them.

"Ready?" Dee-Dee asked.

"Sure," said Kelly. "But how do we start?"

"We just ask it something."

"Like what?"

Dee-Dee shrugged. "I don't know. Hey, it's my house and my game, but you're my guest. You start. Go ahead and ask it something."

"Okay." Kelly thought a moment. "Let's ask it something weird. Something neither one of us knows." After a moment, she snapped her fingers. "I'm ready."

The girls rested their fingers on the planchet, then Kelly spoke her question. "What is the middle name of the current vice president of the United States?"

Nervous giggles erupted from Dee-Dee. The teen pulled her fingers away and covered her mouth. Kelly laughed too but asked her friend to get serious. "Let's try again. Tell us the middle name of the current vice president of the United States."

The planchet moved beneath the girls' fingers. Each looked at the other, eyes speaking a mutual question: are you pushing the game piece? Aloud, they reassured each other that they were doing nothing of the sort. The planchet glided across the board and stopped. The glass window on the indicator framed the letter F. Onward the object moved, stopping atop the letters R-E-D and others. Eventually, the object spelled the name, FREDERICK.

"So, is that Walter Mondale's middle name?" Dee-Dee asked.

"I don't know," Kelly said. "That was the whole point of the experiment, wasn't it? We asked it something neither one of us knows."

"Well, now what?" said Dee-Dee.

"Now we find out if our invisible friend is right."

The girls raced downstairs to ask Dee-Dee's mother. The woman was as clueless about the current vice president's middle name as her daughter and friend. Frustrated, Kelly and Dee-Dee returned upstairs. They knelt before the Ouija board and contemplated asking it another question. Before they could decide upon one, Dee-Dee's mother called from downstairs. The girls raced to the landing. Thinking the girls needed the information for a school project, the mother had called a friend and retrieved the Vice-President's name. "It's Frederick."

Kelly and Dee-Dee were amazed. Whatever communicated with them via the Ouija board was correct!

The experience proved too alarming for Kelly. She has never touched another Ouija board since that night. It's fortunate that her curiosity didn't kick into overdrive as a result of the correct answer provided by the supernatural presence. Indeed, many Ouija board users report that spirits will often provide benevolent and correct answers to questions asked by the curious. This is one of the tricks used to ensnare those who dabble with the Ouija. Keep in mind that use of the Ouija board is one form of conducting a séance. Such experiments may allow friendly spirits to talk with the world of the living, but there are no guarantees. Too often, malevolent spirits compete for the attention of those inhabiting the physical world. Any sort of contact via the board is regarded as an open invitation to them and the first step toward creating obsessive behavior on the part of the users. Full-blown haunting can easily follow such seemingly innocent dabbling. In worst-case scenarios, these infestations may actually be the work malevolent entities. Had Kelly and Dee-Dee decided to investigate further, they may have run into trouble in due time. Such was the case with my good friend and fellow paranormal investigator, JJ Sargent. Like so many of us, JJ played around with the Ouija board when he was younger and more naïve. He cut off his experiments, however, when one particular incident nearly killed him.

JJ was spending the night at his friend Rick's apartment when they decided to turn off the lights, fire up candles and engage in a question and answer session with the Ouija board. No sooner had they begun to inquire about the presence of spirits when Rick leveled a cold glare across the table at JJ. JJ asked his friend if he was feeling alright. Rick shoved his chair back and began to pace around the apartment, the candlelight casting undulating shadows around the walls. All of a sudden, Rick bolted for the kitchen. JJ followed. Rick glared at JJ again, opened a drawer and pulled out a long carving knife. At this point, JJ knew his friend wasn't kidding around. Rick's face grew distorted: his eyes bulged out of red-rimmed sockets and his mouth twisted in a perverted leer.

JJ bolted out of the apartment's sliding glass door. He turned around and saw Rick close behind. JJ tried to outrun his friend. Suddenly, something slammed into the back of JJ's head. He collapsed in a dark corner of the parking lot. A second later, Rick was atop him, knife swinging. JJ held up his arm for protection and felt a hot flash of pain blossom as Rick sliced his forearm open. JJ continued to shout at his friend, pleading with him to snap out of it. Rick kept swinging the knife.

Finally, JJ gripped his friend's arm and shoulder and shook him repeatedly. Gradually, sense returned to Rick's face. He cast a confused look down at JJ and asked where they were and what they were doing. It was up to JJ to explain all. As in Kelly's case – and perhaps for even better reasons – this was the last time JJ touched a Ouija board.

It Runs in the Family

You have already heard me mention JJ Sargent in the previous story and in other sections of this book. However, there is much more to tell about JJ. He and I share many interests, among them a lifetime of supernatural experiences. Like my family who seems to have had more than its share of brushes with the paranormal, JJ comes from a family whose members have also been blessed (or cursed, depending on one's assessment) with close ties to Things Fantastic. Some families seem to experience the paranormal in their daily lives more than others. Such is the case with several members of JJ's immediate family.

Maybe such talents are inherited. From a very early age, JJ's mother Katie was gifted with foresight and other subtle extrasensory powers. But Katie was prevented from revealing that she had such powers. Like many people, Katie's parents were petrified of the supernatural. Moreover, they were certain that if the community suspected Katie of having extrasensory gifts, she would be stigmatized and so would her parents. JJ's sister, Serena, remembers her mother discussing this matter. "She was punished on those occasions when she showed that she was gifted," Serena explains. "Mom learned to keep quiet about it because her mother – my grandmother – would tear into her for talking about these abilities."

Originally from Haverhill, Massachusetts, JJ's family moved to Connecticut when he was still an infant. After his parents divorced, JJ lived in the city of Middletown, Connecticut with his mother, his sister and his younger brother. It was in Middletown that JJ had some of his earliest and strangest encounters with the supernatural.

As a young boy in the third grade, eight-year-old JJ had his first experience with missing time. Amazingly, he was not the only boy left befuddled by the incident. JJ was walking home from school with five other boys one October afternoon in 1974 when the group decided to go out and play a round of football in a nearby park. They passed by the railroad tracks and Saint Lucy's Church. En route to the park, the boys stopped by one youngster's home to retreat a football. The friend invited JJ and the other boys into the house to grab a drink and use the restroom before heading to the park.

"We were inside Rudy's house no more – *no more* – than fifteen minutes," JJ stresses, "but when we stepped out of the house, the sun was gone and the sky had turned that gloomy shade of blue-violet that comes right before nightfall. Mind you, this was October, and the days were getting shorter. But still, we had just left school when we arrived at Rudy's house. Classes ended at 3:30. I'd say it wasn't even four when we got to Rudy's, but by the time we came out, you could tell that it was much later. What's both eerie and great about this incident is that there were several of us who experienced the exact same thing! Nobody dissected it, but you could tell that all of us were freaked out when we stepped outside of Rudy's house. The rest of the kids did what I did. I ran home. I got in big trouble with Mom for getting home so late and not calling or anything. But how could I? We were going to go out and toss the ball around for an hour or two. I bet I would've been home at five or five-thirty. Instead, we lost almost five hours! I didn't even try to explain what happened. Later, I learned the other guys didn't either. But we never forgot what happened and nobody can tell me it happened any different." Some twenty-five years later, JJ would experience missing time again, when he and I took our trek through the remains of Dudleytown (see "Haunted New England" in Chapter Two).

"Missing time" is a term that has been embraced by ufologists the world over to explain periods of time in which the victim cannot account for his actions. (Perhaps UFO researcher Budd Hopkins is to be credited for the widespread popularization of the term; Hopkins named one of his UFO studies *Missing Time*.) Sometimes, the victim isn't even conscious that an inordinate chunk of time has elapsed until hypnosis allows her/him to probe a problematic incident. Other times, a related experience, sound or image jars a person into realizing that a chunk of time is missing from her/his stored memories. Such is the case with JJ, who in the context of reflecting upon some of his many unusual experiences remembered the following frightening encounter.

JJ's second experience with missing time was repressed from his memory until we returned to Middletown, Connecticut and he gave me a tour of his old neighborhood. As we drove past thick woods behind a two-story home, a look of shock suddenly washed over my friend's face and he started recounting the following incident. Further, this missing time incident involves a perplexing encounter with a being that may not be human and alive as we define the concepts. JJ vividly remembers being "around eleven, no more than twelve" at the time, so the event took place several years after his first experience with missing time. One afternoon, JJ joined his mother on the front porch of their home. She was busy writing in her journal and JJ asked what she was penning. Katie explained that it was a journal in which she recorded her thoughts about life on the planet throughout humanity's history as well as speculations on the existence of life elsewhere in the cosmos. Intrigued, JJ asked her to elaborate. His mother had always been a voracious reader. That afternoon, she talked about the manner in which the Bible both complements and contradicts conventional historical texts. She stressed that her son should study the world from all perspectives. Eventually, she revealed that she was widely read in ufology. JJ was amazed by some of the incidents that she related to him that afternoon. Long before such speculations grew popular and a familiar part of pop culture, JJ's mother wrapped up their discussion by sharing her theory that perhaps certain individuals were hybrid beings: both human and alien. Katie was then surprised to see an *Oh, that's old news* look cross over her son's face.

"I know *that*, Mom," JJ said.

"How could you?" asked his mother. "What do you mean?"

"That stuff about aliens and men and some of us being half and half."

"But how could you know? I just told you."

"The man told me that a long time ago."

"What man?"

"The man behind our house. In the woods."

Katie stared at her son. According to JJ, it was obvious that she was very concerned for his safety at this point. "John, who is this man?"

"I don't know. He just appears back there, now and then."

"What does he look like?"

"Tall and skinny," JJ said. "He's very white. Actually, he's dressed all in white but his skin is all white too. Very bright. It's actually hard to stare at him for too long. He glows, mom."

Katie's concern turned to fear. "JJ, when does he come?"

"Just now and then, when I'm playing by myself back there."

"What does he tell you?"

"This and that. Some of what you told me. That there are many more like him mixed in with a lot of us. That we should be getting ready and be on guard. That preparations are being made. That everything's okay but we should think about things and make ourselves ready for them."

There seems to be much missing from the saga of Katie, JJ and the glowing stranger in the backwoods. Unfortunately, that is all that JJ remembers of this puzzling bit of missing history. Indeed, he had completely forgotten about the mysterious glowing man and sharing knowledge of his existence with his mother until I started probing him with questions about missing time for this book. As we drove around Middletown that summer evening, JJ showed me where he used to live and where some of these incidents took place. Then he remembered the alien hybrid story as he pointed to a copse of woods. The look on his face was priceless. It was as though in the course of sorting out the contents of a cluttered room, he ran into a long-lost photo album full of faded photos, not all of them evoking happy memories. "I wish I could remember more of that story," JJ said. "But the rest is fuzzy. I remember meeting the man I spoke of, I really do. Back there." He pointed to the woods as we circled the area again. "I can still see him. But I don't know how often, or for how long, or what we talked about, beyond what I just shared with you. Or – and this spooks me to think it – what, if anything, we *did*, besides talk."

JJ and his mother are not the only family members gifted with paranormal qualities. JJ's younger sister Serena remembers that as a young girl, she experienced several unusual events.

"My bed used to shake," she tells me. "It used to shake all the time when I was between ten and twelve years old or so."

This revelation brings to mind the horrible bed-shaking depicted in William Peter Blatty's novel *The Exorcist* and its film adaptation. Such poltergeist phenomena are often recorded in the homes of children moving between the awkward transitional stages of childhood, adolescence and puberty. Along with reports of bed shaking, small objects are said to move of their own accord. Sometimes these objects disappear for a short time; in other cases, they are never seen again. Framed photos and paintings are often knocked off walls and shelves. (I spoke with one psychology professor who provided the following account: "Besides teaching here at the college, I have my own practice. One of the strangest things I've ever witnessed in my long history of treating troubled patients came about when I took on the case of a disturbed young boy. His family claimed that the boy was destroying the house but they had no idea how. I asked them to explain. They said it was best if I saw it happening. I thought it was just going to be a case of anger management and hormones going bonkers and such. No such thing. One afternoon, I was sitting in my office when the boy's mother called. I drove over to their house. The very moment I walked into the living room, every photo and painting mounted to the walls crashed to the floor. Of course, I personally checked each photo, painting, frame and peg. The wires were still solidly affixed to the back of the frames and the nails and pegs were still on the walls. I'll never forget that incident.") Serena's story also involves a painting but her tale is even more problematic than the psychologist's anecdote. "There was a painting of Jesus hung in my bedroom," she says, "and its eyes used to move back and forth, side to side. This happened all the time. It wasn't an optical illusion or one of those cheesy magic pictures that are designed to do that. You could sit there and watch its eyes moving left to right, right to left."

The most recent member of JJ's family to be imbued with supernormal gifts is his young nephew, Jay. This young seven-year-old boy has had to face death several times throughout his young life. Many children learn about death through the loss of pets. Jay has experienced the loss of a beloved dog and cat, but in the span of a year, he had to contend with the loss of a favorite uncle and grandmother. Further, Jay's father has battled cancer off and on throughout Jay's young life. Thanks to the nurturing love provided by his parents and siblings, Jay has managed to cope with personal loss admirably; nevertheless, the past few months have brought forth frightening revelations from the mouth of JJ's young nephew.

Everything was fine until the passing of JJ's mother. His little nephew Jay took the loss very hard. Things didn't get any better when animals in the family's Waterbury, Connecticut neighborhood started to disappear every few days. The stiffened corpses of cats and dogs were soon discovered by frantic pet owners. On the surface, the animals appeared to have suffered little trauma. Two weeks into the problematic events in the neighborhood, little Jay's dog Katie turned up missing. Her body was found a day or two later. Katie's death proved the last straw for many in the neighborhood. An autopsy was ordered and shocking news followed: Katie and the other dogs and cats had been poisoned! Naturally, little Jay wasn't told what happened to his dog but his parents grew increasingly concerned about their young son. Jay's mental state worsened a few months later, when an uncle passed away.

Serena and her husband decided to move the family. Jay and their other children felt unsafe in the neighborhood (the pet poisoner was never caught); perhaps a change of atmosphere might do everyone some good, they reasoned. The family left Waterbury and found a sprawling, three-story home to rent in nearby Meriden. Unfortunately, this move only brought a depressing and frightening turn for the worse in Jay.

The young boy began to exhibit extremely troubling behavior at the Meriden home. The first symptom of trouble came with Jay's refusal to spend any time alone. In the past, he always enjoyed the company of his siblings and friends, but he was also quite content to play alone, in his bedroom or some other room of the house. Such was no longer the case in the Meriden home. For the first time in his life, Jay grew clingy. He insisted on being in the presence of at least one of his parents at all times. He refused to go to his upstairs bedroom by himself. As the weeks passed, he insisted on crawling in between his parents and sleeping in their bed. Finally, Jay's mother Serena confronted her son and asked what was wrong. The boy burst into tears and refused to talk. Serena coaxed him into confiding in her.

"I can't talk about it," he said. "You'll be mad at me."

Serena promised not to be mad. She vowed to listen carefully and try to help Jay with any problems he was having.

Between sobs, Jay finally told everything: "I see a lot of people in this house," he said. "Kids. An old man. They're in my room upstairs, mostly. And in the front yard. They're like you and me but they're not. They're dead, Mommy."

Of course, anyone who has seen *The Sixth Sense*, a disquieting film and a powerful ghost story, will find parallels between the film and little Jay's story. However, Serena shields her children from such films. She insists that Jay has never seen *The Sixth Sense* or any such film. Yet Jay persisted with his story.

"Something bad happened here," he said. "Now they want to take me with them. I'll be in my room and the old man says, `Come here, boy. Let's go.'"

"And the kids?" Serena asked. "What do they want, baby?"

"The same thing," said Jay. "To take me away. They come into the yard when I'm playing out there. They say, `Come on, Jay! Let's go!' and they run toward the street and look back at me. I'm not dumb, though. I'm not going with them!"

As fantastic as Jay's story may sound, it is hard to completely dismiss it, especially when we consider that other members of the young boy's family are psychically gifted (his late grandmother, his mother Serena and his uncle, JJ). In a forthcoming section of this chapter, we will continue to explore the connection between childhood and the supernatural (see "The Haunting of Innocence").

Haunted Artifacts and a Spirit of War

There is a distinct possibility that items from certain historical locations and periods are more likely to be associated with psychic manifestations than others. War brings turmoil and death. Perhaps this is why stories of ghosts are often linked to battlefields and warships. The same holds true for artifacts that are associated with war. My friend Nanci tells the story of her boyfriend Jeff and his father's trunk of German artifacts:

"Somehow or another, Jeff's father managed to get a hold of many German war items. An old German flag, scores of German war medals, a bayonet, a soldier's helmet and a lot of other stuff. Even the trunk itself was smuggled around from station to station and brought back from Germany. The trunk ended up in my boyfriend's house. One day we were hanging around the spare bedroom where the trunk is located. Jeff's nephew took down the lamp that sits on the trunk, opened the chest and pulled out the old German flag within it. He actually hung it up in that bedroom, then closed the trunk and replaced the lamp. It was close to lunchtime and we left the room to go eat. A little later, Jeff's nephew called us over. He was standing at the door to the guest bedroom where he was staying – the bedroom with the trunk. The trunk itself was closed as he had left it, but the lamp that he had replaced atop the trunk was now back on the floor. We all saw him put it back on the trunk before we left the room earlier. Actually, I wasn't sure he was on the level. I thought he might be playing a trick on Jeff and me. Jeff's nephew replaced the lamp and we left the house for the rest of the afternoon. When we returned from our outing, I went to the bedroom and checked the lamp. It was back on the floor! I was shocked. This time, *I* replaced it atop the trunk. That evening, I returned to the bedroom and found the lamp sitting on the floor again. I've always been a bit psychic. This time I sensed that a soldier associated with at least some of the items in the trunk was using the lamp to draw my attention. I thought he was asking for help, so I did what I could for his soul. I said some prayers and told him everything was okay. The war was long over and he should rest now."

Nanci has often spoken to me about her psychic abilities. Her story continues in the next section of this chapter.

Precognition and "Second Sight:"
Blessing or Curse?

Through the centuries, certain men and women have claimed to be able to see into the future. From prophets to mystics, from Nostradamus to the twenty-first century fortuneteller who practices around the corner, certain individuals lay claim to possessing precognitive abilities. Many of these people are outright frauds. They seek to take advantage of the insecure and unstable and those with low self-esteem. They profit from telling lies and lace their predictions with theatrical shows that incorporate smoke and mirrors, tealeaves and crystal balls. Other people seem to have actual precognitive abilities. They can predict the future with uncanny accuracy. True: anyone who studies a certain situation carefully and familiarizes her/himself with the facts and the players can make a fairly educated guess about the way that things are going to turn out. But there are times when a person gets information that seems to contradict the way a person's life is likely to unfold. In a short time, that information seems to come to pass. The people who receive these perplexing "visions" seem genuinely gifted with second sight.

What to do with this ability? Some people relish it, while others see it as a curse. Some offer advice based on what they see, while others refuse to say anything for fear of being ridiculed or tampering with the game plan that God or Destiny has mapped out for us. The ethical and moral dilemmas that are brought to the forefront with "second sight" are plentiful. (Stephen King's *The Dead Zone* is one of the best books to examine the ethical and moral quandaries associated with this ability.)

In "*It* Runs In the Family," we learned that one young girl was punished for revealing her ability to foresee future events. My friend Nanci claims to be gifted with precognition or second sight. But is this ability really a gift? Nanci herself questions whether being able to see into the future is more of a hindrance than a help in her day-to-day life. On several occasions, Nanci has been privy to forthcoming events in the lives of friends and relatives. She often wrestles with the knowledge and usually prefers to keep it to herself. Still, there have been a few occasions when she has confided in those involved in her premonitions. Most of the time, Nanci is met with startled laughter and staunch denials – only to have these people get in touch with her later, perplexed and wondering how she predicted a surprising and unpredictable event that they experienced.

I'm one of those people. A few years ago, Nanci came over for a visit. Shortly before leaving, she informed me that I would soon be moving. I told her that she was mistaken, that I had no intention of going anywhere.

Nanci laughed. "You'll see," she said. "You'll be out of here very soon, Oscar. Trust me."

Trust her I do, but I was certain she was terribly mistaken on this point. As things turned out, it was I who was mistaken. A series of unexpected events were set in motion whereby it became necessary for me to look for a new place to live. Within weeks of Nanci's prediction, I had purchased a condominium and left my old apartment behind!

If all of Nanci's premonitions involved such lightweight predictions as moving, she wouldn't be troubled with her ability. However, on more than one occasion, Nanci's second sight has allowed her to foretell the approach of death.

"It started with my younger sister," Nanci explains. "My parents were divorced and Becky was no longer living at home. She was living in New York with my grandmother. I was living with Mom in Connecticut. Becky was sixteen at the time. It was Christmas Eve and she stopped by for a visit. I remember we had a good time but I was a bit agitated. Suddenly, I knew why. When Becky was standing on the front porch, getting ready to leave, I knew that it was the last time I would see her alive. I knew this for a fact. I grew very frightened. I wanted to tell her to be careful. I wanted to warn her – but for some reason, I said nothing. It doesn't make a lot of sense, does it? I just watched Becky leave. I was so sad and frightened but I felt even worse when the phone rang in the middle of the night. It was the police. My sister was dead. She died of a drug overdose."

Nanci wrestled with grief throughout the following year. Her sorrow was compounded by the fact that she had sensed her sister to be imperiled on the night that she dropped by for a visit. Nanci chastised herself for not having warned Becky.

"But what would I have said?" she asks. "Becky, you're going to die, don't go? Be careful? What? I was young – seventeen – and I didn't have a clue if what I felt was real or not. And something else: the more I thought about it, the more I wondered if even if what I felt *was* real, did I have the obligation or right to warn her? Would I be interfering with something cosmic? Some big God plan or something? I have no answers. All I know is that I felt a lot worse the following Thanksgiving."

It was almost a year since the tragedy involving Becky. Nanci and her family still grieved for her sister. On Thanksgiving Day, Nanci's Uncle Hank stopped by the house. He was in a hurry to get home to visit with his girlfriend but he wanted to say hello to the family after working part of the day. Once again, a powerful feeling of precognition hit Nanci when her uncle made it to the front door. "He was standing on the porch, in the exact same spot where Becky stood on Christmas Eve, the year before. I was hit with a terrible premonition: I saw him dead. I knew it would happen soon. I knew it just like I knew that my sister Becky was going to die. God, how I wanted to say something to him, but for some reason I couldn't bring myself to voice it. I tried but I couldn't. Something shut me up. Or rather, something held my tongue and told me not to talk. It's garbled, yes, but it's the best I can explain it."

Uncle Hank left Nanci's house and hurried to his own home. He wanted to be there when his girlfriend arrived. Unfortunately, she was running behind schedule and arrived at the house later than she was expected. When she got there, she found Hank sprawled on the kitchen floor, dead from a massive heart attack.

One of these premonitions would surely be enough to rattle the most stoic of individuals, but two would be much tougher to dismiss as coincidence. Nanci needed no further convincing that her questionable gift of second sight was very much a part of her spiritual makeup. Nevertheless, a third incident occurred a few years later.

"Nothing else happened for a long time," Nanci says. "Oh, little things, sure. I predicted that friends would move or come into a little money or meet a future boyfriend or whatever, but nothing on a big scale that involved death and dying. Not until recently. It had been six years since I predicted my sister's death, five since I saw my uncle's death approaching. I was working in a restaurant at a local hotel last year. The night grew late on several of us who were closing. Then the bartender finally left. As she turned around to wave goodbye to us, I zeroed in on her face and her wave. I saw a weird aura around her and I got a terrible feeling. This wasn't a positive light. I knew that she was going out to meet death. I really did. Once again, a part of me felt that I should say something, but another part of me said, 'Hold your tongue, Nanci.' We got the call within the hour. Tina lost control of her vehicle and went into a ditch. She was killed instantly."

Nanci's stories provide us with one of the most complex of ethical dilemmas. What are we to do when we feel that some great misfortune is about to befall a friend? Should we say something even if it makes us look ridiculous? Perhaps many of us already give in to subtle intimations. How many times do we tell our friends to "be careful" when they leave our house to drive home? How many times do we feel a low-grade, almost unconscious foreboding that compels us to give extra warning to a family member about to embark on a journey? Are some warnings more acceptable than others? As much as Nanci has chastised herself over the years for keeping quiet when she felt something negative approaching her family and friends, she is still not convinced that she should have warned her sister, uncle and friend about her anxious feelings.

"How do I know for an absolute fact that I was supposed to say anything? How do I know that my saying something would have stopped what happened?"

Indeed, in the case of Nanci's uncle, it seems that any kind of warning on her part would not have staved off his heart attack. Nor did her vision reveal the specific source of danger (a drug overdose) that would claim her sister's life. Similarly, Nanci did not see any kind of car accident when she gazed upon her departing co-worker; she merely felt that the unfortunate woman would soon be dead. "How do you warn somebody that you know they're about to die?" asks Nanci. "I'm still wrestling with this problem."

It's an intriguing dilemma. I'm glad I don't have to tackle it. The times that I have predicted something in my future or the future of a close friend have not been life and death oriented. I truly do not envy such extreme precognitive abilities as those that Nanci harbors, and I can certainly understand her lament.

"To this day I'm more turned off by this ability than I am happy with it," she says. "What good is it? I know it's there. But again, what am I supposed to do with it? I don't know if it's a blessing or some kind of curse."

Conduits for the Supernatural

I was at a cafeteria the night before I sat down to write this particular section of the book. My mind was reflecting on two interviews that I was going to conduct with former students the next night. As I approached the soda machine, I had my hands full. One held my dinner tray, the other an empty soda glass. I'd soon have to set down my tray in order to manipulate the ice mechanism on the machine and serve my soda. Suddenly, I wished that ice would start to drop out of the machine to make things easier for me – and it did! Of course, this can easily be explained as a faulty ice dispenser. Or one might claim that the machine was full and simply jettisoning its excess. True enough. But I do find the event fascinating for two reasons: the paranormal was on my mind, as I thought about the next evening's interviews, and I was literally wishing for ice to drop out of the machine a mere second before it started to do so. I return to the notion that those who keep an open mind about the paranormal are more prone to experience it, just as those who reject it completely are likely to walk all their days on this planet without encountering anything out of the ordinary.

Of course, there are always exceptions to the rule. Some people spend a lifetime trying to increase their psychic sensitivity and get nowhere, while others seem to have a natural aptitude for it, whether they want to or not. The latter seems to be the case with Jamie and Genette. These fortunate (or unfortunate, depending on your point of view) young ladies seem to be natural conduits for the supernatural.

For many years, Jamie lived in a haunted house in Bethel, Connecticut. The house is quite old, built near the turn of the twentieth century. As a child, Jamie used to see fleeting images out of the corner of her eye in this home. From time to time, she would hear whispers in its empty rooms and long hallways. No one else in the family heard or saw anything, but Jamie was never comfortable in the house. The family eventually sold the place when Jamie was in her mid-teens. They moved to a nearby condominium complex. It is there that Jamie saw her dead grandmother on several occasions.

"She hadn't been gone very long," Jamie says. "We lost her the year before. Mom and I took it very hard. One night I was in my bedroom reading, when I saw movement in the hallway. I was shocked. Standing there, just as solid as you and I, was my grandmother. All of a sudden, I heard my mother scream. She had walked into the hallway from her own bedroom. She was seeing her own mother in the hallway. Then, just like that, Grandma wasn't there anymore. It's not like in the movies. No slow ghostly fadeout. She was just there one second and not there the next. But we both saw her. I'm so glad that Mom walked out of her bedroom when she did. Otherwise, they would have accused me of seeing things again, as they used to when I was a kid living at our old house.

"Mom didn't see my grandmother's ghost again, but I did. Once, I was standing in the bathroom in front of the mirror, and I saw her come up behind me and I actually felt her put her arms around me. I didn't feel scared. Not at all. Another time, I saw Grandma standing in the kitchen. I'd just put out some ingredients to make cookies and I was at the refrigerator, getting a couple more things. When I closed the fridge, grandma was standing by the counter, looking down at my cookie fixings. Then she disappeared.

"I asked somebody at work about it. This woman is very spiritual. She said that my grandmother missed the family and may not be completely at peace. She told me to talk to her and pray that her soul finds peace. I started doing that, telling Grandma that we would eventually join her but that for now she should rest in peace. I prayed and talked to her every night for weeks. She stopped coming around. I've never seen her since."

Not her grandmother, perhaps, but Jamie still sees the occasional ghost. Before moving to California, she witnessed phantom images at her workplace in the town of Bethel. She also had a remarkable multiple encounter while vacationing with her family in Florida.

"We were driving down to Key West one summer," Jamie explains. "It was humid but cool on this day. The Florida highway was flat. To the left was ocean. To the right were fields with the occasional marshy area. I was about sixteen or seventeen at the time and sitting behind my mother. It was the middle of the afternoon. As we passed by one soggy field, I saw a woman in the distance, walking parallel to our car. She was beautiful, with long flowing golden hair, wearing a white smock and long white skirt to her ankles. She was obviously pregnant. I wondered what a pregnant woman was doing walking out in the middle of nowhere. We drove on about five or ten miles, when I looked out to another field and there she was again, walking! I was torn between saying something and keeping quiet. Maybe it was just a coincidence, but two blond haired and very pregnant women dressed in white? I wasn't even convincing myself. So this time, I kept looking out the window. Minutes and miles passed. And then I saw her again! She was still walking, oblivious to the passing cars in the distance from her. Then my mother cried out, 'There's that lady again!' Relief washed over me. Somebody else saw what I saw. We told my Dad what we'd seen and he thought we were both nuts, but I don't care. Like the incident involving my grandmother, my mom confirmed that I wasn't going crazy, and that my experience was real."

Jamie's best friend Genette has also had multiple encounters with spirits. Like Jamie, Genette has never actively tried to engage the supernatural. "I've never even studied it," Genette stresses. "Even after the weird stuff that happened to me, I haven't gone out and read more about it. I avoid it, really. But it just seems to find me."

Genette has traveled the roads to and from Danbury and Brookfield for many years. There is one particular lane heading into Brookfield that has a number of old towering farmhouses in ruins. Some of these deserted homes are built very close to the road, as used to be the custom in days gone by. A few seem about to collapse in on themselves, such is their state of decay. One clear and warm evening, Genette was using this particular road to get home from work. Her friend and co-worker Amy accompanied her. The lights of Genette's Jeep lit up the winding, twisting lane. A nearly full moon lit up landscape and old houses as the young women passed them by. As they approached one of the oldest abandoned structures, Genette thought she detected movement within it. A moment later, something stepped onto the rotting porch.

"It was a man – or what was left of a man," Genette explains. "He was tall and very fat. That's the best way to put it. He was dressed in a red and black checkered shirt and blue overalls. But what really scared me, besides the fact that he was clinging to one of the old pillars in front of this falling down mansion, was his face. It was pasty white and streaked open with red lesions! Amy screamed. I told her, we're going back to make sure we saw what we saw. She begged and pleaded with me not to turn around, but I did. When we drove back, this guy was lurching into the middle of the road and blocking our path! Then he was gone. He just disappeared."

I asked if she was sure.

"Well, I drove right over the spot where he was standing. Yes, I'm very sure."

A few years later, Genette was visiting friends in South Texas. The group decided to drive into Mexico for a few days. The last night of her stay proved to be one of the most frightening of her life.

"We were camping out and having a great time. One night I woke up and the world look beautiful. The moon was out and it was a clear night. I couldn't go back to sleep for some reason or another, so I decided to grab my jacket and a flashlight and walk around a bit. When I was a good distance from the camp, a woman stumbled out of the brush and confronted me. I was petrified but I managed to mumble a question. I asked her if she needed help. She didn't say a word; she just kept staring at me. Then I froze. Her eyes turned blood red and she kept staring. The woman radiated evil. I've never felt that before or since that night. It seemed to me like she was just a glowing repository of evil. Those red eyes – I'll never forget them. I turned around and ran back to camp. Halfway back, I turned and swung the flashlight behind me. The woman was gone. She shouldn't have been there to begin with. We were out in the middle of nowhere. But she was there earlier, then gone."

Jamie and Genette continue to have troublesome encounters with entities. Neither relishes these run-ins; neither cultivates her psychic abilities. At the same time, neither woman seems able to stop her convergence with the unknown.

"It's no gift, as far as I'm concerned," Genette observes. "It's just a part of me, I guess."

Her words echo Nanci's assessment of her second-sight talent.

Spirits That Visit Before They Are Born

My friend JJ vividly remembers being a child in Massachusetts and traveling on a bus with his mother. This was not uncommon. His mother made frequent trips by bus around Haverhill and Gloucester, since the family only had one car. However, this bus ride was special, not for the stark orange quality of the late afternoon sunlight or the chatter the other riders made aboard the crowded vehicle, but because of the woman holding an infant in her arms. The baby grew cranky and his mother sensed his hunger. She reached into her blouse and pulled out a large, milk-filled breast. She offered it to her son. The baby sucked hungrily at the nipple until the bus stopped at the top of a hill. Then the woman fixed her blouse, carefully gathered up her infant and walked up a steep slope toward a brownstone.

Years later, JJ was reminiscing with his mother and brought up the incident. His mother was shocked. "You can't remember that!"

"But I do," JJ protested. "I remember everything about that day." He proceeded to repeat the story.

His mother was visibly shaken. "You simply can't remember that," she repeated. "That happened to me."

"But I was there, too," JJ insisted.

"Well, sort of," said his mother. "I was pregnant with you at the time. You were far along – but you weren't born yet! I saw the woman nursing an infant on the bus. You couldn't have."

Did JJ arrive before his time? This incident is shocking and raises some fascinating questions about the soul. First of all, there certainly seems to be some type of spiritual essence that survives our physical death. Although some ghosts act completely indifferent to their audiences and more closely resemble spiritual film footage than actual entities, other apparitions react to the presence of witnesses. Thus, it seems as though there is a spiritual life force that exists beyond the physical. However, how and when is the energy that will become our spiritual essence – our soul – brought into being? Is this spiritual energy an extension or creation of a mother and father's life essence? If not, how and when is it assigned to our particular corporeal body? Is it only at the moment of birth that this spiritual energy enters our body? Or is it there from the moment we are conceived? If so, does the soul reside in a mother's body as a baby grows within her? The implications of JJ's memory are both wondrous and perplexing. It seemed that his spirit was already present around his mother even before he fully came to term.

A related incident involves another former student of mine. A few months before Jessica was born, her grandmother had a vivid experience that seemed far more than an ordinary dream. As she lay in bed one evening, Jessica's grandmother saw an angel materialize and hover over her bedside. The angel came in the form of a baby girl, with golden hair and wings. Neither Jessica's parents nor her grandmother knew the gender of the forthcoming arrival, but a few months later, Jessica was born, complete with golden hair.

"My grandmother believes I came to see her before I was born," says Jessica.

Her grandmother may be right.

Haunting of the Innocent

The following incident has been imprinted in my head with hyper-real clarity since the day it occurred, even though I couldn't have been more than five years old when it happened. I was out playing with a few neighborhood children. We were chasing each other around my yard and into my next-door neighbor's yard. The man who lived there was a bachelor and away from his house more than he was home. Dusk settled over the neighborhood. The yards and trees took on violet hues. Still we played on. I remember standing in my neighbor's yard and looking back at my parents, who were wrapping up some yard work. Dad finished rolling up the garden hose and Mom was putting spade and hedge trimmers away in the tool shed. Other parents called to their own children and my friends raced home. I did the same. I ran through my neighbor's unkempt lawn. And then something jumped out of one weed-infested patch.

To this day, I see the image with disturbing starkness: a disembodied human foot leaped toward me. In retrospect, it was clearly a male appendage – large and bulky with dark (perhaps diseased) fingernails made all the more grotesque by the bone-white skin of the foot itself and the shocking crimson of the flesh-ragged stump above the ankle. I was so surprised by this hideous appendage that I stumbled and fell inches from it. Instantly, the foot began a rapid up and down, heel to toes bounce toward me. I screamed in terror and used my own sneakered feet to push myself away from this abomination. Still the disembodied foot advanced, bouncing vigorously toward me. I screamed again and burst into tears. Finally, I hoisted myself up and turned around and ran straight into the arms of my mother. In the distance, I spotted my father racing out of the tool shed. My parents questioned me. Without hesitation, I told them what so frightened me. Mom and Dad flanked me and took me by the hands. I resisted, but they insisted on taking me to the spot where I encountered the phantom foot. We got there. They made a thorough search of the knee-high grass. Only after doing so did they insist I must have been mistaken. Today I am grateful that my parents didn't make a quick judgment and simply dismiss my story as the insane ravings of a frightened little boy. They made it a point to show me that they combed weed patches and high grass in search of the object of my terror.

I was so young that I told my parents exactly what I had seen when they questioned me. I wasn't old enough to weigh the consequences of making such an admission. I didn't consider that I might sound like a lunatic to them. I simply recounted that which seemed extremely real to me at the time – and which still seems real to me, some thirty-five years later. I described the incident literally, like the innocent child that I was and as many children respond to the supernatural.

When I discussed the many hauntings in the Crest District, I recounted one particular tale that involved a family driven out of their home by a cluster of spirits (see "Innocence Invaded" in Chapter One). The final decision to vacate the premises came when the family's young son reported "all those people in my room every night...sitting and standing around talking." It's been said that out of the mouths of drunks and children comes the truth. I think there's a great deal of truth in that phrase. It's also been said that the mind of a child is a *tabula rasa* – a blank slate – and as such, we should be ever mindful of the information we choose to share with or keep from the young. But what happens when children are attuned to information and phenomena that their parents aren't aware of? Such is the dilemma Kelly found herself wrestling with when her son Alex began to experience a haunting in his bedroom.

Throughout the year 2000, six-year-old Alex awakened frightened, crying and asking for his mother. Kelly rushed to the boy's side. Alex complained about the man standing by the bedroom door. According to the little boy, this man was tall and slender, dressed in a plain white shirt and black pants. He was losing his hair. The stranger was quiet. He didn't speak. Nevertheless, Alex was frightened by the sentry-like presence of the man standing just inside of his bedroom door. Kelly listened quietly to her son and tried to put him at ease, emphasizing that he was quite safe in the home. Kelly is a staunch believer in the spirit world. As a result, she didn't feel it was right to tell Alex that he was imagining things or hand him the classic line, "There are no such things as ghosts." Nevertheless, Kelly wondered if her son was simply having bad dreams or if he had seen a ghost. She did her best to comfort him without lying to him.

Alex experienced a total of five sightings throughout the year. After a few months, Kelly was grateful that she hadn't dismissed her son's stories as pure fancy. One night after reading to Alex, Kelly drifted off to sleep alongside her son. She wasn't sure how long she snoozed, but she finally woke up. She detected movement near her son's bedroom door and she assumed that her husband had come home from working late. Kelly turned directly toward the door and saw a tall slim silhouette standing just inside the room. The next instant, the shape was gone. Kelly bounded off the bed and raced to the door. She walked into the hallway and called for her husband but the house was silent. She called again. A moment later, she heard light click-clacking sounds approaching from the den. Kelly's Jack Russell terrier Chaucer rounded the corner, followed by her husband's mutt, Holly. The dogs stared at her inquisitively. Had she called to them? They were obviously wondering. The animals' nonchalant mood sent a wave of fright coursing through Kelly. If her husband *had* arrived home, as she initially speculated, the dogs would have launched into their noisy barking, scampering, whining *welcome home* routine. Nothing of the sort had taken place. Yet Kelly was absolutely sure that she had seen a silhouette standing a few steps inside Alex's bedroom. Someone *was* there and vanished. Who was it?

Kelly lives in an old house. At least one previous owner died in the house, but whether the spirit that Alex and Kelly have seen belongs to a former owner remains uncertain. However, by the end of the year 2000, more than one specter may have been detected on the premises. Alex stopped seeing "the skinny man" around Thanksgiving, but early December brought with it an ensemble of specters. One night, Kelly awoke in the wee hours to find Alex standing by her bedside and poking her shoulder. She asked him what was the matter. Her son explained that there were "four or five globes of light" floating around his bedroom. They were very bright and they wouldn't let him sleep.

"I'm not sure if they're friendly or not" Alex explained, "but I have a bad feeling about them, Mom."

Kelly accompanied her son to his bedroom but found no spirit lights within it.

Many people would impulsively blame Alex's sightings on an overactive childish imagination. However, Kelly has always kept Alex from screening horror movies at his young age. Likewise, TV shows and cartoons with overt references to ghosts and possession are filtered out of Alex's viewing. Certainly Alex is not an overly sheltered child but Kelly has wisely decided that her young son is not ready to engage with some subject matter. Given his lack of exposure to the supernatural, Alex's troubles are even more perplexing. Further, Alex's own honest reporting of these encounters adds more credence to his stories.

I believe that it is extremely important to pay close attention to such tales when they come from children. Of course we don't want to ride the Gullible Train and believe any outlandish story told by a child. At the same time, children's minds are not only impressionable but more receptive to innovative modes of thinking and ideas that we tend to dismiss as adults. Young children are more open to the unknown. Most haven't yet been taught to fear it. Perhaps that is why so many of their stories of encounters with the fantastic have the distinct ring of truth.

Part III: Texas

CHAPTER 5

SPECTERS, SOUNDS AND VISIONS:
STORIES BY AND ABOUT
MY FATHER, MOTHER AND SISTER

The Haunted Ranch

I don't think my father ever understood my fascination with ghosts, horror flicks and "things that go bump in the night." While such classic pulp magazines as *Weird Tales*, *Astounding Stories* and other horror and science fiction publications appeared while my father was in his teens, he preferred the Western pulps and devoured as many as he could get his hands on. Of course, I asked him about ghosts and the like from time but he just laughed off my queries. I kept asking, though, even as an adult. Once, riding down the highway on an out-of-town trip when it was just the two of us, Dad opened up. It was one of the few times my father spoke of the supernatural to me. I'm glad it was a long car ride because he had more to say than I expected!

Dad spent most of his youth on a ranch where his father was foreman. The ranch had the curious name of Los Orcones – the Stranglers! It was owned by the Parr family. For many years, the Parrs were one of the political strong-arms in Duval County, Texas. Some attribute Lyndon Johnson's Vice-Presidential election to the Parrs and the enthusiastic vote casting of several thousand dead voters! (How's *that* for supernatural intervention in the physical world?)

"When I was a teenager living at Los Orcones," my father began, "my brothers and I were sent out to locate a baby in the middle of the night."

"A baby?"

He nodded. "You know how it is when you live and get to know a place. All of us were familiar with every sound that could be made out there. Coyotes, bobcats, rattlesnakes. You had to watch your step at all times. The way the wind whipped around the windmill, the stables and other buildings. But every now and then, we would hear a baby crying. No doubt about it. Sounded like the poor kid had been abandoned. My mother would send me and Chayo [my father's nickname for his kid-brother and my godfather, Isaac] out with a lantern to investigate. We did this several times over the years, but we never found a thing. It always seemed like the closer we got to the wailing baby, the further away the sound would drift. Eventually, the baby's cries would fade away and we'd come home empty handed and perplexed.

"The crying came only at night, by the way. My father accompanied us on a few occasions, shotgun in hand, but we never found a baby – or anything else, for that matter. It was the same thing with the fires we saw."

Fires?

"Nothing major, but they looked like distant campfires deep within the brush country surrounding the ranch. I accompanied my father and my brothers – Chayo, Pablo, Roberto – and we would go out and try to find them. Whenever we got close to the flames, they would wink out – *poof!* – gone. It was all very strange to us. Since that time, people have tried to tell me we were seeing fireflies or marsh gas but you know how dry it is out there. And I think I can readily tell a firefly from a campfire."

He paused for a while, then surprised me with another story. "We used to hear stagecoaches, too. The sounds resembled those you hear when you watch a Western movie and a coach goes by at top speed. Chains rattled, tires creaked, a driver cried out, whips cracked in the night and a team of horses neighed and galloped by. Or it sounded as if they did. Of course, even in those days – the early 1930s – stagecoaches had been retired to clear the path for automobiles, but my father and mother remembered the transportation of yesteryear. They both agreed that the sounds in the distance were those produced by a stagecoach."

I asked my father if he ever actually saw a phantom coach.

"No, none of us did. But we all heard it, distant at first as we sat inside the house playing cards or relaxing on the porch, enjoying the night breeze after a long day of working the ranch. Then the sounds grew louder. Everyone would step outside and await the coming of something that never got there. Each of us gazed out into the dark brush country and the road that appeared out of the woods. Nothing ever rounded the bend. Just the sounds. Eventually, they would fade away."

I'm reminded of my experiences in the Crest District. Although several people spoke of seeing an apparition in this neighborhood, I never actually saw anything that might even remotely be considered a ghost. On the other hand, I certainly *heard* my share of phantom voices in Gail's summer residence. The Crest stories and my father's stories of the sounds heard at Los Orcones ranch are good examples of *clairaudient* phenomenon. People who are clairaudient *hear* sounds that are not produced by the physical world as we understand it. People who are *clairvoyant see* paranormal activity that seems to invade the world of the physical. Some people are exclusively either clairaudient or clairvoyant, while others are both. Still other people are by nature neither clairaudient nor clairvoyant but in the course of living their lives, experience both phenomena from time to time. On this rare day when he opened up about the supernatural, Dad described two textbook cases of clairaudient activity.

Benavides, Texas: Haunted Texas Town

My mother and father spent their childhood years on separate South Texas ranches. Mother comes from the Alaniz family. She lived a good portion of her youth in a small ranch community known as *La Rosita* (The Little Rose), near the town of San Diego. Dad is De Los Santos. He grew up at *Los Orcones* (The Stranglers) ranch. (Clearly, my mother grew up on the ranch with the more attractive name!) My grandmothers were housewives. Each had a large family and many chores to attend to. My grandfathers both had classic "Old West" jobs: My mother's father was a chuck wagon cook. He would follow a team of cattle rustlers on the long trails as they herded cattle toward north Texas territories and sometimes beyond, to neighboring states. My father's father was a ranch foreman.

Eventually, the Alaniz and De Los Santos families moved to Benavides, one of many small Texas towns that saw their heyday during the Texas "oil boom" of the 1940s and 1950s and are now in economic decline. Once a thriving community of nearly twenty thousand residents, Benavides' population has dwindled to roughly six thousand citizens in the last three decades. All things considered, those who remain in Benavides enjoy a comfortable rural existence. Entertainment comes from a variety of sources: hunting, high school sports, 4-H club competitions, county rodeos, town fiestas, rattlesnake round-ups, church festivals, and great old-fashioned Texas barbeques. Nor is the town lacking in the technology that has permeated contemporary culture throughout the globe: the Internet is alive and well in Benavides, along with satellite TV, cable, video and DVD rentals, and all the other high-tech 21st Century life amenities (or headaches, depending on your perspective).

Benavides is also within driving distance of several larger Texas cities. Corpus Christi sprawls seventy-five miles to the east, while a two-hour drive to the north takes visitors into San Antonio. In fact, it is these and other relatively close cities (Austin, Houston) that have leeched Benavides and other towns in the area (San Diego, Hebronville and Freer, for instance) of many of its younger citizens. More and more often these days, teenagers leave their hometowns to attend college elsewhere and, except for the occasional visit, stay away.

Even as Benavides is depleted of young residents, its charm grows. I have taken long walks around the abandoned downtown buildings of this town. I have poked my head into the bank and into what remains of the crumbling movie house. I have stopped and walked around the drive-in that my Uncle Marin ran for many years. There's a historicity that sings out of these and other buildings; they hold echoes of the once thriving community. Benavides and countless towns like it hold histories that are ripe for the mining. Do some digging and these towns will yield a treasure trove of fascinating tales, supernatural or otherwise.

Of course, it is the paranormal that concerns us in this book. Already, at least two of the stories I have told have links to Benavides (see "A Demon At Daybreak" and "Vision of the Virgin" in Chapter Two). Likewise, many of the tales in this and forthcoming chapters also take place in and around Benavides. The tellers of these stories remember them vividly. They swear by their recollections. It makes me wonder: if this many stories come out of Benvavides – one small town – how many similar stories could be told about and by people in other Texas towns, or rural American towns in general, for that matter?

Son or Demon?

Before I began to write this book, I made a very rough list of as many personal paranormal experiences as I could remember off the top of my head. A little later, I filled in other encounters as I recalled them. It's no surprise that I blocked this particular experience from my memory for a very long time.

My family's home in Corpus Christi is very small. Because I was a night owl even in my teens, I had to occasionally tiptoe into a bedroom in which someone was asleep in order to retrieve some item or another. Such was the case one late November night in 1978 when I stepped into my mother's bedroom. I left her door open and tried to navigate my way around the room with the light filtering in from the hallway. All of a sudden, my mother sat bolt upright in bed and let out a horrified scream!

"It's me, Mom!" I yelled but Mother kept on screaming and screaming. I moved toward her. She continued screaming and slapped at me, trying to push me away. I fought her and held her close, horrified at this unexpected, horrible outburst. Then she slumped against me and sobbed. I finally let her go. I asked her why she acted as she had. Mother insisted that she hadn't seen me at all – that she saw a tall black horned silhouette moving about the bedroom! My approaching her bed only intensified her fear. My mother said that the only thing she was conscious of was that a demon was floating towards her. Then she saw it grab at her. It was only when I repeatedly shouted, "It's me, Mom! It's me!" that reality ebbed back into her psyche and the terrifying vision dissipated.

Let me stress that my mother is one of the most down-to-earth and sensible people I have ever met. I am not prejudiced by the fact that she is my mother when I make this assessment. Unlike her son, my mother isn't prone to dwelling on ghosts and the proverbial *things that go bump in the night*. I have never seen my mother lose control of her emotions as she did on the night that she mistook me for a demon. This was extremely atypical behavior from her.

There is a sad postscript to this already disturbing story: The day after the incident, my mother telephoned her mother and told her about the horrifying ordeal. My grandmother said that it was a sure sign that Death was approaching the family and that we should all prepare for the worst. Four weeks later, on Christmas morning, one of my mother's brothers died of a massive heart attack.

Of course I understand why I didn't remember this incident when I was drawing up my outline for this book. Who wants to remember the time they nearly scared their mother to death? Worse, who wants to remember a situation in which they are cast in the role of a demon?

My Sister Sees My Father's Ghost

My sister Iris swears that she saw my father's ghost late one night, shortly after she left a friend's house. Curiously, the sighting took place directly across the street from a cemetery, but not the cemetery in which my father is buried. Iris claims she saw my father's ghost in Corpus Christi, yet he is buried in the small town of Benavides. Still, my father lived in Corpus Christi for over forty years. He pretty much adopted the city as his second hometown.

My father was christened Santos, making him Santos De Los Santos – *Saint of the Saints* – a name he despised and saw as a cruel joke. Santos spent his youth working at Los Orcones ranch where his father was a ranch foreman. He didn't receive much formal schooling. Dad was forced to leave his education behind in order to contribute to the family's income. When he grew a little older, he picked cotton for a nickel a pound. This meager amount is practically inconceivable to me but my mother backs up his claim and swears that she was paid the same wage when she was young. When my father reached the age of twelve or so, he picked up a steady eight-hour shift bussing tables at a diner in Benavides for slightly higher wages: a quarter a day. This slap in the face was made even worse by the fact that the owner of the diner often made Dad wait several weeks for a paycheck.

A tour of duty in the U.S. Army during World War II took my father overseas. He visited Paris and was shipped to various locales where he engaged in combat against Nazi troops.

When he returned from the service, Dad spent several years working as a truck driver. In the 1950s, he married my mother and the two moved from Benavides to Corpus Christi. It was in Corpus Christi that my father went from driving trucks to keeping track of the various products hauled in them. Dad spent the next thirty-some-odd years working as a shipping and receiving clerk for a number of companies.

I believe the most valuable lesson my dad taught me was a strong work ethic. I still remember the annoying drone of the alarm buzzer each and every weekday morning at five a.m. I would soon be asleep again but not Dad and Mom. That was their cue to get moving – and they did, until illness forced them both to retire.

Heart trouble and the sudden need for open-heart surgery made my mother give up her cafeteria management job after thirty years of service. Long before she was sidelined, however, my father developed Parkinson's disease. He kept working for a time but severe back trouble combined with the Parkinson's and eventually forced him to retire. Things only grew worse when the Parkinson's began to affect Dad's memory and senile dementia set in. His decline was slow and painful, especially for my mother and sister. I had already left Texas when the worst stages of his illness descended upon him. When my mother could no longer care for Dad in the early 1990s, we put him in a nursing home. Two years later, in 1996, he died of a heart attack. He was seventy-two years old.

Flash forward two more years. The night that Iris saw the ghost of our father was quite ordinary. No thunderstorms. No spooky fog rolling about the seacoast city of Corpus Christi. Iris drove away from her friends' house and stopped at the end of a street. Her headlights lit up countless tombstones that seemed to sprout out of the ground, then grew dimmer in the distance. Iris prepared to execute a left turn. She looked to her left and found the coast clear. When she looked to her right to check for cars, she was stunned to see my father sitting on the right front bumper of her car! He was partially spotlighted by the car's headlights.

As Iris describes it, "Daddy was just sitting there, sort of leaning back on the hood, holding himself up with his arms. He was half turned and his head was craned and he was looking over his shoulder, right at me. The good thing is that he was smiling! He looked happy. More than that. He looked healthy. Not like the sad skinny body he had near the end. He looked huskier. And he was wearing his favorite outfit. Remember that crazy orange-brown plaid shirt he had? He used to wear it with his blue workpants, even after he retired. That's exactly what he was wearing. Then he disappeared."

Why my father chose to visit Iris at that particular moment is perplexing. He certainly got along better with her than he did with me. Perhaps he just wanted to let her know that 1) he had survived death and that 2) he was in a better state than he was in the last years of his life. Truthfully, experiencing my father's slow mental deterioration was more painful than witnessing his physical decline. When his mind began to fail him, my father began to live in the past – before marriage, before his children. He was most often working out in the fields or still in the service. At times, he seemed to return to the present, but only for a minute or two. At least he recognized us all when we visited him, but he spent his time in the land of days gone by. Iris says that in the few seconds that she saw our father again, he seemed healthy and mentally alert. He didn't speak, but the smile on his face and the recognition in his eyes told her a great deal. This is a refreshing message indeed. Thus far, this has been the only time that my sister has seen our father. However, it is certainly not the last time she *heard* evidence of his presence. Nor was Iris alone in experiencing the latter. My mother and I were also privy to these auditory visits.

Daddy's Radio

A textbook example of a clairaudient experience involves my father and sister again, but in a much different situation. Moreover, my mother and I are also a part of this story. After retiring, my father spent many days at home reading the paper and listening to the radio. He had a small set sitting atop a shelf in the kitchen and another radio in the bedroom. Much of the time, Daddy would listen to Spanish stations, but because I was a disc jockey for the English stations between 1980 and 1986, he liked to listen to those, too, particularly when I did a midday shift at an oldies station for a few years. Still, regardless of whether I was on the air or not, if my father was spending the day at home, the kitchen or bedroom radios would be turned on and playing softly.

Dad passed away in 1996 but I'm inclined to believe that he still drops in on the family from time to time. About two years ago, my sister (who continues to live in our Texas home with my mother) began to detect the faint sounds of music playing in our home. This phenomena wasn't restricted to a particular time of day, but it occurred only when Iris was alone in the house. If she were in her bedroom or some other room in the back of the house, my sister heard the radio softly playing in the kitchen. Yet when she went to check out that room, she found it empty and silent. This occurred over a number of weeks. Initially, Iris didn't tell our mother because she didn't wish to frighten her, but eventually, she felt compelled to recount her experiences with the phantom radio. My mother's reaction was extreme relief. She informed Iris that she had been hearing the radio for weeks on end, always in the morning when my sister left for work, the faint tinny sounds emanating from the back rooms of the house when she found herself cleaning up the kitchen. The first few times it happened, Mother was annoyed by the sounds and quickly strode to the back of the house, convinced that Iris had forgotten to shut her shower radio off before leaving for work. However, when she got to the bathroom, she found the radio already turned off. A quick check of my sister's bedroom also found her stereo turned off. Iris wanted to know why my mother hadn't confessed to hearing the sounds. My mother explained that she was alone so much that she didn't want my sister to fear that she was going senile. However, unbeknownst to either my Mother or Iris, I was experiencing the same thing that they were experiencing half a continent away!

I love to kick back and read on the couch, especially on lazy weekend afternoons. One Saturday I was doing just that in Connecticut, when I heard the very faint sounds of music playing close by. I rested the book on my chest and listened for some time. I wondered if I had accidentally set my radio alarm to go off at this hour in the afternoon. Curiosity finally made me get up to look. When I reached the back bedrooms, I found nothing amiss and nothing playing. I shrugged and returned to my reading and heard nothing out of the ordinary for the rest of the day. Sunday afternoon was another matter. Once again, I found myself in the living room (this time grading papers) when

I heard distant music playing. Once again I paused and listened carefully. Unquestionably, the lilting sounds of a tune drifted down the hallway from the bedrooms. Once again, I got up to check on the situation and once again, my search proved fruitless. These events occurred in late November. A few weeks later found me flying down to Texas for the Christmas holidays. Late one night, while engrossed in a novel, I heard the faint sounds of music playing. I thought my sister might have gotten up and flicked the TV on in the living room. Or perhaps she was playing her portable radio softly. When I got up to check, I found the house in darkness and everyone asleep.

Now it was my turn to wonder, as my mother had shortly before, if I was going insane and "hearing voices" that weren't there. I mulled things over and decided I was fine. I knew that whatever I was hearing had something to do with Daddy and with the fact that I had been dreaming about him quite regularly during the past two weeks. I was reminded of the night of his passing. I still think that my father's mind was righted upon his death and that he was trying to communicate with me on the night that he died. At times, my father and I had a rocky relationship. Perhaps he wanted to say goodbye or perhaps he needed reassurance that we'd buried all hatchets between us. In any case, the night that my father died proved especially tough for me to get rest. I was living in Connecticut, many miles from my Texas hometown. I read into the wee hours, then fell into a fitful half-sleep around four-thirty. Shortly after six, my mother and sister phoned from Texas. My father had succumbed to a heart attack. From time to time, I will dream of my father for extended periods of time. On these occasions, I pray for the repose of his soul and talk to him, telling him that all is well and that he should rest in peace. A few nights of such prayers usually make the dreams go away.

I decided not to tell my mother or sister about my phantom radio experiences, but I did reveal that I was dreaming my father on a regular basis. Iris insisted on driving me by my father's grave at the cemetery in Benavides. I'm glad she did. After that visit, the dreams stopped.

Curiously, the entire phantom radio affair reached a climax only upon my return to New England. One night, Iris called me up. "Oscar, when you were down for Christmas, did you ever hear a radio playing in the middle of the night?"

I was stunned by her question. "Once," I replied, "but you'll be blown away by what I have to tell you. Even before I went down, I heard a ghost radio playing in my house, up here in Connecticut." Iris and I exchanged stories. We decided that it had to be Daddy who had come home for the holidays. Before hanging up, I thanked her for taking me to the cemetery to visit our father's grave. My dreams of my father stopped and I knew that he was at peace again.

The Haunted Apartment

In Chapter Three of this book, I told the story of Heidi's grandfather's house and its long and varied history as mental hospital, home for people recovering from tuberculosis and family homestead (see "From Mental Hospital to Haunted House"). In the course of that discussion, I asserted that certain locations are more prone to be haunted than others, simply by virtue of the fact that they have been exposed to more history – more *life traffic* – if you will. The likelihood of a place becoming a receptacle for a restless spirit seems to be compounded when those who reside in a dwelling are both physically ill and spiritually troubled. Since Heidi's grandfather's house was both a sanitarium and a hospital for people with tuberculosis, it may indeed have acquired a ghost or two over the years. This is also very likely the reason why my sister's friend Roland found himself living in a haunted Texas apartment. My sister had the unpleasant experience of seeing the ghost on one occasion but Roland has seen it a number of times. He has also felt it – or something else – accost him in the building.

Many apartment complexes are by their very nature high traffic places. Someone is always either moving in or moving out. However, imagine how much this equation has to be multiplied if a particular complex was once a nursing home. Iris's friend Roland lives in such a dwelling in Corpus Christi. The building has been adequately converted and the apartments are comfortable, but there are still traces that remind residents of the building's past (red and green call lights adorn the bathroom wall; handrails are mounted in various places throughout the apartments).

One night, Iris and Roland returned to his apartment after a night out with friends and settled down to watch a movie on television. The apartment was in darkness, except for the light being emitted by the TV screen. Suddenly, Iris detected movement across the room, by Roland's computer. At first, she thought she was seeing some form of shadow play caused by the TV screen; then the vision soon grew sharper and more disturbing.

"It was a man," says Iris. "Actually, just *half of a man*. He was sticking out from the top of Roland's computer table. Even like that, he was very tall and slim. He was bald-headed and skinny, I think, but he wore a black trench coat and a funny little hat with a broad flat brim. He had a hooknose and he wore a very pinched, sour look on his face. He just stared straight ahead. Not at me. Just straight ahead. I stared at him for several seconds before he vanished."

Iris leaped out of her chair, frightening Roland. He asked what was the matter. She told him exactly what she had just seen. Rather than being met with disbelief or ridicule, Roland sighed with relief and quickly explained that he had seen the exact same figure on several occasions in the apartment. He often appeared in the kitchen, Roland explained. His description of the entity – tall, slim and pale, wearing a black hat and trench coat – matched Iris's exactly.

Roland continues to live in the same apartment. He sees the phantom figure occasionally, but in recent months, there has been a more frightening dimension to the haunting. From time to time, when Roland turns off the lights and settles into bed for the night, he feels tremendous pressure on his chest. He tries to fight the pressure and get up, but the pressure won't go away. He has to struggle mightily in order to rise and even then, it is difficult. Long moments later, the pressure will vanish as suddenly and mysteriously as it arrived, leaving a confused and understandably spooked apartment occupant. Whether the source of this new twist in the haunting is the same ghost that Iris saw on one occasion and that Roland has seen a number of times remains vague. Perhaps it is a residual entity from some other part of the complex. Given the fact that the building was once used as a nursing home, it seems likely that any number of deaths took place there. One thing is certain: the more recent invisible entity that fights to entrap Roland in his bed does not sound like a harmless ghost. Indeed, its action smacks of the work of an incubus or succubus – diabolical spirits that try to sexually invade humans while they sleep (see "An Incubus Attempts A Rape," in Chapter 1).

CHAPTER 6

URBAN AND SUBURBAN HAUNTINGS:
TALES BY AND ABOUT MY
AUNTS AND UNCLES

Psychic Sisters

My mother has always been very close to her four sisters. The sisters seem to share a psychic bond. Quite often, one sister will be thinking of another and will get up to call the other, only to have the phone ring before she can get to it. When the sister answers the phone, she discovers it's the sister she intended to call. Perhaps the story that best underscores how alike the sisters are is related to my wedding day, when my mother and two of her sisters gave me the exact same wedding card. This story is remarkable enough but it grows truly amazing when you consider that each sister bought the card separately, at different stores, in different towns!

The Ghost in the Dining Room

My mother's youngest sister, Caridad (or "Cari," as she is affectionately known), has had her share of incredible experiences, one of which took place shortly after my birth. Sadly, I never knew my grandfathers. My mother's father passed away a few short months before my birth and my father's father left this world shortly after I was born. Although she was a new widow and still mourning the loss of her husband, my grandmother insisted on leaving her home in Benavides, Texas and going to stay with my mother in Corpus Christi the week before I was born. My aunt Cari and one of her brothers drove my grandmother to my mother and father's home, dropped her off and stayed for a short visit. As the hour grew late, the siblings started on the seventy-five mile journey home.

It was a January evening and very late before Cari and her brother made it back to Benavides. My Aunt Cari lived at home with her mother. My uncle lived down the road, but he got out of the car and walked my aunt to the door before driving to his own house. Little did brother and sister realize that an incredible surprise awaited them the moment my aunt unlocked the front door and swung it open. Over the years, this house was added onto a number of times in order to accommodate the growing family. The original home was quite small and built in "shotgun shack" style. That is, the rooms of the house were built in a straight row, one after the other: the front door opened onto the living room, which led into a bedroom, which led into a dining room, which led into the last room of the house, the kitchen. Although additions spread the house left and right as the years passed, there is still a strong essence of the home in its original state. If someone were to open the front door, she would still have a clear view through the original section of the house, thanks to the doors in the living room, bedroom and dining room. Thus, when my aunt opened the door on that January night, she could see through the dark living room and first bedroom of the home, into the dining room, where a small lamp glowed. What she saw in the dining room froze her in her position by the front door. My uncle noticed her reaction and followed her gaze.

"I saw my father," Aunt Cari explained to me when I interviewed her. "Standing by the China cabinet, hands in his pockets, neatly dressed. Plain as day. I saw Daddy standing in the dining room."

"Did my uncle see him, too?" I asked her.

"Yes," my aunt nodded. "In fact, he asked me, 'Cari, are you seeing what I'm seeing?' and I said, 'Well, I see Daddy.' He nodded and said, 'That's what I see.'"

"Did the ghost look at you?" I asked. "Did he say anything?"

"No. He just stood quietly by the China cabinet, with a very peaceful expression on his face. Then he walked around the cabinet and disappeared into the kitchen. Of course there was no one in the kitchen when we checked."

"Were you afraid to stay in the house?"

"Not at all," said my aunt. "It was Daddy. There was nothing to be afraid of."

This is one of the most remarkable paranormal incidents that I have ever encountered mainly because more than one person saw the exact same entity at the same time. While such cases are not unheard of, they are more rare. They also offer stronger proof that something wondrous may have just taken place. It's harder to argue with two people who claim to have seen a ghost than with one person telling such a story. It is much tougher to dismiss such cases as figments of the imagination. Neither my aunt nor my uncle ever saw the ghost of their father again, either alone or together, but the incident remains indelibly etched in each of their minds.

Ghostly Visitations on Christmas Eve

My Uncle Lupe was the first of my mother's immediate family to die. It was a tremendous blow to the many brothers and sisters in the Alaniz family, but it was especially tough for my grandmother to accept that she had outlived one of her grown sons. Despite the love and care bestowed upon her by the rest of her children and grandchildren, my grandmother would never be able to overcome the grief that tore her apart after the death of my *Tio* Lupe. She would follow him into the grave seven short months later. Although the official cause of death was kidney failure, it was clear that spiritual pain had much to do with my grandmother's demise.

My uncle died on Christmas Day, 1978, but his mood took a melancholy turn on Christmas Eve. He began to drink heavily and insisted on staying awake after his wife and children went to bed. Many hours later, my aunt was awakened by loud voices. She got out of bed and shuffled into the kitchen and found her husband sitting at the table, engaged in animated conversation. The only problem was that he was speaking to an empty chair opposite his own!

He spotted his wife and said, "Woman, don't you know how to say hello anymore? Daddy dropped by."

My aunt grew frightened. Her father-in-law had been dead for almost twenty years. She pleaded with my Uncle Lupe to come to bed.

"How can I go to bed with company in the house?" he asked, waving his hand at the empty chair across from his own.

My aunt returned to bed. Eventually, she drifted off again. Much later, she was awakened again by the sounds of talking and laughing. She returned to the kitchen door and her husband turned to her and pointed to yet another empty chair. "Look at this! Mr. Cox dropped by too! Have a seat! Join us." Mr. Cox was my uncle's old foreman at the oil refinery where he worked. He had died the previous year. Again, my aunt tried to convince her husband to come to bed; again, he refused.

The next morning – Christmas morning – my aunt awoke early and found my uncle asleep by her side. She woke him up and they got out of bed and exchanged gifts with their children. My aunt then got dressed and left to visit a few relatives before returning to fix a turkey dinner. My uncle walked into the bathroom to shave and bathe. A moment later, his children heard a crashing sound and forced the bathroom door open. They found him sprawled on the floor, near death, victim of a massive heart attack.

That my Uncle Lupe engaged in extremely bizarre behavior the night before is shocking enough; that he claimed to be visited by his dead father and friend shortly before he himself dropped dead is a clear sign that a paranormal incident took place in the house on Christmas Eve. It seems likely that two spirits came to prepare my uncle for his transition into the spirit world.

The Harbinger of Death

Owls are well known symbols of intelligence. A person with exceptional intelligence is often called a wise old owl. The great 20th century American writer F. Scott Fitzgerald was obviously aware of the connotations of the owl when he wrote his masterpiece, *The Great Gatsby*. Nobody can figure out the mysterious Gatsby but for one man – an inebriated party guest with enormous, owl-eyed spectacles whom the novel's narrator, Nick Carraway, discovers scrutinizing books in Gatsby's library. The owl as a symbol of knowledge isn't restricted to authors of adult texts. A.A. Milne included his version of the wise sage in the form of an owl in his Winnie-the-Pooh stories. Even advertising campaigns have capitalized on the owl as a symbol of intelligence. According to a series of successful commercials, even a wise owl will sacrifice knowledge for the taste of a certain candy: "Just how many licks does it take to get to the bottom of a Tootsie Roll Pop? The world may never know." And at least one bookstore chain has used the owl in its company logo over the years.

Conversely, the owl has also been regarded as a symbol of negativity and misfortune over the centuries and throughout the world. Indeed, there are more ill connotations associated with owls than there are positive. According to many folklore specialists, if a person hears an owl hooting nearby, he is sure to be cursed with ill luck for a long period of time, perhaps for the rest of his life. Moreover, if an owl is heard near the home of someone who is ill or if the creature makes repeated "visits" to the same home, then it is a sign that the bird is acting as a harbinger of death. Such is the role that an owl played in the life of my Aunt Mary and her husband, Luis, in the 1970s.

My aunt claims that a large owl screeched and hooted at her bedroom window for a solid week. The owl arrived in the wee hours and awakened the sleeping couple. Aunt Mary tried to shoo the owl away but the angry bird grew more agitated. It hooted and screeched and tried to claw its way through the screen until she swatted it away with a broom. One week later in the same bedroom, her husband Luis died in her arms of a massive heart attack. After my uncle's death, the owl's visits ceased.

Haunted Highways (1)

My mother's youngest sister, Caridad "Cari" Leonor, encountered a ghost on the eighteen-mile stretch of road between Benavides and the equally small town of San Diego. Cari still lives in Benavides, Texas, where she was raised. Over the years, my aunt has traveled the Benavides-San Diego road on countless trips. My grandmother's health declined slowly but steadily in the last two decades of her life. Aunt Cari undertook most of my grandmother's care and drove her down this particular road to several doctors in Corpus Christi and Alice. Cari also traveled this road on a daily basis on her way to and from her teaching position at San Diego High School.

One night in the 1960s, Cari and my grandmother were traveling the San Diego-Benavides road, returning to Benavides from another doctor's visit in Corpus Christi. It was a clear evening but it had grown late on the travelers, since they had stopped to visit relatives before returning to their hometown. As my aunt's automobile sped down the road, its bright headlights illuminated a small bridge in the distance. The bridge passed over the Narcisenio Creek. As my aunt approached the bridge, she saw a streak of white jet out of the dark shadows on the left-hand side of the road. The streak darted in front of the car and took substance. My aunt swears it was a nude woman with flowing brown hair crossing the road.

Cari screeched the car to a halt. My grandmother hadn't seen a thing but my aunt was frantic. Cari exited the car and used a flashlight to search for the woman, convinced that she may have hit her or forced her to jump off the road and into the creek below. Many long minutes later, my aunt gave up the search. The woman was gone.

Ten years before, one of my aunt's brothers had a very similar experience on the same San Diego-Benavides road. My uncle Cruz was driving down the road with three friends late one night. As they approached a curve in the road that eventually puts drivers on a straight path into Benavides, the driver swerved off the road and sent the car flying into wild brush and railroad tracks. The car rolled over. All three passengers survived, but the driver was killed. Later, when Uncle Cruz and the rest of the passengers were queried, they all swore that their friend had swerved to avoid hitting a beautiful woman who appeared out of nowhere and proceeded to walk onto the highway, directly in front of their approaching car.

Who is this mysterious ghost who roams the highway between San Diego and Benavides? Other people claim to have seen a similar figure, only to have her disappear as their car approached her. Some call her "La Llorona" and still others "La Malinche." *La Llorona* (translation: *The Wailing Woman*) was initially known as *La Malinche* (translation: *The Mean One*) because she was regarded as a traitor. La Llorona is perhaps the most famous ghost in Latin-American folklore. Originally an Aztec, this woman (whose name was either Malintzin or Marina) was eventually acquired by the Mayan Indians as a slave. When Spanish conquistador Hernando Cortez arrived to conquer Mexico in 1500, the Mayans offered the woman to Cortes as a gift. He kept her as his concubine and used her to mollify men in his ranks as well as other conquistadors. La Malinche became invaluable to Cortez in communicating with Native Americans and assisting him in negotiations. Eventually, Mexicans reviled her and viewed her as a traitor for having assisted the Spanish in conquering of their lands. Perhaps it was the Spanish who gave La Malinche the nickname "La Llorona" by perpetuating the myth that she drowned her young children when Cortez was going to abandon her and return to Spain. Regardless of how this woman came to be known as The Wailing Woman, she is said to continue to make appearances throughout Mexico. Eventually, as the legend of La Llorona spread, she was spouted in territory north of the border, into a good portion of the southwestern United States, especially Texas, New Mexico, Arizona and Southern California. Today, there are countless urban legends that tell of people hearing the cries of La Llorona, forever doomed to walk the earth near bodies of water, searching for the bodies of her drowned children.

If La Llorona does make as many appearances throughout Mexico and the Southwestern United States as people say, she is in frequent demand and gets around. Instead, I think that any ghostly apparation seen near a creek – especially a ghost that exhibits any kind of distress – is apt to be labeled La Llorona. I believe that what my Aunt Cari and Uncle Cruz saw was not the spirit of La Malinche but a spirit that is attracted to – and perhaps doomed to – haunt this particular region.

UFOs Over the Haunted Highway

Although ten years and roughly eight miles separate the incidents experienced by my aunt and uncle, the similarities are undeniable. Curiously, the Benavides-San Diego highway attracts more than ghosts. The eighteen-mile stretch that comprises the Benavides-San Diego highway has been a hotspot for UFO sightings over the years.

My *Tia* Lupe was the first person that listened – really *listened* – to my young-boy speculations of life on other planets. I was quite young but Aunt Lupe recognized how deeply I was engrossed in the world of science fiction and paranormal phenomena. When I was ten years old, she gave me a treasure that I still keep close at hand: Edward J. Ruppelt's classic study of the UFO craze of the 1950s, *The Report on Unidentified Flying Objects* (I see the text shelved alongside other books in my study even as I sit here typing). It's not that this particular book proved to be the most influential I've ever encountered on the subject of UFOs. Indeed, Project Blue Book, which Ruppelt once headed, is considered an official debunking agency by some ufologists and a smokescreen by others, designed to keep attention focused away from actual UFO investigations being conducted by the government. Still, Ruppelt's text was the first UFO book I got my hands on, thanks to Aunt Lupe. Here was a text that, by nature of the serious study devoted to its subject matter, validated my belief that such puzzling aerial phenomena deserved attention.

In addition to the treasured UFO text, Aunt Lupe gave me other related gifts: she told me many stories of the glowing discs that appeared in the night sky around the outskirts of Benavides. She had good reason not to dismiss these stories; she herself had witnessed a mysterious light dancing around the small town's night sky. One summer evening in the 1950s, Lupe was sitting out on the front porch of my grandmother's house. As she conversed with her mother-in-law (my grandmother), my aunt spotted a bright light jetting up from behind a patch of trees on the horizon.

"It seemed to soar up from the direction of the church and the town green," Aunt Lupe recalls. "It was very bright and shaped just like a can of vegetables or fruit."

My grandmother and aunt stood up and watched the can-shaped UFO fly around and make rapid 45-degree turns on the horizon. "At times it looked less like a soup can and more like a big glowing oil drum," my aunt explained "It moved here and there and danced around and zigzagged. Then all of a sudden, it took off straight up into the air and grew tiny and winked out."

Such sightings in and around the outskirts of Benavides were common in the 1950s and 1960s, my aunt emphasized. She claims that many drivers cruising the eighteen-mile stretch of highway between San Diego and Benavides frequently spotted mysterious aircraft. One of Aunt Lupe's flying disc stories is particularly engrossing. The story involves her sister and brother-in-law.

As my aunt explains it, her sister and brother-in-law were driving down the stretch of road between Benavides and San Diego one night, heading for the city of Alice. All of a sudden, a splash of light flooded the car and the roadway around them. My aunt's sister and brother-in-law were frightened by the sudden spotlight bathing their vehicle, which was still cruising down the roadway at roughly sixty miles an hour. My aunt's sister looked up and saw a bright round UFO keeping pace with them. A blinding beam of light emanated from the craft and washed over car and roadway. She screamed and yelled for her husband to speed up. "I'm trying," he replied. "But the car's slowing down." My aunt's sister confirmed that her husband had floored the gas pedal but the car was actually losing speed rather than racing forward. When the car slowed to a crawl, the UFO hovered stationary for a few moments. Then the spotlight winked out and the craft shot off into the eastern horizon, leaving two extremely frightened human beings on a lonely South Texas highway.

Other residents of Benavides and San Diego have spotted lights on this roadway. It is also worth mentioning that it was on this same stretch of road that I had my astounding encounter with an entity that appeared to be the Virgin Mary (see Chapter Two, "Vision of the Virgin Mary"). In the next chapter, other haunted highways will be examined, but the San Diego-Benavides highway seems to be a magnet for the supernatural. The locale begs further study.

Holy Statues and the Supernatural

Many Catholics revere icons of the gods and saints they worship. They buy statues of Jesus Christ, Mary and various saints and set up altars and mini-shrines to them. Critics of this practice argue that people are praying to the icon, not the deity or sacred entity which it represents. Those with strong religious convictions argue that they are intelligent enough to understand that the statue is merely that – a representation of a god to be worshipped – and not the god itself. Two women who married my mother's brothers claim to have had supernatural experiences with holy statues. Before my aunt Lupe married my uncle Cruz, she lived in Benavides with her own family. One day, close to the end of World War II, she heard her mother calling her from the other room. My aunt raced to her mother and found her kneeling before a statue of the Sacred Heart.

This particular statue depicts Christ holding his hands up in prayer, raising his eyes skyward as well. A glowing red heart is exposed on his chest. My aunt's mother pointed to the statue's face. Wet droplets fell from its eyes and trickled down its finely sculpted cheeks. The statue seemed to be crying real tears! My aunt's mother was ecstatic because she said she knew her sons were coming home from the war soon. A few hours after this incident, the family and the rest of the United States learned of the Japanese's unconditional surrender. The Second World War was over.

Another aunt also has a story that involves a statue of Christ. My aunt had been going through a very rough time with her faith and with life in general. She found it increasingly difficult to accept the religious doctrine she had been practicing since she was a child. Moreover, try as she might, her prayers didn't seem to be making her life any easier. One Saturday evening after Mass, my aunt stopped by a tall statue of Christ in an alcove off the main foyer of the church. She knelt, lit a candle, prayed silently, rose and rubbed her hands on either side of the statue. While doing so, she asked Jesus Christ to renew her faith. Instantly, my aunt felt her body grow prickly and agitated. No amount of scratching or squirming in her expensive church clothes would alleviate her discomfort. My aunt requested that her husband take her straight home, even though they had planned to go out to dinner. Once at the house, she raced to her bedroom and removed her clothes. In so doing, she made a shocking discovery: her dress and slip were filthy with loose earth! Never before had the dress or slip been in such disgusting states. Indeed, both garments were clean when my aunt put them on, yet as she shook them out, there was so much dirt imbedded in them that it flew all over the bedroom and coated part of her bedspread. (I can't resist the temptation to editorialize here. My aunt's next move was extremely foolish. She admits to sweeping up the dirt and throwing it away! *How could she?* That earth was the ticket back to the faith she was struggling to retain.)

Spirit Lights (1)

Several of my pictures in cemeteries have captured bright balls of light floating about. These glowing globules are called *spirit lights* by many paranormal investigators. Spirit lights can appear in both daytime and nighttime photos. Psychics theorize that the camera actually captures the energy of a spirit in these photographs. Often these lights aren't visible to the naked eye but show up on the film. Skeptics quickly point out that atmospheric conditions are responsible for such light effects. While it is true that weather conditions can affect photographs, I have made it a point to abort investigations if the weather is poor. Foggy and misty nights should be avoided when taking photographs in the hopes of capturing a paranormal presence. In some cases, spirits lights are visible to the naked eye. These lights are by no means exclusively New England phenomena. Many people have encountered spirit lights throughout the world, including South Texas.

As a child, my Aunt Lupe grew up on a Texas ranch near Benavides. It was there, around dusk, that she and her uncles saw floating balls of light skimming around the ranch.

"They looked very similar to an old fashioned lantern," my Aunt Lupe said when I asked her about them. "They appeared many times and they liked to hover around the windmill and the brush country. Many of the old timers used to laugh and say it was some kind of strange bird but the last time I checked, we don't know of any birds that give off bright light, do we?"

Certainly not. My aunt said the lights made frequent appearances around the ranch through her childhood. After floating around for a while, they would wink out or zoom away, especially if someone would try to approach them.

Still, no accounts of spirit lights that I've run across have been as frightening as the encounters that my Uncle Marin had with these lights. Marin was a lifetime hunter. During hunting season in South Texas, he enjoyed getting up early and driving out into the woods to bag a deer. One morning in the 1960s, he arose shortly before four in his Benavides home and headed out to a dense wood near the town. People around the Benavides area call this particular stretch of thicket "La Mota," for some unknown reason. My uncle had hunted in these woods countless times throughout his life, but on this particular morning, something occurred that made him abort his morning hunt. As Marin entered the woods, he spotted a bright light in the thicket ahead. Although the light cast no beam toward my uncle, it shone with extreme brilliance. The globe of light hung stationary about five feet off the ground. My uncle said that it reminded him of an old-fashioned kerosene lantern being held up by someone in the distance but the light seemed far too brilliant to be emanating from such a lamp. (Recall that my Aunt Lupe also described phantom lights as resembling "an old-fashioned lantern.") So bright was the orb that he couldn't even confirm if it was coming from a lantern or some other light source. Uncle Marin recalled that its brilliance prevented him from looking at it for longer than a few seconds at a time.

My uncle called out but nobody replied. He tried again and was greeted by the same silence. Finally, Marin decided to abandon the section of woods and hunt elsewhere. Up ahead, the light tracked his movements and strayed in the direction he was heading. The situation grew tense. Someone was clearly challenging my uncle. Each time he tried to walk in a new direction, the orb followed his movements in the distance and continued to block his path. Finally at a loss and more than a little put off by the whole affair, my uncle decided to scrap his hunting trip.

A few days later, one of his brothers stopped by the drive-in restaurant my Uncle Marin owned for many decades in Benavides. Marin's brother told him of his own aborted hunting trip, due to an unsettling encounter with a bright light in the woods. Marin hadn't seen his brother for several days; he quickly shared his own encounter with the perplexing light. In years to come, both Marin and his brother had other successful hunting trips in the woods called La Mota. There were also other aborted excursions. The brothers encountered the light on several other occasions over the years. At no time did the unrelenting brilliance stand down and give the brothers pass when it made its appearance. On more than one occasion, the brothers tried to approach the light but it would draw back into the woods and never allow the hunters to get closer than twenty or thirty yards from it.

One theory that comes to mind when regarding this light is that it could be a will-o'-the-wisp. Marshy patches of land have been known to produce glowing orbs in a variety of green, yellow and bluish hues. These balls of light most frequently float above marshes and bogs. The latter fact discounts the will-o'-the-wisp theory when it comes to the spirit light in La Mota. South Texas is extremely dry country for most of the year. Further, the brilliance of the light reported in La Mota Woods doesn't mesh with the usual will-o'-the-wisp sightings. Finally, and perhaps most mystifying of all: will-o'-the-wisps do not follow people around, nor do they block a person's passage, as the light in La Mota did with both of my uncles.

As things turned out, my uncles were only the first of many people who ended up seeing the mysterious lights in the woods surrounding Benavides. Soon, other hunters shared their own stories of being followed by lights in the forest. To this day, this phantom lantern continues to appear in the woods around Benavides and on the outskirts of town.

Cryptozoology 2:
Texas Bigfoot, "the Little Penguins" and the UFO Connection

To reiterate, the study of elusive, legendary and unusual creatures is called cryptozoology (see "Cryptozoology: Goat-Man and Big Bird" in Chapter Two). A great deal of the time, cryptozoologists have little more than the stories of eyewitnesses with which to work. If they're lucky, they may also have a few grainy photographs or a poor sound recording to analyze. The capture of extremely unusual or allegedly extinct creatures is rare; corpses are equally scarce. Yet eyewitness sightings prevail.

Over the years, there have been countless reports of strange creatures around the state of Texas. Along with the 1960s and 1970s sightings of "Goat-Man" and "Big Bird" in north and south Texas, respectively, perplexed citizens in the Harlingen and lower Rio Grande Valley areas of the state reported spotting other curious beings. Some of these creatures seemed kin to the Big Bird sightings – incredible avian animals seen swooping through the air over wooded areas and deserted crop fields. However, other creatures in the area seemed to be amazing amalgamations of human and animal. One outbreak of sightings dealt with a beast that sounded like a Texas Bigfoot! The creature was said to be a gargantuan, hairy and misshapen man-beast with enormous strength.

Predictably, most South Texas citizens dismissed these "Big Bird" and man-beast reports as the ravings of drunks and publicity seekers. However, people from all walks of life reported seeing the strange winged and hairy phenomena in the Lone Star State in the 1960s and 1970s. Some of these included serious-minded law enforcement personnel who were called to investigate various sightings. (For a more detailed story of these Bigfoot-like sightings in South Texas, I highly Curt Sutherly's *Strange Encounters: UFOs, Aliens and Monsters Among Us*.)

At the same time that South Texans were spotting Goat-Men and Big Birds and hairy creatures stalking the night, a more widespread wave of sightings was occurring throughout America. More than fodder for cryptozoologists, these sightings involved strange flying discs and their pilots. Astonishing encounters with strange bulbous-headed, black-eyed creatures became increasingly common throughout the nation, especially after the famous Betty and Barney Hill "UFO Incident." Long before Whitley Strieber came forth with his fascinating story of abduction and *Communion* with "visitors" that may or not be aliens, the Hills claimed to have been on a nocturnal drive through the New Hampshire woods when they stopped to investigate a strange light in the distance. It took much time and a psychotherapist to unearth the full mystery of that fateful night. Eventually Betty and Barney Hill remembered being abducted by diminutive creatures. These strangers allegedly took them aboard a spacecraft and conducted a number of physical examinations and experiments upon them. After the Betty and Barney Hill saga grew widely publicized, many American citizens stepped forward with their own scary stories of abduction at the hands of space aliens. Some of these "victims" were less than reputable, but others were as sincere as Betty and Barney Hill in their belief that they took part in something fantastic. The reactions of these witnesses – or victims – were varied. Some were terrified by the experiences; others seemed perplex by the memories that came flooding forth, once unleashed. Almost all the participants were angry over having been treated like laboratory animals, without having given their consent.

Then again, not everyone who sees a strange object or a strange being claims to have been abducted by it. Some people simply report spotting these anomalies. When interviewed, they confess that they were too frightened to investigate any further and raced as quickly as possible from craft and creatures. My Uncle Marin would fall into the latter category on the night that he and several of his employees came upon terrifying wee-hours visitors in the town of Benavides, Texas.

I was a boy when my uncle had his experience. My family was visiting relatives in Benavides. I remember getting up and finding Uncle Marin in the dining room of my Aunt Cari's house. Cari was Marin's sister. The two confided in each other when they were troubled. Even as a kid, I could see that my uncle was not himself on this particular morning. Softly and slowly, he told my aunt a perplexing tale. I only heard a small portion of it before I was hustled out of earshot. My uncle passed away many years ago, but thirty-some odd years after his strange encounter took place, I interviewed my aunt about the incident. Aunt Cari brought me full circle and finished Uncle Marin's story:

"Marin owned his drive-in for many years. He always closed up late – around one o' clock – and drove home anyone who had stayed on to help him close. Usually, it was one or two men. In the summer, it was a couple of older high school boys Marin would hire to help him run the place and cook and close up. The night this happened was very late on a Friday or Saturday. There were four helpers on those two nights because that's when the drive-in was busiest.

"Most of the men had a car, but Marin usually drove the high school part-timers home in his pick-up. It was well after one before they finished cleaning up the drive-in and Marin counted up his receipts and cash. Afterward, he had four young men to drive home. Two got into the front cab of Marin's pick-up and two climbed aboard the back of the truck. The five took off in his truck and drove through the sleeping town. Marin was driving down Main Street, past the closed banks and shops. He was about to execute a turn and take a side street to drop off the first boy when he hit the brakes. The truck's headlights lit up the porch of the town drugstore. This is where his story got weird. Marin swore he saw three or four little men walking across the porch of the drugstore."

"I asked him what he meant by 'little men.'"

"According to Marin, they weren't little people like midgets or dwarfs. They were squat and very low to the ground. Their skin color was a dull gray and they had a funny way of walking. Actually, he didn't call them 'little men;' he called them 'penguins!' They seemed to march or waddle, he said. They turned and stared at the pick-up and then scattered with their strange waddle.

"He was so perplexed by the incident. It troubled him for years. I'm glad Marin wasn't alone that night, though. He saw something very weird and he had four other witnesses to back him up. All of the boys remembered the little creatures. Some put them at two feet tall, some at three. A couple of the part-timers remembered three creatures, while others claimed there was a fourth creature – and maybe even more – in the shadows beyond the headlights. But they all pretty much described the exact same thing: little gray men wandering back and forth with a strange waddle.

"When Marin's headlights lit them up, they scattered into the alleys and shadows behind the drugstore. Marin was very frightened but he tried to put up a brave front for the sake of the boys. They were petrified. The two riding in the back of the pickup insisted on wedging themselves into the front cab of the truck! Imagine! Four guys in the front of the pickup, plus your uncle trying to drive! These were high school seniors – a couple of them even played football – but they were so terrified that they refused to ride in the back of the truck cab.

"I asked my brother if he had reported the incident to the sheriff or anyone. He laughed and said that it would be useless to do so. They would only make fun of him and he was afraid of hurting his business, his reputation and that of the boys. He even admitted that he didn't know if he himself would believe such a story coming from someone else in town, but since it had happened to him personally, he had no choice but to accept it. He seldom spoke of that night again – maybe once or twice over the years, and only to me. When he did, he just laughed and said it was the night he saw the little penguins."

What did my uncle Marin see on that long-ago summer evening in the deserted streets of Benavides? I would venture to say that the supernatural phenomenon he stumbled upon might be associated with the many UFO sightings in and around town during the 1960s. It is curious that UFOs were spotted in deeper South Texas in the 1970s, around the time that people were sighting Texas Bigfoot-like creatures, goat-men andenormous flying birds. Do UFOs and their crew mask their presence by taking on the visage of strange animals? If so, and if we use Dr. J. Allen Hynek's famous scale of UFO categorization as a guide, my uncle may have come close to having a "close encounter of the third kind" – actual contact with an extraterrestrial entity – on the night that he saw "the little penguins."

Our Lady of Guadalupe

Over the years, there have been hundreds of sightings of the Virgin Mary throughout the world. Mexico is no exception. In the land near present day Mexico City, the Virgin made several famous appearances. Today, many Mexicans and Mexican-Americans continue to worship the Virgin under the name of Our Lady of Guadalupe and *La Virgen de Guadalupe*. The Virgin Mary was said to appear around South Texas with great frequency in the 1940s, 1950s, 1960s and even into the 1970s. Some people swore they saw her in the garb and visage that is most commonly associated with the Lady of Guadalupe sightings. Others claimed to have encounters with a beautiful and serene woman dressed in white and pastel blue, complete with shawl or scarf. In most cases, the woman would mysteriously vanish shortly after the sighting. Such was the case at my grandmother's Benavides house in the early 1940s. There, my grandmother and my aunt Fidela had an encounter with a figure they swore was the image of *La Virgen de Guadalupe*.

My grandmother and aunt were moving through rooms located in the front of the house when they spotted a bright light emanating from one of the back bedrooms. They turned and saw a woman dressed in green and red robes. Mother and daughter exchanged surprised looks that confirmed what the other was seeing: the Virgin Mary in her

Guadalupe visage. Then the apparition moved through the open door of one bedroom into another. When Grandmother and Aunt Fidela went to the back bedroom to investigate, they found it empty. However, neither woman doubted what she had just seen.

The Confrontational Ghost

My mother comes from a very large family (eight brothers, four sisters). Among the siblings, a majority claim to have experienced paranormal phenomena. The light that blocked the path when two of my uncles went on a hunting trip isn't the only confrontational entity that the family has encountered. About twenty years before my uncles had their run-in with the phantom light, two other uncles had a far more disturbing experience with a feisty entity. This spirit came not as a globe of glowing energy but in the guise of a man.

It was a clear cold December night in the 1940s. On foot, my Uncle Felipe raced home from a friend's house. His steps fell softly on the side of the pavement as he trotted up a small incline on the Texas road. Another mile or so and he would spot the glowing lights of Benavides in the distance. Felipe knew he should have started home earlier, but it had been a tough workweek and he felt he was entitled to have a little fun on a Saturday night. Earlier, he had caught a ride to his friend's house. The two had driven the short distance from Benavides, down the Benavides-Freer road and turned off onto the gravel road that led them to the ranch where several more of their friends lived. When the friend with the car called it a night at eleven and drove back to town, Felipe opted to stay on. Together, he and his other friends partied until a little after two in the morning.

Felipe dreaded the walk home. The five-miles didn't seem at all far by car, but walking the distance after a night of drinking and whooping it up made the trek seem interminable. As he trotted on, bracing himself against the chilly night wind, Felipe wished he had stayed at his friend's house rather than trek back in the 40-degree temps. He had one bailout option: he knew his great-aunt and uncle lived a short distance away, in an ancient isolated ranch house beyond the thicket of woods to the east. The gravel road leading to his *Tia* and *Tio's* house was coming up soon. Still, Benavides was closer now – the outskirts of the city no more than three miles away – and he was making pretty good progress.

As Felipe got to the top of the slow ascent in the road, he spotted an oncoming figure walking briskly toward him in the distance. As they drew closer, my uncle could tell the shape belonged to man. He was tall, wore a dark coat and a small hat on his head. In those days, when many people walked long distances, it was common courtesy when faced with such a situation to move across the road and give the stranger generous pass. My uncle did just that and continued tramping toward Benavides. A moment later, he was surprised to see the figure cross the road and continue walking briskly toward him. Felipe crossed the road again and continued on his way. Once again, the stranger mimicked my uncle's movements and crossed the road. Felipe grew nervous. The furthest thing he wanted tonight was a fight. For the third time, he crossed the road. The figure was nearly upon him, but still far enough to cross the road yet again and head straight toward my uncle. At this point, Felipe had come upon the narrow gravel road that would take him to his great aunt and uncle's home. He turned onto the road and broke into a run. He didn't stop or look back. Before long, he made it to the front porch of the old house. A few loud knocks later and he was seated safely inside the small wooden home.

My uncle kept the disturbing incident to himself for several days. One afternoon, his older brother Rafael announced that he was going to take a walk to their aunt and uncle's house beyond the outskirts of town and invited him along. Felipe declined and told his brother about the incident. Rafael laughed at his brother. He teased him for chickening out of a fight and told him he should have let the stranger have what was coming to him if he wanted to get in his face that badly. "He better not try any funny stuff with me," my Uncle Rafael said. "He'll be awfully sorry."

Rafael made it to his aunt and uncle's house without incident. While there, he helped the older couple with a number of chores around their property, then dined and chatted with them for a good while before starting home. His aunt tried to talk him into staying the night. She told Rafael that his brother had showed up in the wee hours a few nights before looking petrified. Felipe claimed that nothing was wrong and that only exhaustion had forced him to seek shelter at their house for the night, but his aunt knew better. My uncle explained his brother's trouble on the road. Once again, Uncle Rafael laughed at the situation and Felipe's reluctance to confront the bully. In spite of the couple's invitation to stay the night, he headed home shortly after ten.

It was another clear and cold night – in some ways a carbon copy of the evening when Felipe walked the lonely road. Rafael felt good. The walk in the chilly breeze was invigorating. He had a belly full of home-cooked food in him and the spring of youth in his step. He almost wished the weirdo would make a second appearance on this night. Rafael was a scrapper and proud of it. And come to think of it, just in case the bully did show up my uncle decided to fortify himself for an attack.

The outskirts of the town dump were nearby. Rafael veered off, trotted down a narrow road and kicked around until his boot jabbed something strong and solid. He reached down and picked up a long slender pipe. Weapon in hand, Rafael returned to the main road.

He was about two miles from Benavides when he spotted a stranger heading his way. It was his brother's bully, all right, looking just as Felipe described him: tall, with a small cap on his head and a dark coat. The man kept his hands in his pockets. His face was a black mask in the darkness. Rafael walked a few more yards toward the stranger, giving him the opportunity to cross the road and grant him safe passage. When the stranger didn't offer the courteous gesture, my uncle decided to do so. He trotted across the road and continued toward town. A few moments later, the stranger joined him across the road.

Now Rafael was certain that the approaching figure was the same man who scared his brother senseless. My uncle gripped the pipe a little tighter. He would give him one more chance to be civil, but *only* one more. . .

Once again, Rafael crossed the road; once again, the stranger, drawing ever closer, did the same. My uncle decided that the bold stroller had just bought himself major trouble.

The stranger continued coming toward Rafael and he continued striding toward the stranger. Within seconds they were upon each other, at which point my uncle reared back and let swing full-force with the pipe.

The punch lines of myriad ghost stories have prepared us to guess what happened next. Many of us would assume that the pipe swung right through the stranger. Nothing of the sort happened. My uncle said that he felt the pipe hit its mark. It smashed across the stranger's right shoulder and upper chest with stunning force. My uncle prepared to swing again but the stranger turned toward the nearby woods and raced toward the thicket. It was only then that fear descended upon Rafael. When the figure turned away from my uncle, he ran onto the grassy area on the shoulder of the road and through the barbed wire fence – *through the barbed wire fence* – into the woods beyond. My uncle was stunned by what he saw. Surely, there was some mistake. Perhaps that part of the fence had been taken down. He walked over to the fence, reached and touched the prickly wire. He felt the fence stab his fingers. He reached lower and found the center strand. Several inches from the ground, the third hazardous strand of barbed wire was strung between fence posts.

My uncle dropped the pipe and ran most of the way back to town.

This is a disturbing tale that retains element of classic cases of the supernatural manifesting itself in isolated regions. At the same time, the incident varies significantly. The ghost not only appeared solid, he felt solid. Rafael spoke of the blow the stranger sustained when he slammed the pipe across his shoulder and chest. Yet the same entity could also make himself amorphous and proved it by passing through a potentially deadly fence. The tale reminds us that not all ghosts can be explained as visual psychic residue or images that have been imprinted upon a particular location. Some spectral visions behave as if they are very much alive – and a few evince an aura of danger.

In the forthcoming chapter, I will discuss another (earlier) incident that took place on the same road between Benavides and Freer, Texas. It is equally disturbing and it may involve the same specter.

A Haunted Home on the Range (1)

To reiterate a point made earlier in this text, people who are more open-minded about the paranormal are more likely to experience it in day-to-day life. Such is the case with my Aunt Lupe, who, along with her mother, witnessed the statue of Jesus weeping at the climax of the Second World War (see "Holy Statues and the Supernatural," above). My aunt also spotted bright lights that looked like "floating lanterns" around the family farm on the outskirts of Benavides and can-shaped UFOs doing impossible zigzags in the night sky. Aunt Lupe was also witness to the appearance of a beautiful ghost on a number of occasions.

My aunt lived on a ranch on the outskirts of Benavides when she was a child. The ghost she saw inhabited a house on an adjacent property. This house had long been abandoned and fallen into a state of disrepair. My aunt and her cousin Luis used to enjoy playing in the house, choosing to ignore the potential hazards surrounding such a dilapidated structure. One day as she and her cousin raced through the old home, my aunt came across a tall red-haired woman standing in the kitchen. She looked over at the children, smiled at them and invited them in. Rather than accept her invitation, Lupe and Luis chose to leave the property. They raced home and told their parents about the incident but when the grownups went to investigate the building, they found it empty.

My aunt claims she had several more encounters with the beautiful red-haired woman. As Aunt Lupe recalls, the woman never seemed distressed but rather wore a peaceful look on her face. Perhaps the most striking sighting occurred when the property was finally purchased and renovation began on the various rooms within it. Since some of the workers were related to my Lupe, she and her cousin Luis found themselves playing in the house from time to time, even as it was being repaired. One day, the workers tore down a major portion of one of the interior walls in order to widen the living room of the house. When the workers broke for lunch, my aunt and her cousin stepped through the gouged portion of the wall and into the dimly lit extension. Inside the strange room, they saw the woman once again. She was seated on a rocking chair and swaying serenely back and forth. She smiled at the children and beckoned to them with open arms. Lupe and Luis raced out of the house and got the attention of the work crew. Predictably, when several of the men raced into the house to investigate, they found a vacant rocking chair and an empty dwelling.

Over sixty years later, Lupe's granddaughter, Lina, would have her own encounter with a ranch-house ghost. Unlike the flaming hair apparition, however, Lina's ghost cast an evil pall throughout its surroundings. My aunt felt only serenity emanating from the redheaded spirit. (Lina's story appears in the next chapter, under "A Haunted Home on the Range (2).")

The Mall Ghosts

Corpus Christi, Texas continues to grow in population and overall size. Every time I visit my hometown, I take a drive around. The drives get longer as the city sprawls further out in every direction except the Gulf of Mexico. Today, the city boasts well over three hundred thousand citizens and a strong manufacturing, refinery and shipping industry. Not surprisingly, the retail and restaurant businesses also thrive in the "sparkling city by the sea." Thirty years ago, when I was still a boy growing up in Corpus Christi, the city was considerably smaller and less populated. Rather than the two major shopping malls and astonishing number of shopping plazas that line both sides of South Padre Island Drive, citizens of Corpus Christi had only the Padre Staples Mall in which to do most of their shopping. It was at this mall that my Aunt Lupe had a daytime encounter with two ghosts.

It was late in the afternoon. Lupe, her husband, two daughters and future son-in-law had spent a long afternoon shopping at the mall. Diana, my aunt's oldest daughter, would soon be marrying Weldon, and there was much to prepare for the anticipated event. They walked down a side corridor and headed for the car. Then my aunt spotted a bathroom by the exit doors and decided to use it. As she tells the story, things grew strange shortly afterward:

"I was standing at the sink, washing my hands. Then I looked in the mirror and fixed my hair. All of a sudden, everything went white and brilliant, like someone had turned on many spotlights. In the mirror, I saw something pass behind me. I turned around and there was a little girl. She was tiny! The first thing I thought was – how did this child get in here? Nobody else was in the restroom at the time and I hadn't heard the door open or close. I also thought this girl was far too young to be allowed to go into the restroom by herself. The child looked up at me with pleading eyes and asked if I could help her go potty. But the thing is, she didn't really speak aloud. I heard her very clearly. She asked for my assistance – "Lady, would you help me use the toilet? My daddy is waiting outside but he can't come in here. Please help me." – but she never spoke verbally. It was all mental! Then the child moved into the stall and I helped her with her dress and panties. I was in a confused state because the room was still filled with a brilliant light. Also, the mall was busy at the time, yet nobody had come in or out of the bathroom. When the girl was finished using the toilet, I helped her again and then she walked to the door and reached up for the handle. Then she turned to me and gave me a smile and once again, she spoke to me mentally. She said, "Thank you, lady" but her lips never moved. I heard her but the room was silent. I watched her go out the door and then, as quickly as it came, the blinding light vanished and the dimmer glow of the bathroom lights returned. I stood there in shock for a moment, then I raced out the door. [Husband] Cruz and [daughters] Diana and Gladys were all waiting there for me. [Future son-in-law] Weldon too. I asked them what had happened to the little girl. They all looked at me in a funny way and asked what little girl. I told them the one that just came out before me. They assured me that no one had gone in or come out since I stepped into the restroom! I asked if there had been a man waiting for a child outside of the restroom. Once again, they stressed that nobody had come close to the restroom since I entered it. Then I practically ran to the mall's exit doors and stared outside. Far in the distance, I saw the child! She was clasping the hand of a tall young man and walking by his side between rows of cars. Then the man turned and stared at me. After a moment, he smiled and waved his hands. A moment later, I lost them in the shimmer of the sun. Diana came to me and she saw that I was very shaken by something but I didn't talk about the incident. I was trying to find the man and the child but a bright glare in the distance swallowed them up. I never told anyone for many years. I had so many worries at the time. I was sure that if I told everyone the details of my story they would think I was going crazy."

Certainly this qualifies as one of the most unique encounters with a ghost that I have come across. And yet, it makes a curious sort of sense when one considers the background of the storyteller. My aunt Lupe has always been thrust into the role of caregiver and provider. Like countless women growing up in the first half of the twentieth century, she married and immediately assumed the role of housewife. After she married my mother's brother, Cruz, Lupe raised two daughters. When my uncle had a severe heart attack and was laid up for years, Lupe watched over him night and day. After my uncle passed away in the early 1980s, my aunt continued in her role as caregiver, watching little nieces and nephews while their parents worked. Eventually, she would also help keep watch over her granddaughter, Lina. How interesting that even ghosts called upon my aunt for assistance. Why they chose such a location and time for an appearance remains baffling (what would ghosts need with bathrooms designed to deal with physical bodily functions is beyond me), but it is interesting to note that the ghosts seemed to be testing my aunt's willingness to assist people in need, even under awkward circumstances. Perhaps the answer lies not so much in the activity that took place during the encounter but with Lupe's own self-assessment of her mental state at the time: "My husband was very sick, Diana was going to be married soon, and Gladys was still just a little girl. I was very tired and nervous. I didn't tell anyone about the experience – I refused to talk about it for a long time – because I knew that everyone would think I was going crazy." Perhaps whatever visited my aunt on that day at Padre Staples Mall came not to frighten but to bolster her faith and underscore that she would continue to be very much loved and needed in the role as caregiver for many years to come. Today, the encounter only serves to affirm my aunt Lupe's already strong faith in a deity and an afterlife.

CHAPTER 7

A GATHERING OF GHOSTS AND STRANGENESS: COUSINS AND FRIENDS EXPERIENCE THE PARANORMAL

The Native American Spirit

In an earlier chapter, I described my father's clairaudient experiences at *Los Orcones* (translation: *The Stranglers*), the ranch where he grew up. Several other unexplained incidents took place on the property. Eventually, the De Los Santos family moved to nearby Benavides, but my father's sister married a worker on the ranch and remained to live and raise a family there. My aunt and uncle had several children. Two of these children shared some astounding stories with me in later years.

One of my cousins told me of an "Indian" that appeared on the ranch in the 1960s, when she was growing up there.

"The first time I saw him," Abbie explained, "I was playing on a trampoline outside the house. It was dusk, but you could still see pretty well. I was bouncing high up in the air when all of a sudden, I saw somebody creep out of the brush in the distance. He looked like an Indian. He was crouched low. I saw him dart toward a tree and stand there, watching me. I grew very frightened."

"How do you know he was an American Indian?" I asked.

"The way he was dressed – or not dressed – and what he was carrying. He was very dark and bare-chested, except for a sling across his chest. I think he had a pouch across his back, maybe for arrows, but I can't swear to that. I do know he was carrying a bow. The only thing he wore was this leather loincloth, like Tarzan, you know? On his feet, he wore tall leather moccasins, more like boots."

"I would've probably been scared senseless," I said.

Abbie nodded. "Oh believe me, I was. I tried hard to stop bouncing on the trampoline but it took several seconds. When I did, I saw the Indian dart behind the trunk of the tree. I knew that I would be in trouble with Mom and Dad if I went in and told them a crazy story about an Indian on the property and they came out to find nothing. So instead, I did what I still consider to be both a very brave *and* foolish thing. I actually made a long arc around the yard so that I could see behind this tree, but from a distance. It was getting darker, but you could still make things out without trouble.

When I finished my half-circle, I was standing near the woods and could see behind the tree. The Indian was gone!"

"Are you sure? Maybe he moved around the tree as you made your semi-circle."

"I thought of that, so I did something even braver – and dumber. I think maybe it was because something in the wind told me the Indian wasn't really there. Not there like I was there. I ran right to the tree and ran around the trunk quickly. The Indian had truly vanished!"

Abbie saw the Indian on several other occasions, as did other people who lived on the ranch. At one time, various Native American bands associated with the Coahuiltecan tribe populated the region around South Texas. The De Los Santos family arrived from Spain and settled in extreme South Texas, but many Mexicans in the region were quite resentful of the Spanish arrivals (this was not a Spanish inquisition, but certainly, a Spanish *imposition*). As a result, the De Los Santos family uprooted and moved further north, although they still remained in the region known as South Texas. After founding the tiny village of San Pablo and settling in, the De Los Santos family engaged in frequent skirmishes with Native Americans who were either inhabiting or conquering this region of Texas.

To reiterate a point made while discussing Native Americans and their questionable association with the hauntings in Corpus Christi's Crest neighborhood (see Chapter One), the Coahuiltecan bands native to this region of the state were comprised predominantly of passive hunter-gatherers. However, these Indians were forced to fight to keep their territory when the Apaches swarmed down from their northern territories and engaged them in battle. The Apaches invaded Coahuiltecan country because their own territory was invaded by the Comanche. These aggressive Comanche created the domino effect that eventually resulted in skirmishes between the Apaches and the Coahuiltecans. The Coahuiltecans fought to keep hold of some of their land. They also pushed deeper into the South Texas region that was occupied by various Mexican and Spanish settlers. This included the territory where the De Los Santos family founded San Pablo. Perhaps the Coahuiltecans were the unluckiest participants in this territorial skirmish. Is it really any wonder that these noble people eventually disappeared? Consider the encroachment faced by the Coahuiltecans: Apache invasions from the North, Mexican and Spanish intrusion from the South and diseases brought in from the east, when the Spanish sailed in from the Gulf of Mexico. The Coahuiltecans resisted as much as they could. That included numerous fights with the De Los Santos's. Over the years, my cousin Umberto has filled several bags with arrowheads found on the dilapidated De Los Santos property in San Pablo. The ancient homestead has triangulated holes at the top that were built right into the house on the upper level. My ancestors used these holes to stick their rifles out and fire upon their Indian attackers during countless skirmishes.

I provide this brief slice of De Los Santos and Native American history to emphasize that contra any recent sugar-coated accounts seeking to conceal the aggression that was a part of the territory in the 1800s, skirmishes between Native Americans and settlers throughout South Texas are grim reality. With that in mind, perhaps some of the stories told by the ranch hands at Los Orcones ranch should not be quickly dismissed. As rumors of an Indian spirit spread, the old ranch hands recalled talk of a particularly nasty battle that took place on and around the property many years before. According to Abbie, several old-timers told her that one particular Native American had the misfortune of being captured on the ranch. The settlers inhabiting the property that would eventually become Los Orcones ranch buried the Indian alive on the property. Is this why the ranch eventually acquired its disturbing name? More important, was the spirit of the Native American who was buried alive on the property haunting its current inhabitants?

Within weeks, several others spotted the Indian. Sometimes these visitations came in broad daylight, sometimes at night. The most disturbing of all involved my youngest cousin who lived on the ranch. One night after bathing, Lana stood by the mirror in her room, combing out her wet hair. When she turned to pick up her nightgown, she saw a dark and longhaired man framed in the window, staring in at her. The man was bare-chested. Lana screamed. A minute later, her father and brother were outside, combing the property. Their search yielded nothing. Eventually, the sightings of the Indian ghost grew less frequent but didn't disappear completely. Both Abbie and Lana caught their Native American spirit staring at them from distant buildings and thickets of woods from time to time. Eventually, it was they who left the ranch, not the ghost.

Phantom Flames

Like Abbie and Lana, their older brother Jorge lived at Los Orcones. He also worked on the ranch. One night after putting in a long day's work, Jorge cleaned himself up and walked down the long and narrow road that led to the main highway. Once there, he knew it would be easy enough to hitch a ride into nearby Benavides. Halfway down the unpaved road, Jorge's intentions were radically derailed by a phantom flame.

As my cousin walked down the dark and isolated road, he spotted a dancing ball of fire in the distance. The fire didn't seem to be stationary. Moreover, it was headed directly toward him. Jorge stopped walking and simply watched the flame. He trotted across the road and watched in astonishment as the bright fireball did the same thing and continued floating toward him. Jorge felt fear wash over him. He turned around and headed back to the ranch. A short time later, my cousin ventured a gaze to the road behind him. The bright mass of flames was giving chase! These dancing tongues of fire (Jorge later described them as a roving campfire, moving low to the ground) drifted forward ever closer, until the lights of the ranch house appeared in the distance. At that point, Jorge turned around and watched the flames disappear.

It's no surprise that Jorge decided to stay home that night. He also kept the experience to himself, fearing that his siblings and fellow ranch-hands would make him the butt of many jokes. Indeed, my cousin didn't venture off the ranch until the following Saturday night. This time he caught a ride into town with a visiting friend of the family. In town, my cousin visited his friend Esteban and eventually, the duo decided to walk across town to visit another mutual acquaintance. They stayed until long after midnight and then started walking back. It was a clear night and the cool breeze kept them energized. Very soon, something else contributed to the spring in their step. As Jorge and Esteban made their way down darkened streets of the sleeping town, they were confronted by an eerie sight in the distance: a cluster of phantom flames danced about the ground, blocking their progress. Esteban grew immediately curious; Jorge, on the other hand, grew immediately terrified. Until the moment he saw the flames a second time, my cousin believed that he had either imagined them or been frightened by some natural phenomenon. Now there seemed to be no question but that the flames were connected to the spirit world. The ghostly fire had the power to leave the ranch.

The duo decided to backtrack. When they reached the main street, they chose another road to walk down in order to get back to Esteban's house. As they moved down the new road, the phantom flames suddenly appeared in the distance and floated fluidly toward them! It took several more attempts down several meandering detours before they finally made it back to Esteban's home.

Jorge spent the night at his friend's house. The ordeal was over for the night but not for good. Over the next few weeks, these phantom flames haunted him both mentally and physically. They appeared quite often and, except for the incident that involved Esteban in Benavides, Jorge was always there when he encountered them. Sometimes he was in an isolated part of the ranch when the flames sparked up in the distance. Other times, he was close to some of his fellow workers, in a shed or stable, when he caught a glimpse of the floating fire. On still other occasions he was far away from the ranch, as he had been on the Saturday night when he and his friend were prevented from walking home from the bar. Regardless of location, however, the phantom flames made frequent appearances. Equally disturbing, the ghostly fire began to appear to Jorge in the daytime. Now even the light of day wasn't necessarily safe.

Eventually, Jorge told family and friends about the phantom flames. The term "nervous wreck" is a cliché phrase these days, too often tossed about, but it's a good description of my cousin during this period of time. It seems almost laughable that a strapping young man in his late twenties would be reduced to a babbling, bedridden bundle of fright, but that's what happened to my cousin. He spent a couple of weeks in bed and got better eventually, but his full recovery took years. Today, he doesn't see the flames anymore but he remembers them all too well.

Is there a connection between the phantom flames that haunted Jorge and the blinding spirit light that prevented my uncle Marin from hunting around in the woods from time to time? Admittedly, both stories are similar. Though described as very different phenomena, both involve mysterious light sources that prevented people from crossing certain boundaries. Of the two, the phantom flames seemed to operate in a more aggressive fashion. The bright light in La Mota woods never chased my uncle Marin; it just prevented him from going any further by tracking his movements and remaining just out of his reach. Conversely, the ghostly fires that haunted Jorge seemed to wish to reach him for some reason or another. It is tempting to read both phenomena symbolically: orbs of bright light are often associated with goodness, while flames are often associated with the demonic. But labels can be slippery, often borne out of frustration. Are Jorge's phantom flames the same ones that my father was sent out to investigate, on the very same property, some four decades earlier? Are the flames connected to the Native American spirit spotted by Jorge's sisters around the same time? Perhaps. Or maybe not. Most of us want irrefutable facts, certitudes, understanding and closure when it comes to interpreting life. These qualities are largely absent when studying the paranormal. Currently, there are many possibilities but no definite answers to explain the phantom flames of Los Orcones Ranch. Such is the way the matter is likely to remain.

Spirit Lights (2)

In the previous chapter, I discussed the appearance of spirit lights and chronicled the experiences of my Aunt Lupe and Uncle Marin with such lights around the Benavides area. Those who have seen them have often described these mysterious glowing orbs as similar to old-fashioned gas lanterns. The sightings of such lights around Benavides and its outskirts extend several decades into the past. However, in more recent years, others, including three of my cousins, have seen the lights.

My cousin Ross lived in Benavides for many years. (Eventually, he would move to Corpus Christi, as so many of my relatives from both sides of the family have.) While still living there, he dated Katie, who lived in nearby Freer. Katie would eventually become his wife, but not before their living in separate towns led Ross to experience one of the most frightening periods of his life.

During the time he was courting Katie, Ross found himself traveling the road between Benavides and Freer quite frequently. The towns are relatively close to one another, separated only by fifteen miles and a lonely road. The Benavides-Freer road is very dark at night. Wild Texas brush country lines either side. When he had a night off from work, Ross would make the trek to Freer, spend time with Katie and then head back. Quite often, it was after eleven when he left his girlfriend's house. Late one night when he was driving back to Benavides, Ross noticed a glowing white orb moving toward his car. Initially, he thought it might be a motorcycle heading down the middle of the highway, straight toward him. As the light drew closer, Ross was amazed to discover that the illumination seemed to emanate from a large round disc that pulsated with incredible brilliance. The light drew closer than a hundred feet from Ross's car, then it paced itself with Ross's speed. If Ross sped up to try to catch the light, the disc seemed to propel itself backward at a faster rate. Similarly, when Ross slowed his car, the light slowed as well. According to Ross and others who have seen this light, the orb is blinding and merciless in its pacing. It comes within a hundred feet of the car and then remains at that distance, only to vanish as the car approaches the Benavides or Freer town line. Those who have seen the light insist that it is no mirage or trick of the headlights. Indeed, one late night, Ross steeled his nerves long enough to stop completely on the lonely highway and shut off his headlights. The glow in front of the car remained, waiting for Ross to continue his trip home! Others who have witnessed the light insist that it paces the car not from the front but from the side. They watch the bright orb moving through the brush country, sometimes on the right of the car, sometimes on the left. The light illuminates barbed wire fence and bushes and trees and then winks out as the harried traveler approaches town.

In the case of my cousin Ross, it was he who capitulated and gave ultimate pass to the light. After several anxiety-filled weeks during which his nocturnal trips included many encounters with the ghostly orb, Ross started to visit Katie during the afternoon and he made it a point to leave Freer well before sunset.

The phantom light has made its appearance on the Benavides-Freer highway for at least four decades. Most recently, in the wee hours of the first day of 2002, the light appeared to my cousin Olinda and her boyfriend as they drove home from a New Year's dance. After alarming countless witnesses in the twentieth century, the spirit light has crossed over into the new millennium and is likely to continue to perplex travelers for years to come.

Haunted Schools

The little girl was twelve years old. She sat in the classroom located on the second floor of Benavides Elementary School. The building was not air-conditioned and on this early May afternoon in the 1960s, it was stifling. Try as she might, she found it hard to stay focused on the teacher's droning lecture. Her mind wandered as did her eyes. The girl's desk was located in the row closest to the windows. She gazed at the bright baking world below: the sun baked dry grass and shimmering pavement and –

The girl sat bolt upright in her desk, her eyes riveted to the distant parking lot by the water tower. There, an ornate white carriage was parked, together with a team of four well-groomed and ready horses. The girl tried to blink away the vision but it did no good. It looked like something out of a fairy tale, a surreal Cinderella story. Then the teacher broke her concentration and the girl turned to answer a question. When she returned her gaze to the open window and beyond, the ancient coach was gone.

The girl in this story is my cousin, Maria Elva. She is a fellow paranormal enthusiast who is very open-minded about the subject. As a result, Elva has experienced various unexplained phenomena over the years, several of which took place in and around schools. For some reason or another, countless education sites have long histories of being haunted. Perhaps it is the countless students that pass through their halls and classrooms and dormitories. Many of those students are troubled. Some are ill. Some die or – more disturbing – take their own lives while they are attending these schools. A few actually die on the premises. Detractors claim that most school hauntings can be explained away by one factor: students have lively imaginations and love to conjure up spooky stories. Maybe so, but there are far too many stories and eyewitness accounts to dismiss all or even most haunted school stories as the fictional products of lively storytellers.

Elva's first encounter with the supernatural – her vision of the old fashioned horse-drawn carriage – took place as she sat in a schoolroom. Curiously, some of her more recent experiences also revolve around a school building. Hebronville is a small South Texas town that is close to Benavides. For many years, Elva lived in this town and taught at the local elementary school. Hebronville Elementary has long been purportedly haunted. Elva has been alone in the school and heard the sound of footsteps and doors slamming. On one such occasion, she stepped out into the hallway to investigate and saw the double-doors at the end of the long hallway slam open. "It was like someone pushed them hard and they slammed open," she says. "But nobody pushed them. I watched them slam open by themselves."

There have also been reports of a tall thin man dressed in a black suit – some say it is an old-fashioned tuxedo, complete with tails – roaming the school's dim hallways on late afternoons and evenings. Some students even claim to have caught the man on film, in some of their group photographs. Indeed, the distinguished looking man chose to make an appearance during a photography fundraiser one evening around Christmas. At the time, hallway gates designed to prevent people from wandering through the building after hours closed off some parts of the school. However, a hall monitor spotted a distinguished gentleman walking on the other side of one of the hallway gates. The school employee noted the man's fancy wardrobe – his old-fashioned tuxedo – and quickly assumed he was there for the picture-taking session. She tried to get his attention by waving and calling out to him. She told him he was in a closed section of the school and asked if he was lost and looking for the photo session. The man completely ignored the hall monitor and continued to walk down the hall. The hall monitor's frustration turned to terror when she watched the man walk right through another hallway gate and disappear down a corridor.

Another extremely disturbing story involving the ghost of Hebronville Elementary concerns a young boy out of class on a bathroom break. Ricky was in the fifth grade at the time. He was on his way back to class when he noticed a tall, slender and elegantly dressed man standing by the door to his room. As Ricky approached the door, he took note of the stranger's fair skin and piercing blue eyes. They seemed to bore straight into Ricky. Ricky stood for a moment and was about to ask the stranger to please allow him to enter the classroom, when the man suddenly turned and walked right through the door. Ricky stood in stunned silence. After a moment, he cautiously opened the door. The teacher looked up, as did a few of the students. Ricky's eyes combed the room. The stranger was nowhere to be seen. Ricky stopped by the teacher's desk and quietly asked if anyone had preceded his entrance. The teacher looked annoyed and said no. Ricky took his seat but for the remainder of the afternoon, the boy swore that he heard and felt someone breathing softly upon the back of his neck.

Rural or urban, the reputation of some schools remains shadowy when it comes to paranormal infestation. My mother worked for the Corpus Christi Independent School District for many years. While working at Windsor Park Elementary, my mother met and introduced me to Lisa. Lisa is married to Billy, who works as a maintenance man for the school District. In the early 1990s, Billy was a custodian at Ray High School for a short time. Like Hebronville Elementary, Ray High School has a longstanding reputation for being haunted. Most of the unusual experiences are concentrated around the auditorium and cafeteria wings of the school. Some go so far as to blame the activity on a death that took place in the high school (more about that soon). Many of the stories revolve around one particular section of the school, the combination auditorium-cafeteria.

When Lisa's husband was hired to work at the school, his supervisor quickly put him in charge of cleaning up the cafeteria on a nightly basis. Grateful for the work, Billy didn't complain. One night, Billy prepared to wax the cafeteria floors. He pushed some tables aside, dismantled others and began to stack rows of chairs against the walls. All of a sudden, Billy heard a wave of electronic sound coming from the loudspeakers of the auditorium. He paused and looked to the far end of the cavernous room, where a solitary microphone rested atop a slim metal stand. A program had obviously taken place in the building earlier in the day. Billy continued to stack chairs atop one another. A few minutes later, he heard a *thunk-thunk-thunk* sound, as though someone were testing to see if the microphone was on. Billy decided to check for himself. He walked over to the mike, tapped the windscreen, and heard nothing. The sound system was turned off. Then Billy heard a clanking sound behind him. He turned and witnessed the most shocking sight of his life. A few yards away, one of the metal-legged cafeteria chairs rose smoothly and steadily by itself. It hovered in mid-air for a few seconds, then floated to the half-completed stack of chairs that Billy had been working on before walking to the microphone.

Billy raced out of the cafeteria and sought out his supervisor in another wing of the school. Nervous and agitated, Billy decided to be frank with the supervisor and tell him what he saw. Did the supervisor think he'd gone crazy? "No, I believe you," the supervisor told him. "It's why none of the old hands work the cafeteria, why people keep quitting on us and why we hired you. Nobody wants to work that room. Everyone who does has a story to tell within days. They either demand to be transferred or they quit.

"I've got a lot of folks working here with a lot of seniority," the manager continued. "I'm afraid you have to stick to the cafeteria or request a transfer to another school."

Billy soon joined the ranks of the transferred.

Although most of the paranormal activity around Ray High is reported to take place in the cafeteria, in recent years, other reports have begun to circulate. These usually involve the sighting of a dead student who is said to wander the empty halls of the school from time to time. My old friend and fellow ghost hunter Sam attended Ray High School. He remembers the tragic death of the student who supposedly haunts the school. According to Sam:

"It was 1976 and there was a football pep rally in the gym. The place was packed to the rafters with students and teachers. I mean jam-packed. Everyone was fired up because our football team was up against Miller High, our archrivals. The band was going nuts, the cheerleaders were yelling, jumping and looking fine. It was so loud in there. We were really fired up. Our colors were red and white. Miller's colors were yellow and purple. The cheerleaders were leading us in this crazy chant, 'Make them eat those yellow balloons!' We were yelling this phrase over and over, while from the top of the gym – Ray has a very, very high gym – two guys were tossing down yellow balloons and the gym floor was filling up with them. I turned to yell something into my friend's ear, when all of sudden, I heard a deafening *SPLAT!* I turned back to the gym floor and right away, it was clear what happened: this poor guy – one of the two guys tossing the balloons from the ceiling, over thirty or forty feet in the air – lost his footing on the catwalk and fell. He just narrowly missed landing on a cheerleader. There he lay, totally motionless, on his side. One moment the place was rocking and the next, you could literally have heard a pin drop, it got so quiet. Nobody moved for a few seconds, then teachers and coaches flew to this guy's side. He didn't move a muscle. Later that night, we were all shocked to hear that he passed away in the hospital. He was all broken up inside. He died from internal bleeding."

For almost two decades, Sam has worked for both city and state university libraries. Since that time, he has assisted high school students on research assignments and through them, he has heard of the series of sightings that continue to take place in his old alma mater. Even today, Ray High School students claim that the ghost of a student who was killed during a pep rally haunts the school. Employees at the high school are understandably reticent to discuss the matter with students. Indeed, one young man asked Sam if the student death story was simply a rumor or an urban legend. Sam assured him that it wasn't.

Who haunts Ray High School? Is it one ghost or many? One thing is certain: it seems that the school is undergoing immediate rather than residual hauntings. Many parapsychologists divide hauntings into these basic categories. *Immediate hauntings* are instances during which the paranormal entity is present at the time that it is experienced by the human being. *Residual hauntings*, on the other hand, are cases during which an individual sees, smells or hears a long dead individual. These stunned witnesses are privy to a paranormal pantomime. Rather than apparitions, the witness may be seeing an image of a tableaux that long ago unfolded and is now simply a psychic echo of the actual event. The more we learn about our great planet Earth, the more we recognize that we know so very little about our home. It has been theorized that the earth has certain properties which capture the psychic imprint of events that have transpired. These events may be shocking or they may be "slice of life" in nature. (Have you ever accidentally pushed the wrong button on a camera and wasted a shot? Perhaps this is what occurs in the latter cases.) Residual hauntings are then played out, over and over, like some feedback loop of film or videotape. They may depict a long dead person engaged in the act of experiencing something tragic, or simply going about their daily lives. However, the live human being who witnesses the haunting is usually terrified by the invasion of the spiritual dimension.

That a young student lost his life tragically at Ray High School is indisputable. However, the question remains: Are the stories of an apparition roaming the halls and classrooms of Ray High School little more than rumors and urban legends? Talk to those who claim to have seen inanimate objects take flight around the cafeteria or a stranger walking through brick walls and rows of lockers and they will argue otherwise.

Strange Events at the University Library

Like ghosts and grade schools, ghosts and colleges and universities seem inevitably linked. Maybe it's that most schools are high traffic areas where many people of all walks of life and all sorts of mental states come and go. I know that each of the colleges that I attended or where I taught has had its share of ghost stories associated with it. For example, I earned my Master of Arts and Ph.D. degrees in English at Ohio State University in Columbus. The English Department was located in an old building that was said to harbor a ghost. Today, I teach at Western Connecticut State University. Countless students have told me about an alleged suicide that took place on campus, in the early part of the twentieth century. This suicide is said to be responsible for unexplained manifestations in the university's women's dormitory. Then there are the distinct sounds of a baby crying in White Hall that have been heard by many students. Thorough searches of the building yield nothing. But perhaps the strangest of stories center on Berkshire Hall.

Berkshire Hall is home to the Departments of English, Communication & Theatre Arts, and Athletics. The building is shaped like a giant goal post that has fallen down. For many years, a story has circulated that when the western wing of the building was built, workers quietly removed several old graves that were found around the site. This particular wing would eventually hold the Communication and Theatre Arts Department, along with a nice auditorium where they hold most of their performances. Every great theatre seems to house its share of ghosts. Appropriately enough, this is where the ghost of Berkshire Hall has been most frequently cited. It is always fleeting and always late at night. For some years, janitors refused to work that particular part of the building alone. One Danbury policeman that was hired to guard the gym at night when weekend trade shows were held there tells an interesting tale about his dog. The officer used to bring his German shepherd with him on such nights. The dog walked comfortably throughout Berkshire, but it absolutely refused to go down the long corridor leading to the theatre.

Back in Texas, the university where I earned my Bachelor's degree offers an extremely disquieting ghost story. Before Corpus Christi's university became part of the Texas A&M system, it was known as Corpus Christi State University. I attended the school when it was still good old CCSU and I had quite a fulfilling time there, earning my Bachelor of Arts in English before heading off to Ohio State. While at CCSU, I finally quit my disc jockey job after seven years of being in the radio business on either a full-time or part-time basis. I got a part-time job at the university library and for a couple of years, my best friend Sam became my boss. They say close friends shouldn't work together if they want to remain close friends, but Sam and I disproved that theory many times over. Maybe it's because we've had a lot of practice, working in the city's public library system while in our teens and working for the same radio stations through our mid-twenties.

While working at the library, I met a quiet, unassuming cataloguing technician with a passion for films that even surpassed my own obsessive love of the art. Jim Holmes knew movies back and forth and sideways, too. He watched all of the major first-run flicks and loved to critique them. Jim didn't seem to favor any genre. His tastes ran the gamut. You could usually find him spending his lunch hour poring over a film journal or talking film with fellow buffs around the library. I spent many fifteen-minute breaks engrossed in film discussion with Jim Holmes.

Years later, in the spring of 1994, I was working in New England and had a few minutes to relax in my office before attending a faculty meeting. I downloaded email and found a post from Sam. Sad news: Jim Holmes had committed suicide the day before. It seemed like the strain of losing his mother proved too much for Jim, a bachelor who lived with her and took care of her. I was seized by a sudden pounding headache. Jim was more acquaintance than close friend and I hadn't seen him for several years, but I had always enjoyed conversing with him. I did my best to send positive energy out to Jim's soul, tried to shake the pounding out of my head and went to my meeting. I heard no more about Jim Holmes until several years later. Once again, Sam provided me with an intriguing story that involved an apparition:

"A few years after Jim's death, the reference librarian came in one early morning and went through the routines we all went through if we were the first to arrive in the building. She turned on the lights, fired up the copy machines and prepared for the day. While standing by the copiers, she thought she saw a fleeting image dart behind some shelves near the computer area. She walked over to the computer stations. They would be her next stop anyway. Everything seemed okay. So she booted up the computers and returned to her desk. This was still about ten minutes before the library officially opened and she still had the entire place to herself. The front doors were locked. All of a sudden, she heard the familiar sound of one of the copiers whirring. She walked back to the nook where all the copiers were positioned and sure enough, she found a copy in one of the trays. She looked around the machine and between the copy door and the glass where originals are set out for copying. Both the shelves around the machine and the glass panel atop the machine were empty. The only thing she had was the copy. Centered in the middle of the page was the name, 'JIM HOLMES.'"

The new librarian knew nothing about Jim, let alone his suicide. She certainly rattled the rest of us when we got there that morning. What a story.

"Of course, that's not the first time something quirky happened at the CCSU library," Sam said. He then recounted another perplexing tale that for all intents and purposes has the earmarks of an impish prankster, dead or otherwise:

"This happened at the end of fall semester," Sam recalled. "It was the semester following the one in which Jim Holmes took his own life. It was right before Christmas break. The students had finished up and the library was basically a morgue. I remember being the butt of an outlandish practical joke, if that's what it was.

"I was working 8 to 5 and we were on skeleton crew. I came in and opened up the place in the morning. Together with Security, I was the last to leave at night. Shortly before five, after all the machines had been shut down and the place straightened up, I would make a final round upstairs and make sure everyone was out of the building. I inspected student study rooms, carrels, bathrooms, and other little nooks where students liked to curl up and read. I didn't expect to find anyone. Like I said, we were just entering the interim between semesters. But you never know. One night, I trotted up the stairs to make my usual sweep of the top floor. I rounded the corner of the stairwell and there before me, on the shelves near the stairs, someone had taken every other row of books on two of the massive bookcases – a total of about six shelves, three per bookcase – and shoved all the books from the extreme right to the extreme left. Not only that: these rows of books that had been shoved to the right had also been turned completely upside down! It was some kind of nutty prank, let me tell you – like someone with superhuman strength had simply grabbed the huge row of books, swung them about in their arms and turned them completely upside down, then lined them up again on the right hand side – and very neatly too, I might add."

Sam sighed and knew he would be hard-pressed to leave the building at his usual quitting time. As quickly as he could, he rearranged the books and left them in their proper order. Walking around the top floor and making his rounds, Sam pondered the event. Because semester classes were over, the library had been very quiet and empty that day. Moreover, some of the upstairs walls of the library were made of thick glass. As such, he had a partial view of the tampered bookcases from the ground floor's circulation desk, where he worked. Surely, he would have spotted the joker in the midst of engaging in such a deed? Still mystified, Sam joined security downstairs and together, they dimmed the lights, set alarms and locked up the building.

Another shock awaited Sam the next morning. Once again, the same books on the same shelves were shoved to the right and neatly arranged upside down! Yet Sam had been the first in the building. Had someone managed to remain inside and not tripped up any security alarms? Sam remembered giving both floors of the building a thorough inspection. He even checked bathroom stalls in the men's and ladies' rooms. What was going on? Once again, Sam rearranged the books on the shelves. This time, he kept closer scrutiny of the rare patron who came into the building. He also kept an eye on the upstairs shelves throughout the day. When he closed up the library that night, he made doubly sure to check closely for any hidden stragglers. Sam left the books in their proper order but the next morning showed further evidence of mysterious after-hours antics in the library. Someone had taken great troubles to repeat the prank. This time Sam called campus security and explained the situation. The officers assured him that nobody entered or left the building between the time he closed it and the time he reopened it. Sam was insistent. The upside down books on the shelves said otherwise. And there the mystery rested.

I wonder if these perplexing incidents are the products of a restless spirit or a mischievous human being? It's hard to say. I remember Jim Holmes fondly. He had a great sense of humor but I knew that he wasn't a very happy person. I think that one of the reasons he loved movies with such a passion was because they were his primary source of escape from a lonely and troubled personal life. I am disturbed by the fact that he took his own life. Jim had great stories to tell (I remember especially the enthusiasm with which he told of his personal encounter with "a real live movie queen," Katharine Hepburn) but he wasn't overly boisterous or prone to pranks. On the other hand, after hearing these stories from Sam, I wondered if Jim was at peace. Once again,

I wish his soul positive energy and hope that he rests in peace.

Haunted Highways (2)

There is a fascinating book on urban legends by Jan Harold Brunvand. The book, *The Vanishing Hitchhiker*, takes its title from one of the most famous urban legends that has migrated throughout the country in one variation or another. The story usually concerns a hitchhiker that appears on the side of the road. When some unlucky traveler stops to give the hitcher a ride, he sets himself up for a big surprise. The hitchhiker remains in the car for a short time, only to vanish on the driver. Another variation of the story is slightly more startling: a lone driver suddenly realizes that he is no longer alone and that a phantom passenger has suddenly invaded his automobile, either in the front seat beside the hapless driver or in the previously empty backseat. Still another (and elaborate) variation of the vanishing hitchhiker story focuses on a beautiful young woman looking for a ride by the side of the road. A handsome young man picks her up and offers to take her as far as the dance he will be attending in the nearby town. Coincidentally, the young woman claims she too is headed for the same dance. Driver and hitchhiker attend the dance together and have a great time. Sometime in the evening, the hitcher mentions that she is cold, which prompts the gallant driver to lend her his coat. When they leave the dance, the driver asks where the woman wishes to be dropped off. She tells her impromptu date to leave her in the exact same location, in the middle of the lonely highway. The driver complies and it is only later that he realizes that he has left his jacket with the pretty damsel. He returns to the area the next day and spots a farm in the distance and drives there. The woman who answers the door is shocked to hear the man's story. She tells him that she did indeed have a daughter, but that she was killed many years ago on the highway in the distance, at the exact location that the man claims to have picked up a woman. The woman then leads the man to a small graveyard in the back of the property. There, draped over the daughter's tombstone, is the man's sport coat!

I remember listening to these stories as a kid. For years, young people in my neighborhood claimed to know the exact location where the driver in the latter story picked up his pretty hitchhiker. Others claimed to personally know people who had picked up vanishing hitchhikers on Chapman Ranch road on the outskirts of Corpus Christi. Still others claimed that they themselves had been driving down Chapman Ranch road when they suddenly realized they had an unexpected passenger in the car. Whether the stories about the Chapman Ranch road are true or false remains a mystery. However, it does seem as if they have been greatly influenced by the classic "vanishing hitchhiker" urban legend that has been circulating around America for many years. The story has even been re-told in a song. On the other hand, the stories I have related earlier in this book that focus on the road between San Diego and Benavides are not rooted in classic urban legends (see Chapter 5). Both my aunt and uncle had separate incidents involving a mysterious beautiful woman roaming the road in darkness. Indeed, my uncle almost lost his life as a result of his encounter with the phantom beauty. In both cases, the ghostly female seemed to have vanished into thin air. Moreover, several other relatives had strange encounters on other lonely Texas highways.

The old saying tells us that "Out of the mouths of babes comes the truth." If so, then the words uttered by a distant cousin at the age of six are astonishing. Eva and her parents, Felix and Amanda, were driving from Benavides to Freer on a cold February morning in the mid-1930s. Like the Benavides-San Diego highway, this particular road has a long history of sightings attributed to it. It is on this road that my uncles Felipe and Rafael had their amazing encounters with the confrontational ghost. A decade earlier, that same entity may have already been making its presence known on this road.

Felix and Leonore sat in the front of their sporty black sedan, complete with wide running boards on either side of the vehicle. Little Eva sat in the back seat. The day was cold and overcast but dry. As the family cruised along, they spotted a solitary figure walking along the shoulder of the highway on the passenger side. The figure was dressed in a long black overcoat. A wide-brimmed black hat obscured most of his face. It was obvious, however, that the man was walking toward them. A moment later, the sedan reached the strolling man. As they zoomed past him, something truly incredible happened: with impossible grace and speed, the stranger leaped onto the running board on the passenger side of the car and stood perfectly erect, his black coat pressed against the car's front window! Amanda watched the man through the window and screamed. However, only little Eva, sitting low in the back seat because of her diminutive six-year old figure, had a view of the man above his torso. From her low position on the seat, the little girl stared up at the strange man's shoulders and head. Only a few seconds passed between the time the stranger performed his reckless stunt and the time that Felix slammed on the brakes. But it was already too late. That man had already let go of the automobile's rooftop and jumped off. The car screeched to a halt. Felix executed a careful U-turn and backtracked a few yards, then parked the automobile on the shoulder of the road. He crossed the highway and combed a long stretch of ditches and woods. Up and down he walked. Several minutes later, he returned to the car. Try as he might, he could find no evidence of the madman who dared pull the wild – and seemingly *impossible* – stunt. Felix executed another U-turn and the trio continued toward Freer. Father and mother discussed the incident quietly. They suspected that their daughter was greatly disturbed by the whole affair and they didn't wish to alarm her any further. Eventually, Eva spoke up. She sounded quite composed and matter-of-fact, given the circumstance. Her question, on the other hand, immediately sent another shock coursing through her parents. "Did you notice," the girl asked, "that the crazy man didn't have any eyes?" The parents asked her to explain. "He didn't have any eyes," Eva repeated, "just big black holes where his eyes were supposed to be."

Another incident involving a haunted highway takes place several decades later and involves my cousin Diana. Diana is the older cousin who happened to be in the car with me on the night that I saw a vision of the Virgin Mary reflected on my car window (on the haunted stretch of highway between San Diego and Benavides, I might add). Diana's father – my Uncle Cruz, who had a haunted highway encounter of his own (see Chapter 5) – suffered from heart trouble for many years. One summer night in the early 1980s, my uncle had his final fatal heart attack at his home in Corpus Christi. My first cousin Gladys was with her father at the time, as was loyal wife, Lupe. Older sister Diana had since moved to Austin by this time. EMTs arrived at Cruz's Corpus Christi home and radical first aid measures were induced. As the ambulance sped away with her father, Diana was notified of the grim news. Things didn't look good, her mother warned her; she better get down to Corpus Christi quickly.

Diana and her husband Weldon wasted no time. No sooner had she hung up, then they were in their car, shooting down the highway and heading south. It was a stormy night in Texas. The rain pelted down upon the speeding car in sheets. As Weldon and

Diana drew closer and closer to Corpus Christi, the rain intensified. Diana took the rain as an ominous sign, little realizing that she was soon to be confronted by another, more blatant signal that all was not going well with her dad. Suddenly, the driving rain ceased and the car drove through a short dry stretch of road. Diana spotted a figure on the side of the road. The man wasn't a hitchhiker. He stood with his hands in his pockets. He was dressed simply, in a white T-shirt and khaki slacks, and seemed most unprepared for the cool, stormy evening. In fact, he seemed quite calm and dry. As soon as they passed this figure, the storm resumed and rain slammed the car more forcefully than ever. For a moment, Diana tried to deny the obvious: that the man on the side of the road not only looked exactly like her father but was dressed as her father liked to dress, in a plain T-shirt and khakis. However, it was all too obvious to ignore for very long. Diana strongly suspected that the man on the side of the road was not a nocturnal stroller but an apparition. She suspected that she saw her father, who came to meet his daughter halfway between Austin and Corpus Christi in order to say goodbye.

Is it any great surprise that roadways are haunted? It shouldn't be, if we consider the risks we take every time we get into a car and speed off from point A to point B. Even the safest of drivers can grow careless. Moreover, to a great extent, we are at the mercy of every other driver who happens to be on the stretch of road we use – his reactions, driving experience and overall health become an issue. Similarly, there's always the risk of mechanical failure in our automobiles, even with constant maintenance. The more sophisticated the technology, the easier it is to malfunction and these are often malfunctions that we are powerless to prevent. Human beings inhabit homes and sometimes, for whatever reason, they die in the home and elect to reside there as spiritual entities. They feel comfortable in the home and do not wish to vacate it, or perhaps they were unprepared to die and are struggling with the transition between one form of life and another. Similarly, countless accidents happen on the roadways of the world. People die suddenly. They may have been completely unprepared for the rupture from the physical world. As such, they wander the roadways, seeking some kind of peace and solace in their travels.

There is a distinction worthy of mention which separates roadway ghosts from those residing in homes and buildings: unlike other paranormal phenomena that I have studied, I have rarely encountered stories about haunted highways that involve malicious or diabolical entities. (The exception may be the confrontational ghost that seemed to provoke my uncles, but even this ghost didn't stick around for a long altercation.) Even one of the more frightening cases of the appearance of a ghost by the side of the road seems more like a case of confusion: There is a sharp curve in the road on the eastern outskirts of Alice, Texas. For many years, people riding on the bus between Alice and Corpus Christi have seen a man suddenly appear as the bus rounds the aforementioned curve in the road. This ghost usually appears at night and most of the witnesses have described the apparition's body as transparent. Sometimes he materializes standing near the front of the bus, sometimes at the back of the bus, and still others, sitting next to a frightened passenger. Many witnesses describe this apparition as looking very sad. Others claim that he looks just as frightened and surprised as they feel. Clearly, this is very likely the spirit of an individual who died suddenly and who remains confused and earthbound.

Another variation on this particular theme sounds more like an urban legend but talk to enough people in Benavides and you will find several who swear they are telling the truth. Over the years, several people claim to have stopped and picked up a hitchhiker close to this curve on the highway. Their passenger turns out to be a well-groomed young man in a soldier's uniform. When they ask him where he is heading, the traveler replies that he is going home to Benavides. The drivers are often perplexed. Longtime residents themselves, they can't understand why this man is a stranger to them in such a small town. The soldier remains evasive. When driver and hitcher arrive in town, the soldier usually asks to be dropped off mere yards within the town line or near the first gas station. Most disturbing of all: moments after the soldier gets out of the car and thanks the driver for a ride, witnesses swear the man simply vanishes!

Ultimately, roadway ghosts may be among the most innocuous of ghosts to encounter, but most people who have encountered them stress that a passive attitude makes an entity no less frightening.

Last Visit

Like Diana, my cousin Maria Elva believes that she too was visited by one of her departing parents. It was Elva's parents who had the unsavory experience of being visited by an agitated owl the week before her father's death (see Chapter 5, "The Harbinger of Death"). On the night that he died, Elva was sleeping at my grandmother's house. She remembers being awakened by the presence of someone in the bedroom. Elva felt someone sit down on the mattress at the foot of the bed. She didn't turn around to see who it was, but she didn't feel fright, either. Finally, when Elva was about to roll over and confront her nocturnal visitor, my aunt Cari entered the bedroom and switched on the lights. Elva was shocked to find no one but my aunt in her bedroom and certainly no one sitting on her bed. Before she could voice her bewilderment, she was given the sad news that her father was very ill. Long after her father had been rushed to the hospital in Alice and declared dead, Elva remained haunted by the incident in her bedroom in the moment before Aunt Cari arrived with her news. To this day, she remains convinced that her father's soul stopped by my grandmother's house for one last visit with his daughter before departing this physical realm of existence.

(Worth mentioning here is the fact that Elva's younger sister Nelda is the exact opposite of her older sibling and has no interest in the paranormal. In fact, she goes out of her way to avoid it. Nelda refuses to stay in the room when Elva and I launch into an enthusiastic conversation about the supernatural. She has no stories to contribute and claims that nothing remotely out of the ordinary has happened to her. Together, the sisters make a good example of the way in which those who remain open-minded are more prone to experience supernatural phenomena. Elva remains engaged in the subject and has had several paranormal experiences over the years. Nelda, on the other hand, is clearly closed off to the paranormal and keeps it at bay with the *thanks, but no thanks* vibes she projects.)

The Reluctant Astral Traveler

Some people claim to be active practitioners of *astral projection*. This is a term that is used to describe out of body experiences. The individual concentrates on putting himself in an extremely relaxed state of consciousness, then envisions or *projects* his soul outward. People who have out of body experiences often describe instances in which they visit friends, relatives and faraway places in this spiritual state. Most people find that it takes much practice to engage in successful astral projection sessions. Even those who eventually master the technique place themselves in great danger if they leave their physical form unoccupied for too long a period of time. According to those well versed in occult study, disembodied spirits and demonic entities never given a physical body in the first place hunger to possess a vacant corporeal form. As a result, a person who is engaged in a session of astral projection may return to find her or his body inhabited by a rogue spirit.

I remember that Gail's father had a number of books on astral projection on his bookshelves in the Crest District (See Chapter 1). The events in that haunted house, however, turned me off to reading about the subject for several years. Indeed, if it weren't for the wondrous experience of a close friend, I may have put off studying the subject indefinitely.

Ref's story changed my mind and prompted me to investigate. Ref is a man who prefers to live and breathe in the so-called "real world." His pleasures complement the everyday man's: sports, music, family and community. Although I've known him since high school and we were close friends for many years, the paranormal is an area of interest that we most definitely don't share. Ref is so close-minded about such incidents that even after hearing the many stories I have to tell about the Crest District, he even chose to buy a house in this neighborhood and still resides there! To this day, Ref has only one paranormal story to tell and it involves a case of accidental astral projection. This happened before he bought his own home and still shared a house with his parents and brother. On the morning after he experienced this curious incident, Ref called me up. He was very excited and anxious to share his story with me. He knew that I would be intrigued by it. I was. Almost twenty years later, he reflected on the event. His story remained virtually a word-for-word retelling of his first recounting of the event.

"I was exhausted when it happened to me," he began. "You remember my schedule back then. I was going to school in the early morning, putting in a whole day on the job, returning for night classes. I remember getting home and staring at a pile of books on my desk. I got so depressed. I had tons of homework but I was running out of night to sleep! I finally just said, 'screw it all' and went to bed. I fell asleep almost instantly. All of a sudden, I remember sitting up in bed. I looked behind me and saw myself, sprawled out and fast asleep! I floated up and away from the bed and saw my entire body. Then I looked out the window and I remember feeling so invigorated. Out there, there wasn't any homework or responsibilities or anything. Just the yard, the trees, the moonlight, the sky. I thought to myself, 'That's where I want to be' and I started to drift toward the window. But I stopped. I made myself stop. I looked back and watched my body sleeping and I knew I better not go. I felt fear. I remember drifting back to my body and thinking that I belonged inside it. Then I started to cough and squirm and I realized I was in my body again. I sat up and my head was tingling, the way your arm or leg feels when it falls asleep. I ran my fingers through my hair. I was thirsty, thirstier than I've ever been in my life. I got up and I drank three glasses of water at the sink. I knew that I hadn't imagined it, that it wasn't a crazy dream. A crazy experience, definitely, but not a dream."

Ref's experience prompted me to finally seek out those books on astral projection. I read up about the subject and was surprised by one particular fact: several of the books mentioned that it was important for the astral traveler to keep a glass of water by her/his bedside because the experience dehydrates the body and travelers almost always wake up very thirsty! Another point associated with Ref's experience that is worth considering: out of body experiences might be unconsciously induced by moments of stress or shock. Most of us have heard the assertion that mind, body and spirit are connected, but certain experiences – particular moments of crisis or fatigue – tax that connection. In such instances, we may experience a rupture between these parts of ourselves. We certainly experience such dysfunction when our immune system grows weak and we fall ill. The same may be true of our spirit's ties to the body, when it is in the throes of extreme fatigue and stress. Certainly this describes what Ref experienced on the night he had his out of body experience. One final clarification: it is inaccurate to state that Ref had an experience that involved astral *projection*. Ref didn't project his spirit into the cosmos; rather, he was a reluctant traveler.

"The Little Doctors"

Today, my ex-brother-in-law Adam is a successful lawyer but I still affectionately remember the playful youngster that he was a few short years ago. Adam, Sam and JJ are my brothers and friends. Though we aren't related by blood, the spiritual ties I share with this trio are stronger than those shared by many family members. It's significant that each of these men shares my interest in the paranormal and that each has at least one remarkable story to tell. JJ and Sam's stories are scattered throughout this book. Adam shared a most remarkable story in an interview I conducted with him recently. Elsewhere, I mentioned my belief that UFOs, extraterrestrials and the paranormal may be connected. Adam's curious tale further substantiates my claims.

> **ADAM:** My parents own a cottage by a small lake in Canada and we'd go and spend our summers there, as soon as Dad and Mom finished teaching. Behind the cottage is this golf course. Overall, it's pretty isolated. I hated going to Canada in the summer. My parents always thought it was because I was bored, but the truth of the matter is that I hated to go there because of the little doctors.

> **OSCAR:** I've heard you mention "little doctors" before, from time to time, but you never really elaborated on them. Care to tell me the whole story?

> **ADAM:** Sure, but let me back up. Yes, I hated to go to Canada because of the little doctors, but my recollections of this story actually begin in New York – in Little Neck, where I grew up. You know my dad. He loves to go try out new restaurants and hit fruit and vegetable farm stands. Even as a little kid, I remember we used to drive deep into Eastern Long Island on spring and early summer weekends. As I grew older, I didn't mind accompanying him on these food runs, except for the times that we passed by this one particular store. It had a bunch of pasty white figures that looked to be playing tennis. I think it was a sporting goods store. One entire outside wall had been painted into a mural with these long and white, elongated, doughy looking people swinging rackets and bats and tossing balls.

They weren't realistically painted but they weren't cute cartoons, either. They looked like ghosts or something else to me. That mural never ceased to trigger something inside me. It scared the bejeezus out of me. When I got into my teens, I suddenly remembered why. I felt like throwing up when the memory all came back to me. Or rather, memories – of Canada and them.

OSCAR: Them, as in those little doctors you mentioned?
ADAM: Exactly. My parents never got it. I used to scream and kick and go crazy every year before we left. They owned a small cabin by a lake up near Owen Sound, Ontario. There was a big golf course on some campgrounds right behind the cabin. In front of it was the lake. The place is really isolated. Very few lights out there at night. The night sky is gorgeous. You can fall asleep with your eyes open, no kidding. But I never slept. I just lay in bed, waiting for them to arrive.

OSCAR: They came to the campgrounds?
ADAM: Yes, into the cabin.

OSCAR: Who else was present?
ADAM: Everyone. But they were asleep. These doctors never woke anyone else up.

OSCAR: How do you know they were doctors?
ADAM: Well, I don't know that for certain. I'm just going by what I saw and what they did. All I can tell you is that from the time I was five to about the time I was ten, each and every summer, I would awaken and find them in the cottage, in my bedroom. They would float to my bedside, these funny, doughy-faced, pasty little doctors. They would carry me out of the cottage and to the golf course behind it. We'd go on the green and it was like a trap door or something because all of a sudden we would be going under the earth and they'd shut the clump of earth over our heads and it would be pitch black. Then they would work on me.

OSCAR: This is absolutely incredible! I've heard you mention 'the little doctors' before, but you never gave me the details.
ADAM: Every word is true, as I remember it.

OSCAR: What happened between the time you were taken into the earth and the time they worked on you?
ADAM: I have no clue. All I know is that my memory goes from pitch darkness to my lying on a bed and they're standing over me and looking down and doing experiments on me.

OSCAR: Did these creatures – or whatever they are – resemble the classic Space Alien face that is now a staple of global pop culture?

ADAM: I can't say for sure, but I want to say no. The only thing I remember is that their faces were grossly malformed and pasty white. There were no definite features of any sort that I can recall. Certainly no big teardrop eyes, like you see on the alien drawings you're talking about.

OSCAR: Did you ever see any kind of lights in the sky or a ship?
ADAM: Never. Nothing like that. Just the little men in their lab coats and the golf course.

OSCAR: And after the examinations or experiments were completed?
ADAM: I don't remember them ever taking me home. All I remember is waking up and looking out at the sunny early morning light and bursting into tears because I knew it really happened and it would happen again every now and then throughout the summer and nobody would believe me if I told them anything.

OSCAR: So you kept it to yourself all this time?
ADAM: Over the years my parents heard me yelling and screaming about hating Canada because of the little doctors, but yeah, except for those tantrums, I clammed up about it. Then I forgot all about it for several years – from around the ages of eleven through fourteen. Then I saw that nutty building mural one summer and everything came flooding back. And then Whitley Strieber put out his *Communion* books. I know that a lot of people slammed him for those books but to me, they were a major relief. It was like, yes, somebody else experienced something very similar to what I remember experiencing for several of my childhood years.

OSCAR: And you never tried to contact anyone at all about your situation?
ADAM: What for? I'm telling you, the world is primed for ridiculing anything it doesn't understand. I'm doing fine as a lawyer now. I have a large clientele and a good practice. If anyone heard me spouting off about little doctors and experiments underneath golf courses and such, people would be running for the hills in the opposite direction. This is as close as I'll come to sharing my story with anyone.

A Haunting on Padre Island

Scott was a high school buddy who got into radio a year or two before I did. He lived with his divorced mother in Corpus Christi. Eventually, Scott's mother remarried and the family moved into a beautiful two-story home near the Padre Island National Seashore. Padre Island is an enormous, hundred-mile stretch of beach that meanders from Corpus Christi down to the southern tip of the state. People up and down the Gulf

Coast flock to "The Island" for weekend getaways. Because Texas is such a warm state, the beach is used virtually year-round in some capacity or other. Tourists love the area and use it to get away from colder northern climes. Spring-breakers descend upon the beach by the thousands. Real estate runs for a premium in the area, even though prospective buyers are made aware of beach and saltwater erosion. The trade-off is worth it, most decide. The smell of the sea, the blowing tropical breeze and the proximity of the beach are irresistible to some.

Of course, Padre Island is also filled with history. It was here that pirates landed on the island for respite and replenishment of resources. Some say there is still treasure buried beyond the shores of the island, beneath one of the countless sloping sand dunes that obscure most of the beach from the highway. Ghosts of these long-dead pirates are said to haunt Padre Island. Many of the locals claim to see them roving near the flickering flames of bonfires or lurking in the thick sea grass that sprouts alongside the sand dunes. The Spanish conquistadors also landed on Padre Island in search of treasure. Some ships brought priests to the area to convert the so-called "noble savages" to Christianity. Like Padre Island and its phantom pirates, today, many missions throughout Central and South Texas are said to be haunted by the ghosts of these missionaries and Native Americans who, justifiably, were reluctant to give up their own belief systems and often rebelled at the enforced conversion to Catholicism. Looking over the rapidly developing and ever-increasing tourist-invaded area that Padre Island has become, it is a little harder to envision the landscape as it was a few short centuries ago but the presence of those bygone days is still visible with a little imagination.

The home into which Scott and his family moved was one of several built in a new development on the island. Houses and condominiums are growing congested in some parts of the Texas Gulf Coast, but this particular home still retained some degree of isolation. Moreover, Scott's new home had an added bonus: a dock and inlet as a backyard, where the family kept a small boat tethered and ready for short cruises up and down the marina. The home had all the earmarks of being a paradise, the last place anyone would want to get rid of. Yet that is exactly what Scott's parents did less than a year after moving in. Scott's mother had always dreamed of living near the ocean but she gave up the dream because it never included the supernatural.

Like Gail's summer home and the houses in Corpus Christi's Crest District, this abode was quite new – certainly not the type of dwelling that most of us envision when we think of a haunted house. And yet, the disturbances in the home started soon after the family moved in. They began as little more than disquieting feelings – the sensation that all was not right in the house. It was brightly lit and spacious, yet there was a cloistered and oppressive feeling that invaded the spirit if one stayed there for too great a time. Scott's mother was alone in the house much of the time. She grew uneasy both during the day and at night. Scott felt the same disquieting presence in the home shortly after moving in. Only Scott's stepfather never felt anything unsettling in the home. On the other hand, he was an insurance salesman who traveled around the state three or four days a week. As such, he spent the least amount of time at home.

It wasn't long before Scott and his mother talked about the weighty oppression each felt in their new domain. Both were relieved to have discussed the situation with the other. They provided one another with validation that they weren't simply imagining strange feelings in the home. They decided to make the best of things and told each other that maybe the house needed a party to liven things up.

I remember several of those parties well. Scott's mother and stepfather invited their friends and acquaintances. We invited fellow disc jockeys and other people that we met in the course of working for the radio station. Everyone seemed to have a great time and the atmosphere in the house during these affairs was a far cry from the times when Scott or his mother was alone in it. Unfortunately, Scott said that the festive mood in the home always dissipated with the end of the party. It wasn't that his parents were experiencing marital difficulties, either. "Something just didn't seem to click in that home," according to Scott.

Eventually, Scott's mother took a more active role in her husband's insurance business and she started to travel with him. It was a way to escape the long days alone in the atypical house. On many occasions when Scott's parents were away, I joined Scott at the house for barbeques, gabfests and movie marathons. However, no matter how late these get-togethers wrapped up and in spite of Scott's open invitation to have me stay the night, I always made it a point to drive back home. Like Scott and his mother, I too felt ill at ease in the house (although for a long time, I didn't know that they were experiencing similar feelings in the home). As a result, I preferred to spend long hours conversing on the deck and looking out at the marina. Yes, the view was great, but it wasn't just a question of aesthetics. The house unnerved me.

The longer Scott and his family lived in the house on Padre Island, the more he and his mother preferred to spend their time outside the home – on its deck or away from it. Eventually, Scott filled me in on the feelings that he and his mother were experiencing in the house and I better understood my reluctance to spend the night there.

Had the disturbances in the house remained at this problematic level, perhaps the family would have elected to keep the residence longer than they did. Unfortunately, the haunting intensified. Many people would surely regard the activity in the home as minor at best, but combined with one another, they were disturbing enough to convince Scott and his mother that they should abandon their dream home. Scott's mother heard the first unexplainable sounds in the house: shufflings and thunks coming from the upstairs bedrooms. Softly at first, then louder. When she went up to investigate, she found everything in order and the rooms, empty. When Scott was alone in the house, he too heard unexplainable sounds emanating from the upstairs rooms and other areas of the house. Again, a search of the house found nothing out of the ordinary. On a number of occasions, both Scott and his mother had the uneasy feeling that they were being spied on. This may sound like the deluded thinking of two paranoids, until one factors in the auditory phenomena that Scott and his mother were experiencing. Appliances were found on at various times when Scott and his mother were sure that they had been turned off. Ceiling fans would be found on in empty rooms, even after Scott or his mother double-checked that they were off. Already frazzled, the final blow came one night when Scott's mother was awaiting the arrival of her husband. Scott came downstairs and joined his mother in the living room, where they sat and watched television. The hour grew later and the stepfather failed to arrive. Finally, a few minutes before eleven, the loud whirring sound of the electric garage door opening filled both Scott and his mother with relief. It was short-lived, though. The sound of the garage door closing never came. Scott and his mother waited a minute, two, three. After five minutes, they grew extremely uneasy. Was his stepfather taking in the evening sea breeze? Scott wondered. He walked over to the door that led into the garage and listened. All was silent within. Then he pulled a pistol from a small cabinet. Steeling himself, he opened the garage door. The interior was completely dark. Scott flicked the light switch on and stared in disbelief: one car was still missing and both garage doors were closed! Yet both he and his mother had been in for hours and they were absolutely certain that both doors had been shut since mid-afternoon. No sign of his stepfather, no sign of an intruder, yet something had caused the sound of a garage door opening to resonate throughout the house.

Scott's family moved back into Corpus Christi. His mother and stepfather bought a condo on Ocean Drive. They had a balcony that faced the Gulf of Mexico, so the ocean was still nearby. If the condo wasn't exceptionally roomy, it wasn't haunted either. I was a frequent guest in both places and I was never troubled by any negative vibes in the condo. More important, Scott and his family weren't either.

A Haunted Home on the Range (2)

A large ranch house on an isolated part of a ranch offered rent-free: it seemed like the perfect set-up to my cousin Lina and her husband Jake. The wealthy owner of the ranch liked the newlyweds and even helped them with moving expenses. The couple couldn't believe their good fortune. By living rent-free, they could save up for their own place while Lina attended school and Jake worked as a foreman on the ranch in Dripping Springs, Texas. However, within weeks of moving in, the dream set-up became a living nightmare.

Ominous signs of things to come manifested themselves as early as move-in day. While unloading boxes, Lina and Jake heard a loud crash in the kitchen area. It sounded as though a broom had fallen onto the loud wooden floor. They checked the kitchen and a few other rooms but found nothing except stacks of boxes. The two returned to the arduous task of unloading the large moving van. A little later, they heard the sound of a door slamming but when they checked, the doors to all the rooms were open. Later still, lying on the couch, Lina and Jake reflected on the sounds they heard while unloading. They decided to blame ongoing settling as the culprit. The house was built in the early 1900s and had seen its share of decades and inhabitants. It was sure to have creaks and groans that they would have to get used to. Of course, creaks and groans are one thing, but these noises combined with the other strange phenomena proved quite unnerving. For example, on several occasions, Lina and Jake heard the sound of chairs scraping the kitchen floor. When they inspected their dining table, they found everything in order and the chairs in place.

A few weeks after they moved into the house, Jake's younger sister arrived for a visit. Unlike the couple, twenty-year-old Jenny is a night owl who loves to stay up late. One night, between three and four in the morning, Jenny was sitting on the couch and watching a film on television when she felt someone run thick cold fingers through her hair. The sensation was unmistakable but she tried to dismiss it. When it happened again, she was even more conscious of the long stroke of the fingers as they shoved themselves into her hair then moved downward. Jenny grew frightened. She felt helpless. Should she awaken her brother and sister-in-law? Would they think her crazy? Before she could decide upon a course of action, the phantom fingers raked through her head a third time. At this point, Jenny turned on all the lights in the living room and sat up the rest of the night.

The number three figures significantly into this incident (the invisible entity stroked Jenny's hair three times; the haunting occurred between three and four in the morning).

As I mentioned earlier, various investigators of the supernatural have pointed out that the demonic often makes its presence known with variations on the number three. Three bears strong religious significance in the Catholic faith. By using the number three to make its presence known, Evil mocks the Holy Trinity and the Divine. (Recall that my former girlfriend Lindsey's "wizard" repeatedly jabbed her on the shoulders using clusters of three jabs.)

Jenny wasn't the only guest to experience an encounter with the supernatural in the nearly century-old ranch house. Indeed, Jenny's experience was tame compared to the horrors experienced by the next guests, several weeks later. Lina's cousin, wife and two-year-old daughter arrived for a visit. Once again, Lina and Jake thought it best not to tell their company about the bizarre experiences occurring in their home. Sometime after the trio (another "3" associated with the house) drifted off in the large guestroom bed, the television came on by itself. Lina's cousin awoke to the raucous sounds of a popular sitcom being rebroadcast. He got up to shut off the unit. A few hours later, his frightened wife nudged him awake, requesting that they trade places. He asked the reason for the strange request. "First, let me tell you, I didn't dream this," his wife replied. "I just woke up with a man hovering over me and staring down at me. I saw him clearly. He had a dark beard and a mustache and he was wearing dirty overalls." The two incidents would be enough haunting for anyone in one night but there was still more to come. When the couple finally calmed down enough to drift off again, they were awakened by their young daughter. Earlier, the girl had been sound asleep between them. Now she was sitting up in bed, engaged in animated conversation with an unseen entity.

The sounds in the house increased. Both Lina and Jake grew more uncomfortable when they were alone in the home. One night, Lina awoke for some inexplicable reason and listened as the sound of footsteps shattered the stillness of the night. The steps seemed to originate in the kitchen and grew louder until they stopped just outside the couple's closed bedroom door. Lina and Jake's master bedroom is sunken and the step leading down into it makes a funny squeak when a person first steps on it. The sound is repeated when the step is free of weight again. Suddenly, the sound of someone stepping onto the step filled the silent bedroom. Lina and Jake held onto each other but the second sound that announced the presence had stepped down into the bedroom never came. Instead, a loud and new set of footsteps could be heard outside the shut door. Once again they seemed to emanate from the kitchen. While the previous steps had been loud and surefooted, this second wave of sound betrayed a lazy shuffling movement that grew louder until it stopped directly outside the bedroom door. All of a sudden, a loud crash could be heard from inside the closet, which was directly to the side of the bedroom door. Jake had had enough at this point. He jumped out of bed and turned on all the lamps in the bedroom. It was empty. He opened the door and found the hallway equally empty. The young husband raced through the house, turning on every light as he did so. He discovered nothing, but an oppressive presence hung heavily in the newly lit domain. When the couple returned to bed, they left lights on in each room of their house, including the bedroom. For good measure, the bedroom television was left on, too.

Lina and Jake knew that it was time to speak with the owner of the ranch. They wanted to know more about the history of the place. As they made their request, they felt more than a bit sheepish. After all, the man was Jake's boss; moreover, he was letting them live on the property free of charge while Jake helped him run the large ranch. The owner understood their curiousity. The house had been shut down for years prior to the couple's inhabiting it, he revealed. However, since it was close to a hundred years old, it had housed scores of family members and ranch employees over the years. Then it was his turn to inquire about their curiosity in the history of the dwelling. Lina and Jake confessed all. They needn't have worried about telling their tale; the ranch owner was quite supportive. He asked the couple's permission to bring his pastor to the house in order to bless it. Lina and Jake readily agreed. They stayed with friends that night and the next day, joined the owner of the ranch and his pastor at the troubled house. As the pastor began his prayers, Lina felt a terrible atmosphere hanging heavily over the group, but as the pastor walked around the house, said his prayers and anointed each room with holy oil, the negativity seemed to dissipate. By the time the pastor finished his holy blessings, the entire atmosphere in the home had changed.

Today, Lina and Jake continue to reside in the once haunted house. Whatever restless spirit they initially shared the home with seems to have abandoned it to the young couple. Lina and Jake are lucky: the pastor's prayers and their own strong religious convictions succeeded in pushing the negativity out of the house. Sometimes such blessings prove useless or temporary solutions against persistent entities.

"The Blue Ghost"

Let us journey from the Texas prairie in the last story to the Gulf of Mexico in this one. Specifically, our focus is the great aircraft carrier *U.S.S. Lexington*, now permanently docked in the port of Corpus Christi. The *Lexington* is also known as "The Lady Lex" and, more ominously, as "The Blue Ghost." The ship earned its nickname because of its non-camouflaged blue color scheme and because during World War II, Japanese propaganda repeatedly reported it sunk, only to have the aircraft carrier reappear to wreck havoc during various battles. *Lexington's* planes obliterated their share of enemy aircraft during World War II: 372 airborne craft and 472 grounded craft.

The ship is massive. Its flight deck is 910 feet long. Its maximum width stretches some 196 feet. At one time, *Lexington's* sixteen decks boasted a complement of 1,550 men and women. Most recently, the aircraft carrier served as one of the locations used in the filming of *Pearl Harbor*. With such a colorful past – a past heavily entrenched in battle – it is no surprise that "The Blue Ghost" is also said to harbor a number of spirits.

Stories of phantoms aboard sea vessels are not unusual. Indeed, there have been many reports of phantom ships sailing the oceans with phantom crews. More common, however, are the stories of ghostly inhabitants residing aboard active and non-active vessels. For example, one of the most famous American ships of the twentieth century, the *Queen Mary*, has the reputation for being haunted. Various studies aboard this ship have produced startling results. One of the most informative pieces on the hauntings aboard the *Queen Mary* was a special "ghosts and hauntings" episode of the popular *Unsolved Mysteries* television series.

Like many ships that harbor stories of hauntings, the *Queen Mary* was used in war. During World War II, the ship transported troops to and from overseas. My father returned from the war aboard the *Queen Mary*, sailing into New York harbor when the ship still sported a fourth smoke stack. At the time, the ship was painted camouflage gray, thus earning it the nickname, "Gray Ghost." Could the *U.S.S. Lexington*, also used in war, be haunted as well?

Over the years, I heard many a rumor about the great aircraft carrier's being the site of paranormal disturbances. When I was researching the stories collected in this volume, I decided to investigate "The Blue Ghost" personally. My best friend and fellow researcher Sam and I toured the ship in December 2001. We were fortunate to have Yvonne provide us with an extensive tour of the ship. I've known Yvonne for twenty years. A fulltime librarian at Texas A&M University's Kingsville branch, Yvonne volunteers her time as a tour guide aboard the *Lexington* most weekends. When I broached the subject of ghosts on the ship with Yvonne, she told me that many such stories existed. Yvonne generously volunteered to give me a thorough tour of the aircraft carrier as well as a special "ghost tour" of the ship. The latter included taking me to various locations where paranormal incidents have occurred. Coincidentally, Yvonne's usual volunteer post is the engineering section, where many of the supernatural stories are concentrated.

A fair-skinned, blue-eyed ghost in a white Navy uniform has appeared often in various parts of the engine room. The aircraft carrier is under constant refurbishment. Although many of its decks are now open to the public, some areas on these decks are still sealed off. Still other decks are being prepared for public viewing and will eventually be part of the *Lexington* tour. Understandably, much of the refurbishing work is done at night, when the ship is closed to the public. One night, when only the work crew was on board, one of the workers walked down a narrow flight of stairs that leads down into the engine room. At the bottom of the stairs, he saw a man sitting on a deck chair. The worker didn't recognize the man. Moreover, he wasn't dressed like one of the crew workers. Instead, the clean and well-groomed stranger wore a sporty white sailor suit. The worker was about to make inquiries when the sailor disappeared before his eyes!

This particular apparition – or a similar one – has been seen frequently throughout the engine room. At times, witnesses have walked through a *cold spot* shortly before the ghost made his appearance. (Cold spots – rapid drops in temperature – often signal the appearance of a supernatural entity.) Perhaps the answer to this particular mystery lies in the fact that *Lexington* saw aggressive battles in its day and lost several men to these battles. It was in the very engineering deck where so many sightings have taken place that a torpedo ripped through a bulkhead, killing at least one sailor. Could this be the sailor who now walks the engineering decks of the ship? One of the most popular beliefs among students of the paranormal, is that ghosts remain earthbound because they lost their physical lives so suddenly, that there was no time for any kind of transition between the realms of the physical and spiritual. Ghosts are frequently reported to act confused. They may linger around a certain location because they do not realize it is their time to leave the physical world behind. In other cases, perhaps a trace record of their presence is left behind (for a discussion of *immediate hauntings* vs. *residual hauntings*, see "Haunted Schools" in this chapter). Either of these possibilities seems likely in the case of the ghost that is spotted in and around *Lexington's* engine room; however, given the behavior of the ghost as described in other sightings, a residual haunting explanation holds more credence.

For example, the ship also has four fire rooms, each containing two boilers. One night, a worker was busy in one of the fire rooms when he spotted a fair-skinned man in a spotless Navy uniform walking rapidly down a narrow catwalk. The crewman shouted for the sailor to come back, that he wasn't supposed to be out there – or anywhere aboard the ship, for that matter, given the lateness of the hour. The sailor completely ignored the cries of the worker and kept walking down the catwalk – and right through the thick bulkhead at the other end! A similar incident took place down a very narrow hallway in another boiler room. Once again, a worker on the night crew was sent down to work in the room, only to discover that he wasn't alone. A figure in a sailor suit was walking down the narrow hallway below. The crewman shouted for the sailor to come back, that it was after hours and he was in a restricted area. The sailor paid no mind and kept moving forward – but he *did* get off the ship, walking right *through* the thick wall of the aircraft carrier at the end of the hallway! Perhaps these entities are simply ignoring the humans who call out to them – or perhaps they are not there at all. Instead, maybe these spirits have left a calling card behind, an ethereal image of their physical form from days gone by. Regardless of which story one chooses to accept, too many people have reported incidents of a sailor in the engine room and boiler rooms to readily dismiss them as flights of fancy.

The man in the sailor suit does not restrict himself to the engine and boiler rooms. Overnight guests aboard *Lexington* are usually forbidden, but Boy Scout and Junior ROTC troops are granted special permission to sleep aboard the aircraft carrier from time to time. On several occasions, more than one Scout has awakened to find a man in a sailor suit leaning over his bed, staring down at him. Several of the Scouts and ROTC members have described the man's vibrant blue eyes, light hair and fair skin. All have been greatly disturbed when the man either vanishes before their eyes or walks away and through a nearby bulkhead. A more frightening story comes from one of the den mothers who slept aboard ship. The woman claims that sudden jarring and shaking awoke her. When she became fully conscious, it was to find herself being molested by a phantom in a sailor suit! The woman claims her cries caused the entity to vanish. (Note: I engaged in extensive research of the paranormal incidents *Lexington* and this is the *only* story I came across that boasts the presence of a malevolent entity aboard the vessel. Of course, we might consider the stories of some witnesses who claim they were pushed or shoved by unseen forces. Still, these reports are not on the same par with a molestation claim. Certainly I do not wish to trivialize the woman's story but given the many other tales which describe a more benevolent – or indifferent – ghost, the possibility that the woman was suffering from a nightmare and awakened in a confused and frightened state should be considered.)

Although many of the stories aboard *Lexington* center on the engineering sections, people have experienced paranormal encounters throughout the craft. Take the massive forward deck of the ship, for example. Today, this area houses a large movie theater but at one time, it was the site of a large open area and elevator, where aircraft were loaded and unloaded. It was during such a loading session in the 1940s that tragedy struck and a crewmember was crushed to death. Since that time, many people have reported seeing a phantom crewman wandering around the forward deck. When the theater was being constructed, the work crew – many of whom worked throughout the night – reported light surges in this area. Some members of the crew claimed to see a man in a sailor's uniform strolling the lonely decks nearby. A couple of members of the crew refused to work alone in the area because they claimed to have seen something they didn't care to discuss. Still others swore they saw an apparition materialize and vanish near their workstations. Other workmen felt pullings and tuggings while they worked. When they turned around to see who was gripping or shoving their shoulders, they found no one around. One night, a crewmember came out of a room where he had been working alone. He dropped his tool belt, walked off the ship and never returned. Moreover, when one particular group of inspectors toured the ship, they entered the theater and exited with lightning speed. Initially, employees thought the inspectors were playing some kind of joke on them but the inspection crew was serious and hurriedly left the theater. Their only comment: "We've seen enough in there."

The ship's volunteer lounge is also supposedly host to paranormal activity. The volunteer coordinator frequently finds that items have either been moved around in her office or have disappeared altogether. Volunteers who take breaks in the office have also felt an invisible presence in the room. The entity makes itself known via icy drafts. It also has been known to pull and tug at the clothing of individuals.

There is even a story about the Admiral's quarters. Although an admiral aboard *Lexington* was not part of the ship's regular fulltime complement, a small bedroom was reserved for his visits. Several tourists have claimed to see someone underneath the admiral's bed. Others make no claim to have seen a person but are adamant that they saw some sort of movement beneath the bed. Yet each time, a search of the space has yielded nothing.

Certainly one of the most perplexing paranormal stories associated with *The Blue Ghost* deals with its sickbay unit. The tours aboard the aircraft carrier may be either formal or informal. Some visitors elect to have a tour guide lead their group from deck to deck and location to location. Other guests choose to move independently and at their own pace throughout the ship, using the many informative plaques and nearby volunteers to answer questions. The latter was the case for one family – a father and mother, teen sister and younger brother – who had a run-in with a ghost in the ship's sickbay. From the start of the tour, the young boy was sluggish as he made his way down the ship's narrow corridors and steep staircases. By the time they reached the sickbay deck, the boy was visibly ill. The ship was quite empty on this day but the small group was pleased to find a kind young man in a long white physician's coat in one of the small rooms. The man focused on the boy and immediately expressed concern. He asked the boy to sit on the bed and then lay back. After examining the boy thoroughly, the man advised the parents to get the boy to a hospital immediately. His appendix needed to be removed right away. The family was perplexed by the presence of the doctor. They had no idea that *Lexington* was still functioning in any capacity other than tour site. What else was open and running aboard the ship? Moreover, how would they pay for the doctor's services? These and other questions buzzed through their minds but they were too concerned with their boy's health to stick around and learn the answers. Instead, they thanked the doctor for his assistance and he smiled and reassured the family that their boy would be fine, as long as they took him to the hospital immediately. The doctor's advice proved correct; the boy's appendix was removed later that evening! However, when the father returned to the ship to offer to pay for the most timely diagnosis provided by the ship's physician, he was informed that the aircraft carrier had no such doctor on duty and that sickbay was most definitely closed for anything other than touring! The father of the boy related the previous day's puzzling occurrences. He accompanied various employees to the sickbay and retraced the doctor's steps and relayed the incident in detail. When one of the employees softly suggested that he might have seen a ghost, the father dismissed the suggestion. "He was as real as you and I," he said. "He touched my son. I shook his hand and thanked him for his services." No sign of the doctor – or any imposter – was found. To this day, this incident remains one of the many curious mysteries aboard "The Blue Ghost."

Although Yvonne was quick to point out that nothing unusual has happened to her aboard the ship, perhaps such a boast opened the door for the following incident.

Knowing that Sam and I were to be coming on that day, Yvonne brought her camera along to shoot a few pictures on our ghost tour. She also wanted some shots of herself at various locations throughout the ship and asked us to snap her photo. The first place she requested a solo pose was the engine room, where the ghost in the sailor suit has made many appearances. As she posed for the photo, Yvonne waited and waited for Sam to snap the picture. Try as he might, however, Sam could not get Yvonne's camera to function. Yvonne thought that Sam was joking and trying to scare her. But it was no joke. Yvonne swore that the camera had been fine earlier but now it refused to cooperate. Perhaps it was mere coincidence – or perhaps it was one small form of communication from the spirits aboard *Lexington*. Yvonne is not the only one who has experienced picture-taking problems aboard the vessel. Many guests have complained that the pictures they took in the boiler rooms and engine room didn't develop at all. Instead of images, they got black or white rectangles. This has been especially disconcerting to those who took other pictures aboard the ship using the same roll of film, only to have those shots develop perfectly.

A Mother's Love Is Eternal

So the saying goes and so the evidence seems to underscore. In previous sections, we have heard of departed parents returning to comfort their children in signs of stress. Parents also return to say goodbye before departing this earthly plane of existence. These stories echo the many tales others have told in books that report the special connection some parents have with their children, and vice versa.

My mother's mother grew up in a South Texas ranch called La Rosita. She was part of the Valerio family. Eventually, she would marry my grandfather, who came from another nearby ranch, El Rancho De Las Pintas – or Las Pintas, for short. Even after getting married, my grandmother still visited La Rosita quite frequently. Many of my grandmother's relatives lived in various homes scattered throughout the ranch, including my grandmother's first cousin. Gloria and my grandmother were close. However, unlike my grandmother, who moved off the ranch when she married, Gloria chose to remain on the property after marrying Raymond. Her husband worked as a ranch hand on site and the newlyweds built a home on the ranch and started a family there. Very soon, Gloria and Raymond had a daughter and two sons to raise. Eventually, a fourth child arrived, another girl. Although times were tough economically for Gloria and Raymond, they were quite happy on the ranch and very proud of their children. It seemed as though their love could conquer any sort of economic setback. Unfortunately, a greater obstacle presented itself almost a decade into the marriage. My grandmother's first cousin Gloria took ill and died.

Understandably, the family was devastated. Raymond was especially broken apart. He knew that he had to continue to work fulltime on the ranch in order to provide for his large family, yet at the same time, he worried greatly about the children. Their ages ranged from the eldest daughter who was nine to the youngest, who was four. Various relatives provided the children with assistance but these aunts, uncles and cousins – including my grandmother – had their own families to raise and their own husbands and homes to care for.

Within weeks after Gloria's passing, however, guests who stopped by to check on the children noticed something remarkable about them and their home: both were always spotless. Several aunts and family friends arrived ready to scrub the house down and bathe the kids, only to find the home tidied up and swept, the laundry done and hung on the line, the children freshly bathed and clothed in worn but clean and well-mended clothing. Initially, each friend or relative simply assumed that someone else had arrived and beat them to the general housekeeping chores, but even Raymond became suspicious after arriving home from a long day's work and finding dinner cooked and simmering on the stove. As this happened with increasing frequency, the children were queried.

"Who came by?" they were asked. "Who did the laundry? Who cleaned the house? Who made dinner today?"

Each time their answers were the same: "Mamma stopped by and cooked. Mamma did the laundry. Mamma cleaned up the whole house."

Mamma? Gloria had been dead for months! The children's answer never wavered. *Where did she come from?* Raymond asked his children.

From the eldest daughter to the youngest, each child pointed to the broom closet. "From in there. She comes out and we're happy to see her. She's happy too. She comes out and does work and bathes us. She cooks. She sews for us. When it gets late, she kisses us and goes back into the closet."

The children refused to change their story.

If they were telling the truth, this is a great example of an apparition making positive appearances in our earthly domain. Not once did these children express any kind of anxiety or fear over the fact that their dead mother was returning to visit them. Nor does their story seem to be a prank. Children are innocent and usually tell the truth. Most people agree that kids also make poor liars when they are asked to sustain a lie for very long. Moreover, things get even more tenuous when there is more than one child responsible for maintaining a fictitious story. Yet all four of the children continued to insist that their mother was visiting them on a daily basis.

Perhaps Gloria and her siblings were not frightened by the return of their mother but widower Raymond, relatives and friends were greatly disturbed by the children's stories. My grandmother explained that a priest was eventually called upon to visit and bless the home. He did just that, blessing each room of the small wooden structure. Neighbors and relatives concluded that the ghost was likely restless because she was worried about her kids fending for themselves at such a young age. Still, the combined diligence of the residents of La Rosita and the priest's blessings seemed to be effective. A short time after the priest came to the house and blessed it, my grandmother's cousin seemed to move on to a peaceful rest and was never seen again. But her love was certainly felt in the hearts of her children, who never forgot her and were quick to repeat their amazing story in later years.

CONCLUSION

Synchronicity and the Supernatural

Earlier in the book, I described my incredible sighting of the Virgin Mary. I conclude with an epilogue of sorts to this story. This recent event proved to be the catalyst that convinced me to finally put all these tales together in a text that explores the nature of hauntings and paranormal phenomena. It is also another strange case of synchronicity in my life.

Synchronicity is the occurrence of two events in our lives which we feel must be connected somehow, even though the connection is obscure to us. Try as we might, there seems to be no logical way to connect them to each other. Most of us have had synchronistic moments. They bewilder and intrigue us. At times, moments of synchronicity seem to pile one atop the other in rapid-fire succession. Is there some cosmic force tugging at puppet strings and running the Big Show? Or has our mind picked up a pattern that just happens to be a coincidence and attempted to make something more of it? Each position has its supporters. Certainly when one or two moments of synchronicity occur in our lives, they give us pause and we are correct to scrutinize them carefully. But what happens when we experience a rash of synchronistic events that build one upon the other and continue to form a seemingly complex web of connectedness in our existence?

Let's flash-forward thirty-some-odd years and twenty-six hundred miles from my first encounter with an image of the Virgin Mary, to December 2001 – from South Texas to Southern New England. I'd been going through a stressful and tumultuous few months. Among my problems was my growing suspicion that my creative well had gone dry. It seemed ironic, considering the fact that I had a book being published in the next few weeks. Of course, given the nature of writing and publishing, the span of time between writing the material, peddling it, getting it rejected, sending it out again, getting it accepted (if all goes well) and revising it again (and again) can seem an eternity. In truth, even though the book was due out in another week or two, it had been months since I'd written something creative that I felt was any good. Friends congratulated me on a film article that was also on the brink of being published in the next week or so, but like the book-length manuscript, that article had been submitted and accepted well over a year ago. I lacked scope and vision. I needed a new project – something that would turn me on and get me going at my usual lightning-fast speed. What would do that for me? Where was the idea that would light a fresh flame of creativity within me?

And then, out of the blue, it seemed, my answer arrived at dusk while I was lying on the couch and watching fall shadows creeping across my living room walls and ceiling. I began to reflect on the lifetime of supernatural events that I've either experienced or heard about. The spider web shadow play continued to splash patterns across my ceiling and like the merging shadows, ideas started to intersect and coalesce in my mind. Something – perhaps it was just the final vestiges of sunlight hitting the right chrome car bumper outside my window – flashed a small bright yellow patch at the center of the thin branch shadows. The object shimmered in a bright oval pattern and was gone. No matter. It was there long enough to trigger a wild surge of inspiration within me. Suddenly, I knew exactly what I wanted to tackle as my next project. The result is the book you're holding in your hands and reading.

I can't emphasize how strongly the urge to move forward quickly with this project launched me into action. (Never before have I written a manuscript of this length so quickly – six weeks, plus three for revision – or been so pleased with the results.) I knew that I had to get these stories out. I was sure that others would find them both intriguing and reassuring. I knew that I should include not only my own personal experiences, but the experiences of others. I knew that my book belonged in the hands of those who may have had similar experiences and needed someone to tell them that they weren't going crazy. I knew, especially, that the text would be more than just a simple recounting of spooky stories; it would also offer information on myriad subjects associated with the paranormal. I knew that it would provide no definitive conclusions, but it would contain carefully researched information on the whys and hows and do's and don'ts of Things Fantastic: hauntings, possession, poltergeist activity, clairvoyance, clairaudience, UFOs and their potential connection to the paranormal. I knew that as a lifetime student of the supernatural, I would be able to guide others through a wondrous tour of the unknown. I knew these things and a few short days after beginning the manuscript, I received indisputable confirmation that I was most definitely on the right track. My "thumbs up," if you will, came in the form of a weekend loaded with synchronicity.

Shortly after I began writing the book, my friend Emily invited me over to her house for dinner. After a delicious home-cooked meal, I told her a little bit about my new writing project. I remember that I had just written the Demon in the morning/ Virgin Mary at night section of my story, but I didn't tell Emily that. Not right away.

Emily, whose father is a minister, wished me luck on the project. I asked her if she had anything she wished to contribute to the text.

"I have only one story that you could call supernatural and it deals with the Virgin Mary."

I was stunned but I remained silent and let Emily continue.

Emily proceeded to tell me about a rough time in her life in the 1980s when she felt in dire need of spiritual support. One night while driving down Route 25 in Brookfield, Connecticut, Emily stopped by the Grotto of Our Lady of Lourdes, a meditation garden where icons of the Virgin and the Stations of the Cross are set up around lovely landscaped garden paths and trails. While there, Emily walked over to a pew before a small altar and bowed her head and asked God and Mary to give her a sign that everything was going to turn out alright. Some forty seconds later, Emily got her sign. As she walked back to her car, every single light in the grotto went out! The only lights that remained burning were the many candles flickering around the various statues and stations around the grotto.

I told Emily about my own Mary experience and I thanked her for sharing hers. It was her story that fully confirmed that I was onto something. And since that time, I have had one Mary sighting after another, although not in the blatantly supernatural sense as my childhood vision. But I see Mary icons everywhere: at the store (in books and calendars, key chains and candles and CDs), on television (on documentary specials and other shows with images of the Virgin clearly depicted in the background), at the theater (in several films), in windows (of houses, stores, and outdoor murals). Has my mind picked up on these images because I've come to associate them with the text that I've been working on? Or is synchronicity itself a part of the supernatural world?

Until Emily shared her story with me, I had never heard of the local Grotto of Our Lady of Lourdes, but because I had just written my Virgin Mary book section and Emily's experience dealt with Mary as well, I wanted to visit the place. The day after my chat with Emily was a Saturday, an unnaturally mild December day in New England, sunny with a blue sky and the temperature actually hovering around the seventy-degree mark. It was the kind of day to spend outdoors, which is what my friend JJ and I decided to do when he arrived for a visit that afternoon. As we drove around the area, I told him about my desire to visit the shrine and we set out to find it.

The first weird event of the day hit me shortly after getting onto Route 25. As I drove toward the shrine, JJ and I passed an ancient cemetery on a hill. JJ, as I've mentioned in previous chapters, shares my enthusiasm for the supernatural and pleaded with me to turn around so that we could give the cemetery a cursory investigation and decide whether it was worth returning to with cameras at a later date. I pointed out that it was getting late and that I wanted to find and visit the Grotto before sunset.

"The cemetery has obviously been there a couple of centuries," I said. "It's not going anywhere. We'll come back to it."

"Yeah, I guess you're right," he said. "But I still say we're doing it backwards, visiting a holy place by day and going into a place that could be potentially haunted by Evil at night."

My friend's words startled me. I couldn't believe he had made such a statement. Mere hours ago, in the wee hours of the morning, I had returned from Emily's and written the conclusion of the Mary section. In my conclusion, I discussed our prejudiced way of thinking about Good and Evil. The fact that we've associated each of the concepts with certain symbolic colors, icons and yes, even times of day (Day = Good, Night = Evil) makes us forget that there is far greater fluidity to Good and Evil than our regimented thinking has allowed us to believe.

JJ rattled me even further by adding a postscript to his observation: "Of course, cemeteries don't necessarily have to be haunted with bad stuff, at night or otherwise." This was almost too much for me to contain, but I decided to keep mum about the whole thing for the time being.

Was JJ picking up on my thoughts? Was he not only "reading" my mind but echoes of the text that I had written, which was running through my head at that moment? I am not ready to dismiss such a possibility, especially when it comes to my three closest friends, JJ and Kelly in Connecticut, and Sam in Texas. There have been several times when I am on the brink of calling Sam – actually moving to the phone to pick up the receiver and punch in his phone number – when it rings and it's him. The opposite is also true. Likewise, JJ and I have had some incredible moments of connection. One night we made note of the incredibly lifelike appearances of three mannequins standing inside a store window. The mannequins were so realistically crafted that they were actually somewhat disturbing. A little later that evening, we ended up at JJ's house. At a loss for what to watch, I grabbed a DVD off his shelf. It was a film called *Tourist Trap*. Although it was released in 1979, it's one that this pair of horror aficionados had missed the first time around. JJ had just purchased the film and was anxious to view it for the first time too. We had no idea what it was about except that it involved people falling into peril when their car breaks down in a backcountry road. Imagine our surprise when the psycho in the picture is obsessed with mannequins and uses them to frighten and kill! What are the odds that out of JJ's incredibly large movie collection, I would choose a film heavily involving mannequins in its plot, a short hour after having an extensive discussion on the disturbing visage of some mannequins?

Probably as slim as the following: In spring 2003, JJ and I visited Foxwoods Casino and each spent about twenty bucks on the slot machines. On the way home, we got into an extensive discussion of synchronicity and slot machine winnings just as we pulled up to a slot machine in a furniture store window some eighty miles and several hours after leaving the casino!

What about this incident: Last week, I had lunch at the university and a colleague mentioned the infamous last lines of that great horror tragedy, *King Kong*: "Twas beauty that killed the beast." That same night, I had dinner with my friend Kelly and she quoted the same exact line from the same exact film!

Here's yet another curious example of synchronicity at work: one afternoon, JJ and I were driving to Norwalk, CT and got stuck behind a very slow Sunday driver in a pick-up truck. We were exasperated because the man was doing something like 23 mph in a 45 mph zone.

"Look at this jerk," I yelled. "He's driving like—"

JJ and I both yelled out "MOLASSES!" at the exact same time. Molasses is not a word (or substance) I often use, nor JJ for that matter. So why did we both sing it out full-force and in unison?

Back to December, 2001. The first thing I noticed upon pulling into the parking lot of the Grotto of Our Lady of Lourdes was a car that looked *exactly* like an ex-girlfriend's. I pointed it out to JJ, then dismissed the possibility that she was visiting the same place on this day. For one thing, she wasn't at all religious. For another, it had been ages since I'd seen her. My suspicions proved correct. She wasn't anywhere on the premises.

The next thing I noticed about the Grotto was the peace and serenity that it brought me the moment I set foot onto its beautiful paths. I noticed a small crowd gathered at the main shrine, so I walked down the back paths and stopped by various statues and Stations of the Cross positioned around the trails for visitors to meditate and contemplate. I paused at the far back, where a large wooden crucifix has been erected. Then I moved on to the main Mary shrine, which was empty by now. I signed the guest book and wrote a few words.

Then I studied the altar, where yet another surprise awaited me. The altar was crowded with various statues of the Virgin. Some looked expensive, while others seemed to be cheaply manufactured. Regardless of quality, though, all were surrounded by scores of burning candles. However, none of the statues struck me with the profound impact of the lone-framed painting in one corner of the altar. There she was: the Virgin of Guadalupe as I remembered seeing her in the car so long ago, her body surrounded by a halo of brilliant yellow light, her green shawl draped over her head and shoulders, her body clothed in bright red robes! I scanned the statues. Every one of them showed Mary dressed in whites and pale blues. Yet here was Mary in the painting, looking exactly as she appeared to me when I was a young boy!

There was one more shocking moment of synchronicity in store for us that day. I backtracked and we ended up visiting the cemetery after all. We arrived at dusk. As we pulled into the main gate of the graveyard, I heard someone honk. I turned and saw my ex-girlfriend smiling and waving as she drove past the entrance!

Within a day and a half of writing my Virgin Mary story for the book, Emily shared her own paranormal story with me – a story that also dealt with the Virgin Mary. Less than a day later, I set out to find the holy shrine that she told me about and discovered a painting depicting the very image of the Virgin as I remember her. There were also numerous moments of synchronicity throughout the supremely inspiring day.

It was the sort of day that makes me reflect upon the amazing connectedness of the seemingly random cosmos. A couple of days before, I felt that I was wallowing in chaos. Suddenly, I had purpose and direction again. And I was being nudged by some cosmic force that was telling me to *go, go, go, boy; you're on the right track*. Although the weird interlacing of events startled me, I welcomed the cosmic communiqué. I've been open-minded about the supernatural in the past, sure, but by writing about it and dwelling on it so extensively, I knew that I was opening myself up to the paranormal world more so than ever before.

Not "The End" But "The Beginning"

Three days after we visited the Grotto of Our Lady of Lourdes, JJ returned to the site to take some pictures there. Later that night, he emailed to let me know that when he arrived, he walked up to the main shrine and found the guest-book open to the short prayer of thanks that I wrote to the Virgin! Many people visit the Grotto on a daily basis, at all times of day and night. Before JJ and I left the previous Sunday, the shrine had grown crowded with people again and others had opened and signed the guest book. The odds of JJ's finding it open to the very page that I wrote in are slim indeed. The entire experience further confirmed my belief that I needed to share these tales of the supernatural with others, not in order to frighten but to highlight the wonders of existence as we know it on earth and as we glimpse it when the natural converges with the supernatural.

Whatever great Life Force exists in the cosmos, it continues to communicate with me via images of the Virgin Mary. Throughout the writing of this text I spotted icons of the Virgin repeatedly. When I let the initial draft sit for well almost a year and a half because of other commitments and a very heavy work schedule, the sightings continued. I knew that I was being nudged to return to this project and finish it. Christmas season, 2002 found me in Texas again, visiting friends and relatives. When I stopped by the home of my first-cousin Gladys and her husband Richard in San Antonio, we went out to dinner and had a fine visit together. On the way home, Gladys drove by a shrine to the Virgin Mary that is said to be an exact replica of the Bernadette grotto in Lourdes, France. The astonishing thing about this incident is that Gladys had no idea at all that I was writing a book on the paranormal and she hadn't heard me mention my Virgin sighting since the night it happened (recall that Gladys and her sister Diana were riding in the backseat of the car with me). Yet even as I tried to puzzle over this latest moment of synchronicity involving the Virgin Mary, Gladys shocked me again. She told me that she saw the Virgin in September, when her mother underwent a serious operation!

"I was spending the night in my mother's hospital room," she revealed. "It was very late and the lights were dimmed. Mom was sleeping soundly. I was in a chair when some movement caught my eye. I looked up and stared at the mirror on the cabinet. It was reflecting pale white light. Then it grew clearer and clearer until it became the Virgin. She was turned sort of sideways and holding her hands together in prayer. She was dressed all in white. Then she faded away."

Except for the color of Mary's robes, Gladys saw the exact same thing I saw as a kid riding down the highway that long ago night in South Texas! How appropriate that my beloved first cousin – a cousin who was more like a sister to me as we grew up in Corpus Christi (the Body of Christ) – and I should have such similar experiences.

We're back to one of the most *positive* supernatural images threaded throughout this text: the Virgin Mary. Most people – even those who do not embrace Catholic dogma – agree that the Mary icon is a fine representation of benevolence, compassion and goodness. It is a fine image with which to conclude our explorations.

I hope that you have found this text both entertaining and informative. If you are one of the many people who have had an experience that seems to transcend everyday reality, I hope that these stories have brought you some measure of comfort and reassurance. You are certainly *not* losing your mind. You are in good company with many other rational men and women who have had similar encounters.

More than anything else, I hope that that this book conveys the notion that in spite of the existence of malevolent supernatural forces that may seek to gain dominance in our everyday lives, there is also a tremendous Positive Life Force that we can tap into via these experiences. Think of most apparitions, flying disc sightings and tales of strange creatures not in a negative sense but as testament to the wondrous untapped forms of life that we are only now beginning to understand and that may await our own transcendence.

Peace and positive energy!

APPENDIX I:
RECOMMENDED READING

Listed below are some of the most important texts on the paranormal that I've read over the years. You are probably already aware of the plethora of available material covering the subject. The following books are the keepers, in my opinion. They're a good starting point for the serious student of the supernatural. Together, they provide a strong mini-library of reference material. They fill our minds with wonder and make us ponder the complexities of the cosmos and life in its various forms. Most are non-fiction texts that deal with ghosts and haunted dwellings. However, I have also included a few works of fiction that I believe are important reading for those interested in learning more about haunted dwellings and cases of possession. Because I strongly believe in a connection between UFOs and the supernatural, I have also included important studies in this area. Finally, I have listed a few excellent volumes of Mexican-American, Latino and Native American history, as well as a web site with a focus on Texas Indians.

Haunted Houses, Cases of Possession
and Other Paranormal-Related Phenomena

Allen, Thomas B. *Possessed: The True Story of an Exorcism*. New York: Bantam, 1994.

Anson, Jay. *The Amityville Horror.* New York: Bantam, 1974.

Brittle, Gerald. *The Demonologist*. New York: Berkley, 1981.

—. *The Devil in Connecticut.* New York: Bantam, 1983.

Brunvand, Jan Harold. *The Vanishing Hitchhiker: American Urban Legends and Their Meanings.* New York: Norton, 1989.

Castaneda, Carlos. *The Active Side of Infinity.* New York: Harper Perennial, 2000.

Cavendish, Richard. *The Black Arts.* New York: Putnam's, 1967.

Copper, Arnold and Coralee Leon. *Psychic Summer.* New York: Dial, 1976.

Eason, Cassandra. *The Mother Link: Stories of Psychic Bonds Between Mother and Child.* Berkeley: Seastone, 1999.

Ebon, Martin. *The Devil's Bride: Exorcism: Past and Present.* New York: Harper & Row, 1974.

Editors of *USA Weekend. I Never Believed in Ghosts Until. . .* Lincolnwood (Chicago), IL: Contemporary Books, 1992.

Edwards, Frank. *Strange World.* New York: Bantam, 1969.

—. *Stranger Than Science.* New York: Bantam, 1967.

—. *Strangest of All.* New York: Ace, 1962.

Fuller, John G. *The Ghost of Flight 401.* New York: Berkley, 1976.

Hauck, Dennis William. *Haunted Places: The National Directory.* New York: Penguin, 1994, 1996.

Hunt, Stoker. *Ouija: The Most Dangerous Game.* New York: Harper & Row, 1992.

Lombard, Eric. *By Lust Possessed.* New York: Signet, 1980.

Moody, Raymond A. *Life After Life.* (25th anniversary edition.) San Francisco: Harper San Francisco, 2001.

Pickering, David. *Cassell Dictionary of Superstitions.* London: Cassell, 1995.

Rickard, Bob and John Michell. *Unexplained Phenomena: A Rough Guide Special.* Shorts Gardens, London: Rough Guides, 2000.

Walker, Danton. *I Believe in Ghosts.* New York: Taplinger, 1969.

Warren, Ed and Lorraine Warren, et al. *In A Dark Place: The Story of a True Haunting.* New York: Dell, 1992.

Warren, Ed and Lorraine, with Robert David Chase. *Ghost Hunters.* New York: St. Martin's, 1990.

—. *Graveyard: True Hauntings from an Old New England Cemetery.* New York: St. Martin's, 1992.

Westbie, Constance and Harold Cameron. *Night Stalks the Mansion.* New York: Bantam, 1978.

Wilde, Stuart. *Sixth Sense.* Carlsbad, CA: Hay House, 2000.

Winer, Richard, and Nancy Osborn. *Haunted Houses.* New York: Bantam, 1979.

—. *More Haunted Houses.* New York: Bantam, 1981.

Fiction Texts on Hauntings and Possession

Blatty, William Peter. *The Exorcist.* New York: Harper & Row, 1971.

Jackson, Shirley. *The Haunting of Hill House.* New York: Popular Library, 1959.

Macardle, Dorothy. *The Uninvited.* New York: Bantam, 1947.

Matheson, Richard. *Hell House.* New York: Warner, 1985. [Originally published in 1971.]

—. *A Stir of Echoes.* New York: Tor, 1999. [Originally published in 1958.]

UFOs and the Supernatural

Fuller, John G. *The Interrupted Journey: Two Lost Hours "Aboard a Flying Saucer."* New York: Dial, 1966.

Hynek, Dr. J. Allen, Philip J. Imbrogno and Bob Pratt. *Night Siege: The Hudson Valley UFO Sightings.* St. Paul: Llewellyn, 1998.

Imbrogno, Philip & Marianne Horrigan. *Celtic Mysteries in New England.* St. Paul: Llewellyn, 2000.

—. *Contact of the Fifth Kind.* St. Paul: Llewellyn, 1997.

Jung, C.G. *Flying Saucers: A Modern Myth of Things Seen in the Skies.* (Trans. R.F.C. Hull) New York: MJF, 1978.

Keel, John A. *The Mothman Prophecies.*

Ruppelt, Edward J. *The Report on Unidentified Flying Objects.* Garden City, NY: Doubleday, 1956.

Strieber, Whitley. *Communion.* New York:

—. *Transformation: The Breakthrough.* New York: Morrow, 1988.

Sutherly, Curt. *Strange Encounters: UFOs, Aliens and Monsters Among Us.* St. Paul: Llewellyn, 1996.

Mexican-American and Native American Cultures and History

Hester, Thomas. "'Coahuiltecan': A Critical review of an Inappropriate Ethnic Label." *La Tierra.* Vol. 25. No.4. October, 1998. 3-7.

Mirande, Alfredo and Evangelina Enriquez. *La Chicana: The Mexican-American Woman.* Chicago: U of Chicago P, 1979.

Newcomb, Jr., W. W. *The Indians of Texas: From Prehistoric to Modern Times.* Austin: U of Texas P.

Novas, Himilce. *Everything You Need to Know About Latino History.* New York: Plume/Penguin, 1994.

Ricklis, Robert A. *The Karankawa Indians of Texas: An Ecological Study of Cultural Tradition and Change.*

Wallace, Ernest, and E. Adamson Hoebel. *The Comanches: Lords of the South Plains.*

www.texasindians.com (This is an extremely detailed and informative web site on Texas Native Americans. I highly recommend it as a launching point for those Who wish to continue to investigate the diverse cultures and histories of Native Americans in the Lone Star State.)

APPENDIX II

RECOMMENDED VIEWING

I hesitated to add an appendix of film recommendations simply because of the sheer volume of material that has been committed to celluloid over the years. On the other hand, I felt my book was incomplete without such a list. Here, then, are a few select titles for your consideration. This list is comprised of what I believe are some of the most important and engaging horror films that deal with the afterlife, haunted dwellings and possession. If you are a horror movie fan, it is very likely that you have already screened many of these pictures. However, there may be one or two obscure titles on the list that are worth tracking down. Yes, there *have* been literally thousands of horror films produced on budgets ranging from the shoestring to the ridiculously generous, but listed below are the motion pictures that I believe have made impressive contributions to the horror genre (though not necessarily box office grosses) and the ongoing study of paranormal phenomena. Watching these films can be both entertaining and illuminating.

Amityville Horror, The. Dir. Stuart Rosenberg. MGM, 1979.
Carnival of Souls. Dir. Herk Harvey. 1962.
Changeling, The. Dir. Peter Medak. 1979.
Craft, The. Dir. Andrew Fleming. Columbia, 1996.
Curse of the Cat People. Dir. Gunther von Fritsch and Robert Wise. 1944.
Dark Water. Dir. Hideo Nakata. 2002.
Entity, The. Dir. Sidney J. Furie. 1983.
Exorcist, The. Dir. William Friedkin. Warner Brothers, 1973.
Eye, The. Dir. Oxide Pang Chun and Danny Pang. Lions Gate, 2002.
Ghost Story. Dir. John Irvin. Universal, 1981.
Haunting, The. Dir. Robert Wise. MGM, 1963.
Legend of Hell House, The. Dir. John Hough. 1973.
Others, The. Dir. Alejandro Amenabar. 2001.
Portrait of Jennie. Dir. William Dieterle. 1948.
Possessed. Dir. Steven de Souza. Showtime, 2000.
Seventh Sign, The. Dir. Carl Schultz. 1988.
Stigmata. Dir. Rupert Wainwright. MGM, 1999.
Stir of Echoes. Dir. David Koepp. Artisan, 1999.
Uninvited, The. Dir. Lewis Allen. Paramount, 1944.

ABOUT THE AUTHOR

A native of Corpus Christi, Texas, Oscar De Los Santos meandered his way to New England and stayed there. Currently, he is a professor of English and director of graduate studies in English at Western Connecticut State University. Oscar's lifelong love affairs with quirky stories, science fiction and horror are reflected in his fiction and non-fiction. His other specialties include Modern and Postmodern American Literature and conspiracy theory. Oscar is also the author of *Hardboiled Egg*, a short story collection. *Sailing the Seas of Chronos* and *Black Auras* are the first two books in his *Infinite Wonderlands* science fiction series. A third book in the series – *Kaleidoscope Future* – is forthcoming. As co-author, he has contributed to *Questions of Science, Answers to Life* and *11:11 – Stories About the Event*. Oscar earned his M.A. and Ph.D. from Ohio State University. He is a member of the Science Fiction Research Association and the International Association of the Fantastic in the Arts, and participates in the organizations' annual conferences. Oscar has published articles on science fiction, horror, postmodernism, conspiracy theory, and film. He has also participated in science seminars and forums on cloning and urban sprawl. If he isn't teaching or watching a baseball game, he's writing or playing Frisbee with Bonita, his Jack Russell terrier. Oscar welcomes your comments. Write him at oscar@loonyscribe.com and visit his website at http://www.loonyscribe.com

Also available Summer/Fall 2004 from Fine Tooth Press:

Fiction

Pressure Points by Craig Wolf
Hardboiled Egg by Oscar De Los Santos
The Massabesic Murders by Gypsey Teague
To Beat a Dead Horse by Bill Campbell
White River by Will Bless

Non-Fiction

Breakout by Ronnie Wright

Poetry

Composite Sketches by Lou Orfanella
Balloons Over Stockholm by James R. Scrimgeour

In the Works:

Trickster Tales by JP Briggs
A Poet's Guide to Divorce by David Breedan
Reel Rebels edited by Oscar De Los Santos
Street Angel by Martha Marinara
The New Goddess: Transgendered Women in the Twenty-First Century edited by Gypsey Teague

For more information about these and other titles, as well as author bios and interviews and more, visit us on the web at:

http://www.finetoothpress.com

Printed in the United States
63086LVS00003B/111

9 780975 338872